THE MONOPOLIES AND MERGERS COMMISSION

British Coal Corporation

A report on the investment programme
of the British Coal Corporation

Presented to Parliament by the Secretary of State
for Trade and Industry by Command of Her Majesty
January 1989

LONDON
HER MAJESTY'S STATIONERY OFFICE

Cm 550   £10·30 net

0-10105502-1

Members of the Monopolies and Mergers Commission as at 13 September 1988

Mr M S Lipworth (*Chairman*)
Mr H H Hunt CBE (*Deputy Chairman*)
Mr D G Richards (*Deputy Chairman*)
Mr R G Smethurst[1] (*Deputy Chairman*)
Sir James Ackers[1]
Mr C C Baillieu
Professor M E Beesley CBE
Mr F E Bonner CBE[1]
Mr L Britz
Mr M B Bunting[1]
Mr K S Carmichael CBE
Sir Robert Clayton CBE[1]
Mr P H Dean
Mr A Ferry MBE[1]
Mr P S G Flint
Mr D G Goyder
Miss A M Head
Mr M R Hoffman
Mr J D Keir QC
Mr L Kelly
Professor S C Littlechild
Miss P K R Mann
Mr S McDowall CBE
Mr L A Mills
Mr B C Owens
Mr N L Salmon
Mr D P Thomson
Mr C A Unwin MBE
Mr S Wainwright CBE
Professor G Whittington
Mr R Young

Mr S N Burbridge (*Secretary*)

---

[1] These members formed the group which was responsible for this report (see Appendix 1.1, paragraph 2).

Note by the Department of Trade and Industry

In accordance with section 17(5) of the Competition Act 1980 the Secretary of State for Trade and Industry has excluded from the copies of the report as laid before Parliament, and as published, certain matters publication of which appears to the Secretary of State to relate to the affairs of particular persons whose interests would, in his opinion, be seriously and prejudicially affected by publication and publication of which appears to him not to be in the public interest. Accordingly certain parts of the text, and of one Appendix, have been omitted. The omissions are indicated by a note in square brackets.

No excisions have been made from Chapter 1: Assessment, Complete list of conclusions and recommendations.

Contents

Page

Glossary vii

Chapter 1 Assessment 1
Complete list of conclusions and recommendations

2 Scope and method of inquiry and developments in BC since 1982 .. 14

3 Objectives and business strategy 17

4 Planning, policy and the capital investment programme 24

5 The appraisal of investment projects 44

6 Forecasting 63

7 Management systems 70

Appendices
The numbering of appendices indicates the chapters to which they relate.

1.1 Terms of reference 88

2.1 Submission of evidence by third parties 89

2.2 The BC/CEGB Understandings—a statement by BC 90

3.1 Select Committee on Energy—Inquiry into ESI privatization 93

4.1 Key supply indicators 100

5.1 to 5.11 Investment case studies

5.1 Allerton Bywater Colliery 101

5.2 Asfordby Colliery 104

5.3 Daw Mill Colliery 110

5.4 Dawdon Colliery 114

5.5 Harworth Colliery 120

5.6 Margam Colliery 124

5.7 Markham Colliery 131

5.8 Prince of Wales Colliery 135

5.9 Sutton Manor Colliery 138

5.10 Warsop Colliery 144

5.11 Creswell Colliery, Merthyr Vale Colliery, Cynheidre and Dawdon
Collieries, heavy duty installations 146

7.1 Project control performance 151

Glossary

Advancing face   Where the extraction of coal is carried out simultaneously with the driving of the access roads (gates). The gate roads on some longwall advancing faces may be formed in advance of the face where advance heading machines are employed.

ARA   Antwerp, Rotterdam, Amsterdam—the main coal-importing ports for North-West Europe and used as a basis for price quotations for all deep-water ports in North-West Europe.

ARTEMIS   A network computer system customized by BC to provide physical and financial data to assist project management.

APEX   Association of Professional, Executive, Clerical and Computer Staff.

Avoidable costs   The costs (expressed as unit costs) which would not be incurred if the coal production activity in question were not undertaken. In the case of an existing colliery, taken as the operating costs; when considering major additions of new capacity, taken as being the total costs (ie including capital charges).

BACM   British Association of Colliery Management.

BGS   British Geological Survey.

Capital charges   The capital charge (calculated for existing collieries) represents the cost of capital (at a rate approximating to the rate payable by BC on its borrowings) applied to the written down value of fixed assets employed at, or in support of, each colliery.

CEGB   Central Electricity Generating Board.

CEN   BC Central Area.

CIC   Capital Investment Committee.

C.i.f.   Costs, insurance, freight.

Coal Preparation Plant   A surface installation for the beneficiation and/or screening of coal.

Coking coal   Coal having inherent chemical and physical properties which render it (after appropriate preparation to remove excess extraneous material) suitable for the manufacture of coke. Many coking coals, are, however, also used for general steam-raising.

DCF   Discounted cash flow.

Drivages   Roadways driven to obtain access to the coal or to facilitate the opening out of new working areas.

EBG   Elsewhere below ground.

EFL   External financing limit set by the Government.

ESI   Electricity Supply Industry.

F.o.b.   Free on board.

Gate   Roadway serving a longwall face.

Gate end box   Electrical contactor and associated control equipment contained within a certified flameproof enclosure.

GJ–gigajoule   An internationally recognized unit of heat. The average United Kingdom power station coal contains about 24·5 GJ per tonne as sold, but depending on inherent quality and the degree of beneficiation individual coal qualities vary from under 20 GJ to over 30 GJ per tonne (1 GJ = 1 billion joules. 1 joule = the heat generated by a current of 1 ampere for 1 second against a resistance of 1 ohm).

Heavy duty	Usually applies to powered support, conveyors and power loaders of a type larger, more powerful and more robust than those traditionally used.
Heavy duty supports	Chock shield supports with yield loads of 250 tonnes or more.
IFR	Investment and Financing Review.
IRR	Internal rate of return.
Licensed mine	Small mine or opencast site licensed under the Coal Industry Nationalisation Act 1946 (as amended).
Longwall mining	Progressive extraction of a panel of coal from a long working face usually serviced by a roadway at each end.
Low grade coal	Coal with low inherent calorific value, but the term is also loosely applied to all coals below 20 GJ per tonne as sold.
MAF	Market Adjustment Fund. A term used by BC to describe a number of self-contained and self-balancing suspense accounts established to administer the attribution to production units of market rebates on sales of coal.
MAT	Machine available time.
MOB	Men on colliery books—number of industrial grade men employed by BC at a colliery (including officials and weekly-paid industrial staff).
MINOS system	Mine operating system, involving the remote control and monitoring of equipment and the mine environment by computer, usually from the surface.
mtce	Million tonnes coal equivalent.
mtpa	Million tonnes per annum.
NACODS	National Association of Colliery Overmen, Deputies and Shotfirers.
NEA	BC North East Area.
NELP	North East Leicestershire Prospect—a reserve of coal lying mainly under the Vale of Belvoir.
Net proceeds	Saleable proceeds adjusted for other income (eg service charges and sales of colliery methane) and for the creation or release of provisions for coal stocked or lifted from stock. Net proceeds is offset against costs to arrive at operating profit or loss.
NPV	Net present value.
NTS	BC Nottinghamshire Area.
NUM	National Union of Mineworkers.
NYK	BC North Yorkshire Area.
OMS	Output per man-shift.
OPEC	Organisation of Petroleum Exporting Countries.
Opencast mining	A mining method for working shallow coal seams which consists of removing the overlying strata or overburden, extracting the coal, and then replacing the overburden (spoil).
Operating costs	All costs incurred at a colliery or in support of its operations, including depreciation of fixed assets, and appropriate allocations of Area and Headquarters overheads and services as operating costs. It strikes colliery operating profit or loss by deducting the total operating costs from net proceeds.
Operating profit/loss	The operating profit or loss is arrived at by deducting total operating costs from net proceeds.
ORE	Operational Research Executive.
PC	Project Committee.

Pithead netback	Actual revenue received from the sale of a particular coal to a particular customer after deduction of rebates and any specific transport and handling costs incurred by BC after the coal has left the colliery (or opencast disposal point) weighbridge.
Project ledger	A database for the collection of all financial data relating to each project including approved cost, authorized expenditure, actual expenditure and outstanding commitments.
Retreat mining/working	Extraction of a panel of coal using preformed roadways, either purpose-driven or by the re-use of roads formed by advancing panels, driven to their ultimate boundary (from which coal working commences).
Saleable proceeds	Average net revenue received from the sale of all coals of any given quality standard. (See also **net proceeds**).
SCT	BC Scottish Area.
Shearers	General expression used to describe type of coal-winning machine utilizing drums fitted with pick points rotating in a vertical plane.
SSEB	South of Scotland Electricity Board.
Steam coal	Term commonly used to describe hard coals except coking coals, anthracites, and larger sizes of bituminous coal supplied for domestic use. (However, all types of solid fuels can be, and often are, used for steam-raising purposes.)
SWL	BC South Wales Area.
SYK	BC South Yorkshire Area.
TDR	Test Discount Rate.
Tranching system	A price arrangement under which the agreed tonnage to be supplied is split into a number of tonnage and price 'bands'.
UDM	Union of Democratic Mineworkers.
Washery	A surface installation designed to clean coal in a variety of ways using water as the basic medium. Other mediums may also be added depending on the process. Commonly used in conjunction with other plant (eg crushers and graders) in the beneficiation of coal. (See also **Coal Preparation Plant**).
WES	BC Western Area.
Winding time	The agreed period of time at the beginning and end of a shift within which men descend or ascend the mine.

1 Assessment

1.1. On 14 March 1988 the Secretary of State for Trade and Industry referred to the Commission questions about the investment programme of the British Coal Corporation (BC). The terms of reference are reproduced in Appendix 1.1, which also records the setting up of the Commission Group for the inquiry.

1.2. Section 1(a) of our terms of reference draws our attention to risk and thus to the problems of the future. It is not unusual for the Commission to be told by undertakings referred to it under section 11 of the 1980 Competition Act of the change currently occurring in the industry. In the present case we think that BC is faced by great uncertainties and discontinuities. This has influenced our approach and our assessment.

1.3. At the outset of the inquiry BC told us of its achievements in recent years. Some of the relevant figures are:

	1982–83	1987–88
Cost per GJ of deep mined coal (1987–88 prices)	£2·01	£1·65
Overall output per man-shift (tonnes)	2·44	3·62

Over the same period deep mined saleable output fell from 104 million tonnes to 82 million tonnes, average manpower from 207,640 to 104,355 (actual manpower at end March 1988 was 89,000), the number of operating faces from 574 to 246 and the number of collieries from 191 to 94. BC told us that about three-quarters of the productivity improvement had come from the use of heavy duty supports and other investment and from modified working practices and the remainder from pit closures.

1.4. Although our previous report concluded that much needed to be done, by any standards BC's achievements during the last few years have been impressive.

1.5. The process of change on which BC embarked involved it in, to use its own words, 'turning an institution into a business'. It involved it also in moving from preoccupation with levels of physical output to an emphasis on financial performance—again in its own words 'from tonnes to money'.

1.6. Cultural change of the magnitude which BC needed often requires symbols, slogans, and simple, constantly reiterated targets. Costs in pounds per gigajoule (£/GJ) have become a central benchmark. Together with the 1988–89 financial target of break-even (after interest and social grants) the £/GJ rule concentrates attention on costs—and it also emphasizes usable energy rather than the weight of material extracted from below ground.

1.7. But at a time when BC might have hoped to be able to continue its drive for cost reduction without any increase in the level of uncertainty in the external environment, it is faced with major institutional change. While fluctuations in the international prices of oil and coal and in exchange rates, however severe, have been and are an unavoidable part of its business environment, the announced privatization of the electricity supply industry (ESI) and, during the course of our inquiry, the announcement of a firm intention to privatize BC, mean radical change.

1.8. BC's strategy since 1985 has been to acknowledge the need for flexibility in its planning and to work to a policy of what it calls 'minimum regret'. This means avoiding such irrevocable actions as closing pits which might subsequently be needed or opening pits which might never earn a satisfactory return.

1.9. BC believes that the minimum regret policy is robust. But BC also told us that, if ESI privatization were to result in significantly increased levels of imports, its policy would require an increase in the number of pit closures.

1.10. The present may turn out to have been a time of unique institutional uncertainty for BC. We believe, however, that it has not come to terms with the continuing uncertainties which will characterize its relations with a private sector ESI. We also feel that it has not added to its strong drive towards cost reduction a sufficiently bold, imaginative approach to influencing favourably vital aspects of its business future. We have been surprised by a defensive attitude by BC to possible criticism of some aspects of its decisions and operations—a defensiveness which we think does not sit well alongside a more open, creative attitude to the future. BC has in our view already lost opportunities to consider in detail how it might increase its attractiveness to present and future customers, for example in its response to the threat of future imports.

1.11. Our terms of reference specifically require us to examine the responsiveness of BC's investment programme to change in business strategy and objectives, and the contribution made by the investment programme to achieving its objectives. Against a background of continuing volatility in the commercial environment we have tried to frame our conclusions and recommendations in the light not only of changes in strategy since 1984–85 but also of those strategic changes which we think are bound to prove necessary.

The report: its conclusions and recommendations

1.12. The bulk of our inquiry has been into BC's investment policy and practice during the recent past. That is reflected in the detail of Chapters 3 to 7. We have found that the management systems which BC has in place and the controls which are exercised on the selection of capital expenditure projects are generally good ones. The business planning system, the cost per GJ criteria used to eliminate high cost projects and the discounted cash flow (DCF) investment appraisal methods applied all help to ensure that capital expenditure contributes to BC's strategy of cost reduction. This is not to say that the systems have always worked well or are without scope for improvement. Our detailed conclusions and recommendations, summarized at the end of this chapter, identify matters on which action should be taken.

Priority areas for attention
Strategy and planning

1.13. BC agreed with the Government in March 1987 to seek to break even in 1988–89. It has further committed itself internally to targets which reduce the shortfall in self-financing for the years 1988–89 to 1991–92. These become its 'milestones' for increasing its proportion of self-financing. The figures show an improvement from a shortfall of £274 million in 1988–89 to one of £25 million in 1991–92, with financing self-sufficiency reached in the following year. While we sympathize with BC's worries about unforeseen changes in its external environment, we believe that BC should commit itself firmly to five-year figures agreed with the Government. This commitment will imply an acceptance of responsibility for getting things right if they go wrong, and of the discipline of making up, from further increases in revenue and/or further reductions in costs, any shortfalls which might occur.

1.14. Recommending the precise way in which BC must change its strategic thinking in order to deal constructively with uncertainties and discontinuities recently placed before it is not easy. BC is in our view in danger of being caught at times in a circular argument in which it thinks present policies are robust because any circumstances which would make them fragile and vulnerable are consciously or unconsciously disregarded. If it becomes at Board level able to 'think the unthinkable' BC may as a result be able to develop means of influencing more favourably its future business environment.

1.15. In BC it is the Chairman who fulfils the function of Chief Executive Officer, and, as is appropriate at a turbulent period for the organization, strategy is an integral part of his role. At present analyses of different aspects of the external environment are carried out in different parts of the Headquarters organization, and brought together to permit a corporate view to emerge. The new challenge BC has to meet is the prospect of major discontinuities in its external environment. We think that BC's Board will need to ensure that there is a cohesive system and organization conducive to systematic and rigorous review of future prospects in BC's business environment.

1.16. At local level, as BC's circumstances change, and particularly when the ESI is privatized, BC should consider changing the arrangements so that Areas and mines are called on, within the business planning cycle, for some formal input on their local business environment.

1.17. We found BC now has a comprehensive Investment Appraisal Manual which, if followed in full, should enable it to make sound decisions on individual project proposals. The case studies that we undertook showed too that BC's investment appraisal has noticeably improved in recent years.

1.18. There is nonetheless scope for further improvement. In particular, BC should ensure that greater attention is paid to the need to evaluate fully all practicable options in preparing Stage I submissions. Clear guidance should be set out on how to establish the minimum feasible alternative to the preferred option. This alternative should be used for comparison in the detailed financial analysis of project proposals at Stage II, rather than relying as much as BC does at present on the 'do nothing' option for this purpose.

1.19. In some cases it is important to consider BC's collieries as part of a system. We recommend that BC incorporates in its Manual guidance on how the effects of certain projects on other parts of the system should be taken into account in investment appraisal.

1.20. In examining BC's procedure for appraising investment, and looking in some detail at individual projects, the case which has caused us most concern has been that of Asfordby. In our view Asfordby has at no time been demonstrably viable according to BC's own investment criteria. BC insists that it has. Extensive discussion on this matter has not brought us closer together.

1.21. A further review of the Asfordby project was being carried out as we completed our inquiry. In completing this, BC's investment criteria should be strictly applied.

1.22. If in reaching a final judgment on Asfordby, or indeed other major projects, criteria other than the financial are judged to be important, then these non-financial factors should be made explicit, and judgments on the relative weight of financial and non-financial factors made at Board level.

1.23. Whatever the rights or wrongs of Asfordby's history we believe that an important lesson to be learned is that of the danger of 'piecemealing through time'. By this we mean spending money on a marginal project and subsequently treating the money already spent as a sunk cost. Using this approach almost any project could at some stage become financially attractive. In future, the sort of conditional approval given for Asfordby in advance of showing a satisfactory financial return should not be allowed except when other factors are explicitly judged to be of sufficient weight.

1.24. As part of the process of assessing risk and uncertainty, BC maintains systems for modelling United Kingdom energy demand and international trade in steam coal. We consider that these are useful systems which can make a valuable contribution to BC's strategic planning and to the assessment of its competitive position. However, we are concerned at the limited use which BC at present makes of these facilities. We consider that BC should make more use of its forecasting models. It should broaden their use to allow it to consider the effect of a wide range of possible developments, both in the United Kingdom and elsewhere, on the industry. It should plan a regular programme of 'what if?' analyses to examine the effect on the industry of specific developments, for example ESI privatization, exchange rate movements, competition from alternative fuels and possible rapid growth in world trade in coal.

1.25. The cost per GJ criteria used in the investment programme have been tightened both by not being indexed for inflation and as part of BC's objective of reducing unit operating costs by at least 20 per cent between 1985–86 and 1989–90. We think that any further tightening of the cost per GJ criteria should formally be linked to the BC's latest assessments of the future economic environment and clearly related to a view of BC's future market situation.

Manpower

1.26. We have already referred to the considerable improvements in productivity which have accompanied the major restructuring of the industry over the period since our last report.

1.27. On this occasion our terms of reference require us to consider specifically whether BC 'could improve its performance with regard to ... the efficient use of manpower in achieving the required rate of return on investment projects'. In this context we have looked at and made recommendations on manpower planning, the control of manning levels elsewhere below ground (EBG), flexible working and more generally on the coverage of manpower issues in project submissions.

1.28. Our principal conclusion on manpower is that its treatment in the formal investment process was not always sufficient to ensure that estimates of manpower requirements and productivity were fully justified. As a consequence we feel that it is possible for opportunities to make the most efficient use of manpower resources to be missed. We therefore recommend that manpower issues should always be fully covered in project submissions.

1.29. More flexible working practices can contribute greatly to making the most efficient use of capital equipment. We commend BC's efforts to introduce more flexible working generally and particularly in new mines which require considerable capital investment.

Post-investment appraisal

1.30. We have detailed suggestions about the preparation of Completion Reports. We also recommend that BC subjects about four or five of its completed projects a year to a detailed Headquarters appraisal, considerably more broadly based than BC's Completion Reports. Some recent heavy duty projects would be suitable early candidates.

Project management, planning and control

1.31. There has been a steady improvement in the planning and in the financial and programme control of BC's capital projects, although we think that BC still has some way to go to absorb all the lessons recently learnt about project control. We also recommend some improvement in BC's estimating and monitoring of project costs.

1.32. There should be a career path in project management, so as to encourage the full development, use and retention of expertise. BC should ensure that its proposed central project management function provides this.

Proceeds and capital performance

1.33. Two of the ways in which the financial performance of collieries is measured may have to be changed when the ESI is privatized. The first is the way in which BC calculates pit profits, by attributing revenue after averaging discounts by reference essentially to two categories of coal. This is appropriate at present, but should the number of power generating companies substantially increase, crediting each colliery with its own net proceeds would prevent collieries being isolated from their markets. The second concerns the attribution of fixed and working capital to collieries or groups of collieries. At present BC does not calculate return on capital for individual collieries. Each colliery carries a capital charge, calculated by reference to BC's average rate of interest payable and the written down value of the colliery's tangible fixed assets, which is deducted before striking the 'bottom-line' profit. This may be adequate for the present, but, together with the change to calculation of proceeds, the full attribution of all capital to collieries would permit the calculation of their return on capital employed.

Conclusion

1.34. Since 1984–85 BC's performance has greatly improved. Since we last reported, in 1983, BC's investment appraisal and related procedures have in general improved, although we have been puzzled by the history of the Asfordby new mine project.

1.35. BC has reached a point at which its drive to 'turn an institution into a business', with particular emphasis upon reduced costs, must be combined with a new dimension of management requiring it to adopt a flexible, light-footed response to major uncertainties. BC will in the next few years need great skill if it is to combine reducing costs still further with creating and exploiting opportunities to meet the new institutional and market realities.

1.36. We are required to consider whether in relation to any matter falling within our terms of reference (Appendix 1.1) BC is pursuing a course of conduct which operates against the public interest. We do not find that it is.

Complete list of conclusions and recommendations

Recommendation No.		Paragraph No.
	Objectives and business strategy	
	On BC's own evidence the process of changing the 'culture' of the Corporation from 'tonnes to money' is not yet complete. The dominant current objective of achieving financial break-even in the present year dramatizes the change needed in BC's thinking. From examining the relationship between strategy and investment we have concluded that BC has been right to dramatize its objectives in this way.	3.38
1.	While accepting, however, that a simply-stated financial objective has advantages in focusing attention on the need for short-term financial achievement, **we think that BC should now commit itself firmly to specific, quantified financial objectives for the next five years.** BC is reluctant to commit itself publicly to specific targets for revenue and costs, but has developed internal targets for reducing the shortfall in self-financing for the years 1988–89 to 1991–92. The figures show an improvement from a shortfall of £274 million in 1988–89 to one of £25 million in 1991–92, with self-sufficiency reached in the following year. **All investment projects, and the investment programme as a whole, should be related to these targets.**	3.39
	But commitment to those targets, while a very important discipline, should not be used as an excuse for ceasing the search for greater improvement. BC's stated policy of 'minimum regret' for investment decisions properly, in our view, concentrates short-term attention on cost reduction at existing mines. But such a concentration, together with the emphasis on revenue costs rather than on investment opportunities which flows from the target of breaking even in 1988–89, could lead to the avoidance of bold decisions, the lack of which might be regretted in the longer–term future.	3.40

2.   The minimum regret policy can be meaningful only if decisions to proceed and not to proceed are carefully examined in the light of a sufficiently wide range of possible future situations. We are not convinced that BC has examined sufficiently early an adequate range of possibilities for a future which includes ESI privatization and the intended privatization of BC. **If the five-year targets to which it commits itself are indeed to be robust, BC must now think more imaginatively about the ways in which things can go wrong (in terms of its earlier assumptions) and what it could then do to get back on course.**   3.41

    BC's view is that the appropriate Test Discount Rate (TDR) for its business is 10 per cent for colliery results, and 15 per cent on the margin, after risk assessment, for individual projects. We recognize the practical difficulties involved in establishing the relationship between these rates and the rate of return of 5 per cent which BC is required to maintain on all its investment. We are satisfied, however, that BC currently applies these 10 per cent and 15 per cent discount rates, and that the proportion of its investment programme to which these rates apply is sufficiently large to ensure that an average return of at least 5 per cent is achieved on its new investments.   3.42

Planning, policy and the capital investment programme

    BC has revised its corporate planning arrangements. Its business planning system is now an effective structure for planning and appraising through the Areas' business plans, including those for investment, for each mine. The system provides a vehicle for dialogue between Areas and Headquarters, and is the main means by which BC makes its investment programme follow its strategy. The business planning cycle is also one of the means BC is using to change the culture of management at the level of mine manager and above. The business planning system is thus well constructed to meet the requirements of the main planks of BC's strategy since the strike.   4.75

3.   In BC it is the Chairman who fulfils the function of Chief Executive Officer, and, as is appropriate at a turbulent period for the organization, strategy is an integral part of his role. At present, analyses of different aspects of the external environment are carried out in different parts of the Headquarters organization, and are brought together to permit a corporate view to emerge. The new challenge BC has to meet is the prospect of major discontinuities in its external environment. **We think that BC's Board will need to ensure that the systems and organization are conducive to systematic and rigorous review of future prospects in BC's business environment.**   4.76

4.   However, the business planning cycle does not at present call upon the Areas or mines to provide any formal input on the local business environment. **This has been appropriate to BC's present circumstances. As these change, and particularly when the ESI is privatized, these arrangements will need to be examined, and if necessary revised.**   4.77

5.   In the course of our inquiry BC announced organizational changes, involving a smaller management organization to supervise the collieries in some coalfields. A number of features, including technological changes and rising productivity, have already enabled BC to become a smaller, better controlled organization. **We recommend that BC should, as we assume it will, continue to examine the prospects of further simplifying its organizational structure to enable it better to respond flexibly to a more rapidly changing business environment.**   4.78

BC's system for selecting investment projects relies on colliery unit cost criteria, expressed in £/GJ, to act as a first hurdle. For investments at existing collieries where the increments are small compared with the capital already sunk, the assessment is expressed in operating costs. For major investments in new capacity, total colliery unit costs, incorporating capital charges, are used. Projects surviving these tests are subjected to DCF analysis, and are expected to meet BC's rate of return criteria. This is satisfactory as a system.

4.79

6.   The £/GJ criteria have been progressively tightened in two ways. First, they have not been indexed for inflation. Secondly, greater emphasis is now being given to an upper limit of £1·50/GJ, rather than £1·65/GJ which was the upper limit when the policy was introduced. This reflects BC's objective to reduce its operating costs by at least 20 per cent between 1985–86 and 1989–90. **We think that any further tightening should be linked to the kinds of assessments of the future economic environment we refer to in Chapter 6 and clearly related to a view of BC's future market situation. The total cost cut-off for large projects in new capacity is now the same as the operating cost cut-off for small projects, at £1·50/GJ. Acknowledging that these both approximate to avoidable costs, BC should consider making the former lower than the latter, to reflect the greater uncertainty attached to the longer payback periods of such projects.**

4.80

We accept BC's argument that six-day working at new mines would be commercially advantageous, and we note that this has now been agreed in principle with the UDM.

4.81

BC fully recognizes the commercial importance of maximum utilization of capital plant. To achieve this there are a variety of forms of flexible working which could be employed at existing mines. We commend BC in continuing to explore all options.

4.82

7.   BC has met considerable resistance to its proposals for more flexible working arrangements, particularly from the NUM at national level; but we have been told that there has been considerable misunderstanding of the proposals. It is clearly important that the need for flexible working, in its various forms, is properly discussed and understood by the workforce. **We therefore recommend that the unions should be fully consulted at the appropriate level, and that the objectives, options and proposals should be explained clearly to the workforce at colliery level.**

4.83

8.   Another obstacle to flexible working is the limitation of underground shift length to 7·5 hours plus one winding time in the 1908 Coal Mines Regulation Act (as amended). **BC should seek early consultations with the trade unions, preparatory to making further representations to the Government on this matter.**

4.84

The appraisal of investment projects

BC now has a comprehensive Capital Investment Manual which gives full guidance on the preparation, and submission for approval of capital investment projects. We also found, in the case studies of investment projects that we undertook (the approval dates of which ranged from mid-1983 to March 1988), that the most recent cases showed noticeable improvements in the preparation of investment projects over the earlier cases. Even so, we think that there is scope for further improvement in BC's procedures.

5.88

We found it difficult to form a clear picture of the extent to which BC believes that its mines form a coal supply system—that is, the extent to which the output of one mine is affected by, and in turn has an effect on, the output of other mines. BC told us that for some purposes the mines should not be thought of as forming a supply system. Thus its smaller investment projects, each of which would in itself have a minor impact on BC's total supplies, at particular mines are appraised on a 'stand alone' basis. For other purposes, however, BC does manage its mines as a coal supply system. For example, the procedure by which BC averages the proceeds for individual collieries is a clear indication to each colliery that its financial performance is not independent of the activities at other collieries. This interdependence is also recognized, for investment purposes, in BCs' annual business planning cycle.

5.89

In our view BC's output-related investment projects are not mutually exclusive in that each project will have some effect on the cash flows projected in connection with other projects. Indeed, with the present emphasis on investment only in low cost collieries, each investment project will in principle have implications for the continued viability of higher cost sources unless BC can increase its sales. For many projects this effect will be minimal. In some cases the output effect may be more significant but only in relation to a discrete market (eg coking coal). But for almost all of BC's major output related projects, this interdependence of projects should be explicitly recognized in the appraisal. This interdependence becomes increasingly significant as the number of collieries declines.

5.90

9. **We therefore recommend that BC incorporates into the Manual practical guidance on how to ensure that the relevant 'system effect' of all projects for new or replacement capacity which require Headquarters approval is taken account of in the appraisals of those projects.**

5.91

10. **We recommend that BC gives close consideration to how options are assessed in the first stages of project preparation. There are three matters to which BC should pay particular attention:**

(a) **The Manual requires that a 'sufficiently adequate' evaluation of *all* (our italics) practical options be made in the preparation of the Stage I submission. We found that in a number of the case studies the assessment and choice of options at Stage I was inadequate, and this led to sometimes protracted discussions at Stage II or to significant modifications to the project after approval.**

11. (b) We found that the detailed analysis in Stage II normally relates only to the option which has been chosen prior to the preparation of the Stage II submission and to the 'do nothing' option. We think that the important comparison is with the minimum feasible alternative and that, as BC acknowledged, this is not necessarily 'doing nothing'. **BC should set out clearly in its Manual the basis for establishing what the minimum feasible alternative is for the purpose of its investment appraisal.**

12. (c) **We think that for appraisal purposes a more thorough analysis of the individual elements of composite projects should be undertaken at Stage II. The combination of elements showing the highest net present value (NPV) should form the base case for assessing the merits of alternative combinations of the scheme's proposed components.**

5.92

Our examination of the case studies and the procedures for the approval of capital investment projects leads us to conclude that potential opportunities to make the most efficient use of manpower resources may be missed. In those projects we studied there was in most cases only limited formal coverage of manpower and industrial relations issues.

5.93

While accepting that these issues would be discussed between Headquarters and Area staff, and that not all projects have on the face of it significant manpower implications, we expect that every major capital investment project provides the opportunity for a critical examination of the utilization of manpower resources. The procedures for the submission and approval of capital investment projects, whilst requiring that these issues are covered where relevant, do not ensure that estimates of manpower requirements and productivity for the various categories of labour are fully discussed and justified in project documentation.

5.94

13.

14.

We recommend that those submitting capital investment project applications be required in every case to cover fully all manpower and industrial relations issues and to justify estimates of manpower requirements and performance. We also consider that those responsible for approving projects should critically examine these aspects of submissions to ensure that no opportunity has been missed to maximize the efficient use of manpower resources.

5.95

15.

We were further concerned that the manpower planning system itself could in some circumstances lead to initial overmanning or inflated estimates of manpower requirements. This could arise from the use of the 'non-attendance percentage' in the formula employed for the calculation of essential manpower requirements. **We recommend that the use of this formula for calculating manpower is critically examined in those project submissions where the non-attendance percentage of any category of labour is higher than current target levels.** BC told us that its aim is to reduce the non-attendance percentage to a minimum: implementation of this recommendation may assist in the achievement of that aim.

5.96

Our 1983 report attached considerable importance to the control and reduction of EBG manning levels. We were therefore surprised to note that this had not become a feature in most of the capital investment projects we studied. In most cases this category of manpower as a proportion of the total remained virtually unaffected. We note that BC has been making a continuing effort in this respect and that targets have been set and met. We accept that retreat working and other forms of modern mining technology at the face will (with lower face manning levels) initially lead to an increase in the proportion of indirect labour.

5.97

16.

Whilst fully accepting this, and welcoming the efforts which are already being made by BC, we feel that in the context of major capital investment projects it would be appropriate fully to demonstrate this effort. **We therefore recommend that the EGB issue should be covered in all project submissions, and where appropriate the required levels of EBG manpower should be demonstrably justified.**

5.98

In the closing stages of our inquiry we were pleased to learn that BC had issued instructions to Areas which went a considerable way towards addressing the concerns expressed in paragraphs 5.97 to 5.98.

5.99

In our view the Asfordby Project has always been marginal in financial terms. After allowing for risks associated with the project, the financial appraisals have at no time shown a return which meets the minimum DCF yield which BC has set for collieries. The most recent estimates of total unit costs including capital charges fall well outside the Corporation's present criteria for investment both in replacement and incremental capacity.

5.102

BC has taken a different view and has argued that although initial contracts were let prior to Stage II, approval for further contracts was always conditional on the achievement of improved performance and six-day working. BC told us that the decisions to go ahead have been solely on the basis of the financial prospectus for the project. The results of the latest review were not available during our inquiry but BC told us that it was likely that this would show that Asfordby would satisfy its DCF criteria.

5.103

We are concerned that so much expenditure has been committed to a project over three years during which time it has not been possible to show a strong financial case. This concern is increased by the uncertainty about the revenue that can be earned from Asfordby coal, which is reported to be of a low quality and whose ash characteristics are now of concern to CEGB. ESI privatization may add to the uncertainty surrounding revenue. We understand the reasons why BC embarked on the project in 1984 but we cannot accept the view that the project has been shown to be financially attractive. To suggest so can only undermine the value of the DCF and cost per GJ criteria as instruments of management control.

5.104

17. We accept that the project now has sunk costs and that this, combined with an agreement on six-day working, may mean that the remainder of the project can be shown to be a worthwhile investment. We accept that it would be right for BC to continue with the project if it now meets BC's financial criteria. However we would regard this as a bad precedent for BC to set if the project can, in effect, only be justified by disregarding a significant part of its capital cost. BC has itself told us that it seeks to avoid the 'piecemealing' of projects which can lead to unjustified expenditures. We consider the history of Asfordby may illustrate a problem of 'piecemealing through time', that is spending money on a marginal project and subsequently treating the money already spent as a 'sunk cost'. Using this approach almost any project could at some stage become financially attractive. **We recommend that in future the sort of conditional approval which was given for expenditure on Asfordby, in advance of its showing a sound financial prospectus, should not allowed by the Board, except when other factors are explicitly judged to be of sufficient weight.**

5.105

18. BC agreed with us in principle that the achievement of a wider corporate objective could make worthwhile going ahead with a project which would otherwise be rejected on strict financial grounds. **Where this is the case, we recommend that the wider benefits should be clearly laid out in the project appraisal, and, for a significant project, the responsibility for making such an important judgment should lie with BC's Board.**

5.106

Forecasting

As part of the process of assessing risk and uncertainty, BC maintains systems for modelling United Kingdom energy demand and international trade in steam coal. We consider that these are useful systems which can make a valuable contribution to BC's strategic planning and to the assessment of its competitive position. However, we are concerned at the limited use which BC at present makes of these facilities.

6.31

19.   BC's United Kingdom energy model is updated and forecasts prepared only once a year and other forecasts are prepared to meet particular requirements on an *ad hoc* basis. We were surprised that BC had not made more use of its models to carry out 'what if?' analyses of, for example, possible outcomes from ESI privatization. **We consider that a more frequent systematic use of the forecasting models would help BC management in its assessment of the many uncertain factors affecting the industry.**

6.32

20.   In its 1987 study of world coal trade BC excluded the United Kingdom from its world trade model. While that may have been appropriate at the time **we think that as a general practice United Kingdom coal production and demand should form part of the world trade model.**

6.33

We recommend that BC should:

21.   **—create a system for more frequently updating and running its forecasting models and should incorporate the United Kingdom coal market into its world model;**

22.   **—broaden the use made of its models to allow it to consider the effect of a wide range of possible developments, both in the United Kingdom and elsewhere, on the industry; and**

23.   **—plan a regular programme of 'what if?' analyses to examine the effect on the industry of specific developments,** for example ESI privatization, exchange rate movements, competition from alternative fuels and possible rapid growth in world trade in coal.

6.34

Management systems

The discounts which BC allows, other than those which are quality-related, are averaged over collieries by reference to two main categories of coal, bituminous graded and bituminous non-graded. Three other categories exist, viz anthracite graded, anthracite non-graded and South Wales bituminous, but these all relate to South Wales only.

7.82

As long as the bulk of the coal produced is supplied to some 30 national customers from whichever collieries are best placed to meet the customers' needs most economically, it would make no sense to do other than credit each colliery with proceeds established after deduction of the company-wide average discounts.

7.83

We do not believe that the same considerations will necessarily apply in the future when the ESI is privatized and there may be a significant increase in the number of power generating companies seeking supplies of coal from local sources. We believe that the present policy would result in the insulation of individual collieries from their markets, protecting them from the consequences of their geographic position and the nature and grade of their products. Crediting each colliery with its own net proceeds would enable the true profitability of each colliery to be established, by linking it to its own markets.

7.84

Within the present framework BC has satisfactory arrangements for measuring cost, output and quality against targets for individual collieries, and for monitoring capital expenditure on individual projects and in aggregate.   7.85

The Annual Review provides a formal means by which the decision-taking level can monitor project progress. BC has, since 1985, improved its procedures, and we are satisfied that adequate attention is now given to this task.   7.86

Completion Reports provide a formal means of holding managers responsible for overall project performance (in terms of adhering to time and cost), and for initiating sanctions if this is unsatisfactory. This is an effective way of encouraging well-run projects.   7.87

At the time when many of the projects we examined went out to tender, market conditions were such that prices for the contracts were exceptionally low because of excess capacity in the construction industry. This explains why so many of the contracts were let at markedly below Stage II estimates. BC has now changed its instructions to those preparing Stage II estimates, and they are now required to make their estimates on the basis of the price expected at the time the contract is expected to be let. The previous practice could, in some circumstances, be misleading, and we think this is a welcome change.   7.88

24.   In our 1983 report we commented unfavourably on the way project costs were monitored at Headquarters against Stage II estimates rather than against sums which reflect the prices contracted at Stage III. **BC agreed with us that Headquarters monitoring should be against both figures, and we recommend that this should be implemented.** This will improve control of capital investment in respect of annual expenditure; monitoring against commitment; and monitoring against approval.   7.89

25.   BC's Annual Reviews and Completion Reports currently fulfil a specific and rather narrow role. **We therefore recommend that, in addition, BC establishes a procedure to choose some four or five completed projects each year and subjects them to detailed Headquarters post-project appraisal.** We believe that BC is well placed to conduct such reviews and to ensure that the lessons, both favourable and unfavourable, are disseminated widely among it staff. One suitable area for early review would be recent heavy duty installations. This should provide a solid basis for ensuring that the future of the remaining Heavy Duty Programme, continues to be soundly based.   7.90

We note that BC is shortly to issue a manual on project management; this, which we recommended in our previous report, is to be welcomed.   7.91

26.   There is to be a project management function under central, Headquarters control. **BC should ensure that thereby expertise once developed is retained and used, and that there is a career path through project management in BC.** BC will, nevertheless, continue to need to purchase specialist help in project management and control from outside from time to time, both to refresh its in-house team with new ideas, and to deal with 'lumpiness' in the construction programme.   7.92

The changes BC has made, and continues to make, to its project management improve planning, and financial and programme control. However, we think that BC still has some way to go fully to absorb the lessons recently learned about project control, and may be able to take further advantage of advice from consultants. BC's cost estimating which we commented on in our previous report is still inaccurate, but the errors have been of overestimation.

7.93

27.   BC does not think it worthwhile to attempt to calculate the actual return on capital of an individual capital investment project after the project is complete. **We think that, since the justification for expenditure is ultimately expressed in money terms, the post-completion analysis of the project should always include a financial assessment of the project, including a calculation of the return on capital, and a statement of the contribution to the actual change in colliery performance since the project was approved.**

7.94

We believe that the absence of proper calculations of returns on capital employed for individual collieries is of little consequence at the present time with BC treating its mines collectively as a coal supply system. In these circumstances we regard the inclusion in a colliery's profit and loss account of a capital charge, calculated by reference to BC's average rate of interest payable and the written-down value of the colliery's tangible fixed assets (plus other capital assets used at or in support of the colliery), as a useful reminder to the colliery management that a satisfactory return should be achieved on assets employed.

7.95

However, we believe that this procedure may well be inadequate in the likely circumstances following privatization of the ESI; and the more so in the event of privatization of BC. We believe that BC should now be giving thought to ways in which it could fully attribute fixed and working capital to individual collieries or groups of collieries.

7.96

2 Scope and method of inquiry, and developments in BC since 1982

Scope of the inquiry

2.1. In accordance with the terms of reference our report is confined to the consideration of various aspects of BC's investment programme, including detailed consideration of a number of individual projects. Section 11(8) of the Competition Act requires the Commission to 'exclude from their investigation and report any consideration of any question relating to the appropriateness of any financial obligations or guidance as to financial objectives (however expressed) imposed on or given to the person in question by or under any enactment, or otherwise by a Minister'.

Method of inquiry

2.2. On 14 March 1988 the Department of Trade and Industry issued a press notice which included the terms of reference and invited persons wishing to give evidence to write to the Secretary of the Commission. Invitations to give evidence were sent by us to BC, the Confederation of British Industry (CBI), the Trades Union Congress (TUC), and the unions represented in the industry, and other bodies which might have an interest in the inquiry, including major customers of, and suppliers to, BC. Advertisements inviting evidence were placed in *The Times, The Guardian, Financial Times, Observer, Scotsman, Glasgow Herald, Colliery Guardian*, and *Mining Engineer*.

2.3. Those bodies which submitted evidence are listed in Appendix 2.1. The following bodies attended hearings: BC; the National Association of Colliery Overmen, Deputies and Shotfirers (NACODS); the British Association of Colliery Management (BACM); the National Association of Licensed Opencast Operators (NALOO); the Central Electricity Generating Board (CEGB); the South of Scotland Electricity Board (SSEB); and the British Geological Survey (BGS). The Department of Energy attended an informal meeting with the Commission.

2.4. The National Union of Mineworkers (NUM) was invited to submit evidence but declined. The Union of Democratic Mineworkers (UDM) also decided not to submit evidence.

2.5. Members of the Commission visited BC Headquarters in London and between them members visited those collieries which were the subject of case studies. Some of these visits included going underground.

BC: developments since 1982

2.6. In 1983 we reported on the efficiency and costs in the development, production and supply of coal by the National Coal Board (NCB) (Cmnd 8920, June 1983). Chapter 2 of that report describes the British coal industry at that time. The rest of this chapter sets out developments in the industry since then, bearing in mind that our present remit is limited to the examination of BC's investment programme. Although our terms of reference do not require us to do so, at appropriate places in our present report we note the progress made by BC since our last report, which covers our terms of reference in recommendations 1–24.

2.7. In March 1983 the Secretary of State for Energy announced objectives for BC covering return on assets; aiming at a market share which could be profitably sustained; bringing capacity into line with market share; and reducing costs. These objectives were substantially reaffirmed by the Under Secretary of State for energy in November 1983 following agreement with Mr (now Sir Ian) MacGregor when he succeeded Sir Norman Siddall as Chairman in September 1983.

The NUM dispute of 1983–85

2.8. The NUM imposed an overtime ban on 31 October 1983, and large-scale strike action began in March 1984 at most (but not all) collieries. An NUM Delegate Conference held on 3 March 1985 ordered a return to work without a settlement. BC told us that the 11-month long strike caused the industry:

—a 70 million tonnes loss of production;

—a reduction of 64·5 million tonnes in coal sales;

—the loss of 73 coal faces (15 per cent of the total);

—severe damage to a further 80 faces;

—damage to a number of collieries from which they were unlikely to recover fully;

—a financial cost of about £1,750 million (including £342 million to cover continuing detrimental effects in 1985/86); and

—some loss of loyalty by customers who had found it necessary to identify alternative fuels.

2.9. After the severe disruption to its operations by the industrial dispute, BC took the view that a completely new approach to the future prospects of the industry was necessary. A 'New Strategy for Coal' was outlined to the Coal Industry National Consultative Council and presented in detail to union leaders in October 1985.

2.10. The two main elements of this new strategy were:

(a) phasing out dependence on subsidy and eventually generating the greater part to the industry's investment requirements from internal sources; and

(b) meeting market requirements at competitive prices.

2.11. BC was determined to reduce costs, including overheads, and to maximize output at low-cost collieries and opencast sites. It therefore introduced the cost parameters, based on energy output of coal expressed in pounds per GJ (£/GJ), which were to be used to judge colliery performance, and which we describe in paragraph 3.7 and elsewhere.

2.12. In March 1987 the Secretary of State for Energy settled further objectives for BC with Sir Robert Haslam, who succeeded Sir Ian MacGregor. These followed previous lines but introduced a specific breakeven objective. They are laid out in paragraph 3.8 and discussed thereafter.

Deep mining

2.13. Most of BC's output is deep-mined coal. In 1987–88, to a total turnover of £4,388 million, deep-mined output contributed £3,404 million; and of a total saleable output of 96·9 million tonnes, contributed 81·8 million tonnes. During the period April 1983 to March 1988, 73 collieries were closed; over the same period colliery manpower fell from 202,669 to about 89,000 largely as a result of some 98,500 men accepting redundancy terms. There were 94 collieries at the end of 1987–88, including three new collieries in the Selby complex, which commenced production in January 1988.

2.14. New sites are being developed at present at Selby in Yorkshire and Asfordby in Leicestershire. Other sites prepared for 'green field' development are Hawkhurst in South Warwickshire and Margam in South Wales.

Opencast mining

2.15. Opencast mining represents only a limited proportion of total United Kingdom output although it makes an important contribution to BC's profits. BC's opencast production in 1987–88 was 15·1 million tonnes, contributing £702 million to turnover. However, its contribution to BC's operating profit was £252 million, compared with a loss on deep mines and related activities of £100 million. Opencast coal is of low cost and usually of high quality. BC told us that if it is to achieve its financial objectives it must rely heavily on opencast production. The significance of opencast output is not confined to its profitability and quality; high-quality opencast coal is also blended with low-quality deep-mined coal to make it saleable.

2.16. BC does not extract opencast coal itself. The extraction is carried out by private contractors, with their own workforce. We discuss opencast activities in paragraphs 4.52 to 4.56.

2.17. Deep mining was, at the start of our investigation, organized into eight Areas, each headed by an Area Director. Colliery managers report to the Area Directors through the Deputy Director (Mining). There is also a Deputy Director (Administration). A number of Area functional departments provide services to the collieries. Further reorganization has been set in motion, and from 1 January 1989 the four smaller Areas will be replaced by four Groups. These Groups will report to the Director of Group Operations. The Area Directors report, as will the Director of Group Operations, to the Operations Director, who is also Deputy Chairman. Opencast mining is operated by the Opencast Executive, which reports separately to BC's Board.

2.18. Since 1985 BC's Board has had an Executive Committee under the Chairman and attended by the Deputy Chairman and Executive Directors. Executive Director appointments include those of Technical Director, Commercial Director, Finance Director, Secretary and Industrial Relations Director. The responsibilities of the executive directors are such that, with certain minor exceptions, Heads of Headquarters departments report to them. The Commercial Director also has reporting to him BC's Marketing Department which is organized into marketing regions. BC has taken steps since 1980 to secure a significant reduction in overheads, for example by reorganization of Headquarters departments, and by reducing non-industrial staff. Overhead costs chargeable to collieries have, as a result, reduced from 1982–83 to 1987–88 by some 35 per cent in real terms in total, or by some 20 per cent in real terms per tonne of output.

Supply arrangements with the CEGB/SSEB

2.19. BC has understandings with the CEGB and the South of Scotland Electricity Board (SSEB) for the supply of coal to power stations. At Appendix 2.2 is a summary of the position as BC saw it last autumn. In the spring of 1988, the SSEB declared its intent to terminate the supply and price agreements for BC coal from 1 April 1988 unless BC made further concessions on price. BC was of the view that the SSEB had longstanding contractual commitments to take its supplies for Longannet and Cockenzie power stations from BC. It therefore took court proceedings in Scotland to prevent the SSEB from purchasing or taking any coal (other than its existing stocks) for use at these two power stations from any party other than BC. Following negotiations between the parties agreement has now been reached, without prejudice to BC's claim as to the existence of longstanding contractual commitments, for the SSEB to continue to take coal from BC during the year ending 31 March 1989. No new agreement has been reached for supplies after that date.

2.20. Supplies to BC's other major (and most of its minor) customers are made under individual contracts with BC. While these contracts incorporate BC's standard published terms and conditions, the commercial terms are negotiated in each case.

2.21. We should like to thank all those who assisted in this inquiry. We are particularly grateful to the representatives of BC on whom the main burden of the inquiry fell.

3 Objectives and business strategy

3.1. The Commission are asked in the reference (1)(c) to examine, not BC's business strategy and objectives as such, but:

(a) the contribution made by its investment programme to the strategy and objectives; and

(b) the extent to which the investment programme responds appropriately to changes in BC's strategy.

3.2. We asked BC what it saw as its dominant current objective. It replied that its central task is to 'turn an institution into a business'.

3.3. This task contrasts strongly with previous strategy and objectives. BC quoted 1973–74 and 1979–80 as important dates during the last two decades. At both these times sharp rises in oil prices led to the belief that BC would be hard put to it to dig enough coal. The emphasis was on physical output.

3.4. Since 1984–85 the Corporation's strategy has turned from physical output to financial performance. Our terms of reference thus require us to examine how responsive the investment programme, and investment projects within it, have been to this change in strategy, and what contributions the programme and investment projects have made, are making and are likely to make to achieving the current objectives. Our detailed comments on these matters are in Chapters 4 and 5: here we consider more general issues.

Current objectives and strategy
3.5. Following the disruptions of 1983 to 1985 (see paragraphs 2.9) BC was determined to reduce costs, including overheads, and to maximize output at low-cost collieries and opencast sites. Collieries which had or appeared to have no prospects of making an economic contribution would be examined under the Colliery Review Procedure. Where redundancy was necessary, BC would seek to avoid any individual being compelled to accept it.

3.6. BC considered that the most severe competition would be from imported coal. The range of pithead operating costs which would be competitive over the next 15 years was seen as being between £1·00/GJ and £1·65/GJ.

3.7. BC introduced, therefore several cost guidelines:

(a) collieries unable to produce consistently below operating costs of £1·65/GJ to be closed as soon as possible;

(b) incremental or additional output from existing collieries must have operating costs no greater than £1·00/GJ—to prevent investment in marginal output at higher cost than short-term marginal revenues; and

(c) major project expenditure would be undertaken only at collieries with operating costs below £1.50/GJ—after taking account of costs and benefits of new investment.

3.8. In March 1987, the Secretary of State for Energy settled further objectives for the industry with Sir Robert Haslam. These were, in summary

(a) to achieve financial break-even in 1988–89 after payment of interest and accrual of social grants;

(b) thereafter to generate an increasing surplus on revenue account and so increase the proportion of self-financing;

(c) to earn a satisfactory rate of return on capital and maximize profitability by concentrating on low cost production and those sales which maximized profit on a continuing basis; and

(d) to reduce the operating costs per GJ of mining activities by at least 20 per cent in real terms by 1989–90, compared with those in 1985–86.

3.9. Thus it can be seen that while after 1985 BC introduced several 'cost parameters', expressed as £ per GJ for its collieries, it was not until March 1987 that its Chairman agreed with the Government a specific, quantified target. That target was for financial break-even in 1988–89. The target represented not a change in direction but a sharpening of focus.

3.10. There were during the course of our inquiry no specific, quantified targets for the years after 1988–89 agreed with the Government. BC told us that subject to unforeseen changes in the external environment it had adopted the following specific targets for the shortfall in self-financing for the years 1988–89 to 1991–92:

	£m
1988–89	274
1989–90	283
1990–91	114
1991–92	25

3.11. BC published its 1987–88 accounts on 13 July 1988. The 1987–88 loss after interest on ordinary activities, but before exceptional restructuring costs was £152 million. This compared with the following figures for each of the previous four years:

			£ million
1983–84	*1984–85*	*1985–86*	*1986–87*
(803)	(2,065)	188 profit	(17)

Strategy and capital investment policy

3.12. Following changes in strategy and objectives since 1984–85 BC made what it has described to us as a 'radical reassessment' of its capital investment policy.

3.13. BC told us that it has particular regard to:

(a) the relationship between its capital investment policy and its overall objectives;

(b) how capital investment policy reflects its view on the future marketing position;

(c) its 'cost parameters';

(d) the required rate of return and the assessment of risk; and

(e) the determination of priorities for investment in the light of the above.

In BC's view these matters involve a fairly clear distinction between:

(a) 'capacity-related' investment in major projects in new or replacement capacity, or major changes in colliery infrastructure, where future market prospects (particularly expectations of revenue) are crucial; and

(b) 'operational' investment in plant, machinery and minor projects required for the continuing efficient operation of existing capacity, where the main emphasis is on cost reduction.

3.14. The Government's objectives for BC state clearly that the 'basic objective of BC must be to earn a satisfactory rate of return on its net assets and achieve full financial viability without Government support'. BC must bring productive capacity into line with the principles set out in the 1978 White Paper 'The Nationalised Industries' (Cmnd 7131). BC's policy on capital investment is designed to achieve these objectives.

3.15. So far as 'capacity-related' investment is concerned, BC told us that the requirement to order capital investment so as to bring productive capacity into line with a continuing share of the market under competitive conditions 'should not be interpreted simplistically', because of the range of uncertainty surrounding both the potential market volumes and the proceeds associated with such volumes.

3.16. In 1986, BC gave projections of future United Kingdom coal consumption to the Select Committee on Energy; these were:

1986 (actual)	114 mt
1990	105–115 mt
1995	105–120 mt
2000	105–130 mt

BC still regards these projections as reasonable (although it believed that fluctuations outside these ranges are possible). Within the overall figure, the electricity market will continue to dominate, with most of the range of uncertainty falling on this market, although the industrial market will show some growth if oil and gas prices are high. However, BC's own share of the total United Kingdom coal market will be determined by BC's competitiveness, and will thus be as important a determinant of BC's market volume as the level of United Kingdom coal consumption. There is, therefore, a wide range of possible outcomes in the size of BC's own market, and it would thus, BC believes, be quite impracticable to fix upon a particular level of future demand for the purpose of planning capacity and investment. BC holds, furthermore, that such an approach, even if practicable, would be contrary to its objectives, which are clearly designed to put 'money before tonnes'. BC therefore rejects the notion of planning investment to produce a given target output. As a consequence, it also rejects 'gap-ology' (ie the determination of a shortfall between projected supply and projected demand) as a procedure for determining 'capacity-related' investment.

3.17. BC's approach is, therefore, to seek to make investments which:

(a) reduce costs at existing capacity which is currently or potentially competitive; and

(b) create a new or replacement capacity which will be competitive with other fuels and imported coal.

3.18. Such an approach does not preclude giving due weight to quality considerations or other important 'marketing' factors when considering individual projects. But such arguments are essentially supportive, and are relevant only if the capacity concerned has the potential to produce at competitive cost.

3.19. As investment policy is designed to meet BC's financial objectives, rather than to produce a particular level of output, the key is to produce at economic levels of cost. But what constitutes 'economic' will depend upon the levels of competing prices, which are subject to considerable uncertainty. BC's view is that the main source of the competition (which will largely determine BC's market share) will be internationally traded coal, particularly steam coal. Here, BC believes it is essential to take a longer-term view, particularly as the present low sterling price of international steam coal is in its view not sustainable. BC's published view of the possible price range in the year 2000 is $40 to $55/tonne of 24·5 GJ (or $45 to $60/tonne of average import quality) at Rotterdam assuming an exchange rate in the range of $1·25 to $1·55. There will, of course, be considerable short-term fluctuation outside the range, both in the $ price and in the exchange rate.

3.20. Thus the industry is faced not only with a wide range of potential market volume but also a wide range of competitive costs. At the same time, although BC is actively seeking ways to increase flexibility, there are strict limits to its ability to respond to short-term fluctuations in market conditions. BC therefore has sought to establish 'robust' management rules which will allow it to follow a policy of 'minimum regret' in the face of uncertainty. In order to emphasize the overriding importance of costs, these have been expressed in terms of costs per GJ.

3.21. BC told us that in order to cope with the degree of uncertainty in competitive prices, the rules recognize that:

(a) BC is unlikely to regret *closing* capacity which cannot produce at costs competitive with sustainable world coal prices. But as that price is uncertain, and closures are generally irreversible, the criterion for the upper level of acceptable costs for closure decisions would be somewhat above the 'central' view of the sustainable world price.

(b) By contrast, *commitment of new resources* to provide new or replacement capacity is generally avoidable and may be delayed, so that the criterion for acceptable cost of 'incremental' output would be towards the bottom of the range of competitive costs; since otherwise there would be a probability that marginal cost could exceed marginal revenue, particularly over the next few years.

3.22. Accordingly, when BC's new strategy was promulgated in October 1985, the parameters laid down were (for collieries other than anthracite mines) as described in paragraph 3.7. These guide lines have not been indexed for inflation since October 1985, and have thereby tightened in 'real' terms, reflecting BC's perceptions of the increasingly competitive market environment. Furthermore, BC has been placing increasing emphasis on the £1·50/GJ parameter rather than £1·65/GJ as the *upper limit* of acceptable cost for all collieries by the end of the next five years, broadly in line with BC's central view of the value of BC output against 'sustainable' international coal prices. (Industry *average* operating costs would thus be significantly less than this.) The cost parameters relate primarily to steam coal production, which accounts for 90 per cent of total sales. Somewhat different considerations apply to naturally smokeless fuels, and certain washed domestic and industrial coals which are able to earn a degree of premium value.

3.23. The cost parameters in paragraph 3.7 have been expressed in terms of operating costs, and have been intended primarily as guidelines to Areas on the decisions to be taken during the next few years on the closure of high-cost capacity, and the selection of investment projects (particularly under delegated authority). In the case of the closure criterion, operating costs excluding interest charges represent a reasonable surrogate for 'avoidable' costs. For the greater part of investment undertaken by Areas under delegated authority, interest charges on *new* investment will be only a modest element in colliery costs, so that BC believes no significant distortion is involved (but with great merit of simplicity) in using cost parameter guidelines based on operating costs (that is, including depreciation, but excluding interest charges).

3.24. However, with large capital projects, where capital on new investment represents a significant proportion of total colliery costs on completion, it is not appropriate to use cost parameters based on operating costs. Furthermore, such projects generally have long lead times, involve strategic issues, and will be required to be submitted to Headquarters for approval. Thus, in these cases the focus will be on the colliery result after investment, where BC would aim for a cost no greater than £1·50/ GJ *including* capital charges on new expenditure at 10 per cent real rate of return. However, BC told us that in these cases meeting the cost criterion alone would not be a sufficient condition for project approval. When such major projects are considered by the Capital Investment Committee (CIC) and the Board, the major emphasis will be upon DCF appraisal, including specific risk assessment in the 'most likely' and 'pessimistic' cases.

3.25. The White Paper 'The Nationalised Industries' (Cmnd. 7131, 1978) laid down (paragraph 61) that nationalized industries should treat the opportunity cost of capital as 5 per cent in real terms before tax. However, in BC's view it is clear (paragraph 64) that this was not intended as a Test Discount Rate (TDR) for appraisal purposes, but a rate to be achieved on all investment. Indeed the

White Paper makes specific provision for the industries to adopt higher TDRs to take account of risk, appraisal optimism and the proportion of 'non-measurable' expenditure which is inevitably involved. BC's view is that the appropriate TDR for its business is 10 per cent for the colliery, and 15 per cent on the margin after risk assessment to the extent to which specific risks can be identified. (These will vary from project to project.)

3.26. The real rate of return also governs the extent to which Area Directors have delegated powers to approve capital expenditure. In the case of 'measurable' projects at a colliery, provided that there is a DCF yield of at least 10 per cent, and a current operating cost of less than £1·50/GJ, then the delegation limit is £5 million for projects with a marginal return of over 40 per cent, £3 million if the marginal rate is over 30 per cent, and £1 million if it is over 20 per cent. Less than 20 per cent marginal return would require Headquarters approval, as would projects at collieries operating at over £1·50/GJ where the colliery shows a DCF return of less than 10 per cent.

3.27. Prior to April 1988 the 'base case' in investment appraisals was calculated using current saleable proceeds, but from July 1987 this was to be reduced by 1 per cent per annum in 'real' terms over the next five years, principally in recognition of the likely effect of the terms of the CEGB Joint Understanding, with a further 1 per cent per annum reduction applied as a sensitivity test at Headquarters. From April 1988, BC decided that the 'base case' appraisal should incorporate a 2 per cent per annum reduction in real terms over the years to 1992–93 using current saleable proceeds as a base, in recognition of current uncertainties. But a variety of other contingencies are also applied to proceeds to arrive at a 'most likely' case. Further consideration of this issue will be required in the light of the proposed privatization of the ESI, including the terms of such long-term contracts as may emerge. A further 10 per cent proceeds abatement from 1990–91 against the 'most likely' case has been regarded as an appropriate sensitivity test for use in a 'pessimistic' case in project appraisal. (BC subsequently informed us that its latest practice was to base the 'pessimistic' case at a level some 20 per cent below the most 'most likely' case.)

3.28. BC told us that any determination of investment priorities needs to take account of:

(a) The degree of 'inherited' commitments from previously approved major projects.

The normal priority will be to complete such projects as quickly and effectively as possible. (However, the Annual Review procedure enables a view to be taken as to whether it is still economic to proceed with an uncompleted project.)

(b) The extent to which BC investment is of ongoing 'operational' nature, in terms of normal replacements, re-equipment of coal faces, etc.

In any given year, therefore, the scope for change in the level and composition of the investment programme is relatively limited.

3.29. Thus over the next few years, expenditure on as yet unapproved major projects and new mines will constitute at most 10 per cent of total capital expenditure. A further 30 per cent will relate to the completion of major projects already in place, particularly Selby; but the major component (approaching 50 per cent) will be represented by heavy duty face equipment, and other expenditure servicing operations at existing mines. This reflects the main order of investment priorities followed since the issue of the New Strategy from October 1985 namely:

(a) expenditure to reduce costs and increase productivity at those existing mines able to operate at competitive costs, and to sustain ongoing operations at such collieries;

(b) major projects to provide new and replacement capacity at the best of existing mines when the marginal cost of such capacity is low; and

(c) new mines capable of providing competitive output in the longer term.

3.30. BC told us that in view of the highly competitive market it faces, the policies on capital expenditure developed since the 1984–85 strike represent a significant change in emphasis. In particular:

(a) there has been explicit rejection of output targets and 'gap-ology' as a basis for capacity and investment planning;

(b) investment criteria reflect 'cost parameters' related primarily to meeting competition from imported coal;

(c) the adopted required rates of return are more akin to those required in the private sector; and

(d) a system of priorities has been designed to give greatest weight to improved performance to ensure the optimization of existing capacity.

3.31. In discussing with us its 'minimum regret' policy BC has argued that application of the policy results in investment decisions which are commercially sound in the light of the uncertainties faced by the Corporation.

3.32. We asked BC if it had used 'scenario' analysis in order to test the robustness of its policy. It said that it had employed a consultant with extensive experience of the use of scenarios in an international petrochemical company. He had advised it that in his view scenario analysis could not usefully be taken further than BC had already gone.

Future markets 3.33. BC's analysis of risks concerning, for example, the future international price of coal, and the future of the US \$/£ exchange rate, is discussed in Chapter 6. Within a discussion of strategy it seems relevant, however, to note BC's assumptions about this very important aspect of its future markets.

3.34. Discussing its future business environment BC said, about electricity privatization and coal imports:

Given the dominance of the power station market in BC's total revenue, and the currently very low (albeit unsustainable) level of the sterling price of international coal, the major potential threat to BC's position is large-scale imports of steam coal by the ESI, leading to reductions in both sales volume and revenue per tonne. It is in this context that the privatization of the ESI has to be considered. BC has argued that it will be in the commercial interest of both BC and the ESI to establish long-term contractual arrangements for coal supplies, to take the place of the present Joint Understanding with the CEGB. This is far and away the most important strategic issue in BC's business environment.

3.35. BC's evidence to the Select Committee on Energy is reproduced at Appendix 3.1. The Corporation told us that although the memorandum pre-dates the publication of the Government's White Paper on Privatizing Electricity, it represented a considered statement of the implications of ESI privatization for the United Kingdom coal industry, in the light of the information available at the time of the Government White Paper.

BC's privatization 3.36. We asked BC if it had taken any decisions concerning its own announced privatization. It said it had not, since the Government's intentions had been expressed only recently, and in very general terms.

Conclusions

3.37. Our terms of reference do not require us to comment on BC's business strategy as such. They require us rather (1)(c) to investigate and report on whether it could improve its performance with regard to:

(a) the investment programme's contribution to strategy; and

(b) the responsiveness of the programme to changes in strategy.

In March 1987, the Secretary of State for Energy agreed the objectives with Sir Robert Haslam which are recorded in paragraph 3.8. BC told us that the current objectives are in marked contrast to those of 15 years earlier, when strategy was centred on physical output, and that they represent a major effort to 'turn an institution into a business'.

3.38. On BC's own evidence the process of changing the 'culture' of the Corporation from 'tonnes to money' is not yet complete. The dominant current objective of achieving financial break-even in the present year dramatizes the change needed in BC's thinking. From examining the relationship between strategy and investment we have concluded that BC has been right to dramatize its objectives in this way.

3.39. While accepting, however, that a simply-stated financial objective has advantages in focusing attention on the need for short-term financial achievement, we think that BC should now commit itself firmly to specific, quantified financial objectives for the next five years. BC is reluctant to commit itself publicly to specific targets for revenue and costs, but has developed internal targets for reducing the shortfall in self-financing for the years 1988–89 to 1991–92. The figures show an improvement from a shortfall of £274 million in 1988–89 to one of £25 million in 1991–92, with self-sufficiency reached in the following year. All investment projects, and the investment programme as a whole, should be related to these targets.

3.40. But commitment to those targets, while a very important discipline, should not be used as an excuse for ceasing the search for greater improvement. BC's stated policy of 'minimum regret' for investment decisions properly, in our view, concentrates short-term attention on cost reduction at existing mines. But such a concentration, together with the emphasis on revenue costs rather than on investment opportunities which flows from the target of breaking even in 1988–89, could lead to the avoidance of bold decisions, the lack of which might be regretted in the longer-term future.

3.41. The minimum regret policy can be meaningful only if decisions to proceed and not to proceed are carefully examined in the light of a sufficiently wide range of possible future situations. We are not convinced that BC has examined sufficiently early an adequate range of possibilities for a future which includes ESI privatization and the intended privatization of BC. If the five-year targets to which it commits itself are indeed to be robust, BC must now think more imaginatively about the ways in which things can go wrong (in terms of its earlier assumptions) and what it could then do to get back on course.

3.42. BC's view is that the appropriate Test Discount Rate for its business is 10 per cent for colliery results, and 15 per cent on the margin, after risk assessment, for individual projects. We recognize the practical difficulties involved in establishing the relationship between these rates and the rate of return of 5 per cent which BC is required to maintain on all its investment. We are satisfied, however, that BC currently applies these 10 per cent and 15 per cent discount rates, and that the proportion of its investment programme to which these rates apply is sufficiently large to ensure that an average return of at least 5 per cent is achieved on its new investments.

4 Planning, policy and the capital investment programme

BC's planning cycle

4.1. Following the 1984–85 strike, BC changed its national planning arrangements. There is now an annual cycle which starts in the spring of one year with the Strategic Planning Conference, and concludes in the spring of the next with the delivery to the Secretary of State of the Investment and Financing Review (IFR). Table 4.1 shows the timing of this cycle.

TABLE 4.1 **BC's business planning cycle**

	Key event	Timing
1.	Investment and Financing Review	April/May
2.	Strategic Planning Conference	March/May
3.	Strategic planning exercise	June/July
	(a) Capital Investment Committee reviews with Areas their strategic plans	August/September
	(b) Strategy paper to Executive Committee	October
4.	Five-year Business Plan exercise	October/November
	(a) Five-year Business Plan paper to Executive Committee	November
5.	Area Budgets prepared	December/January
	(a) Area Budgets paper to Board	February/March
6.	Investment and Financing Review	April/May

Source: BC.

4.2. BC told us that the process was essentially iterative, and continuous. We consider below the main elements of the system.

4.3. The Strategic Planning Conference is a two-day conference with a particular theme—the 1987 conference theme was 'to increase the awareness of the prevailing and likely future environment...and...the need for correct and adequate planning...'. Attendance varies—the Area Chief Engineers attended the 1987 conference, but not the 1988 conference, which Area Accountants went to—but always includes all full-time Board members, heads of Headquarters departments and other key Headquarters staff, and Area Directors. Speakers at the conference may include, for example, experts on the world coal situation. The general thrust of the conferences has been to impress on Area Directors the need to cut costs and become increasingly self-financing.

4.4. Following this conference, the Technical Director takes the lead in preparing a paper for the Executive Committee, recommending the approach to be taken in the following planning exercise, and taking up the themes of the conference. In 1988, this paper concluded that:

(a) There are abundant world-wide coal reserves of good quality which can be produced at low cost.

(b) The volume of internationally-traded steam coal would increase significantly in the years to 1995.

(c) Various exercises indicated that, by 1995, the 'sustainable' price of internationally-traded seaborne coal would be of the order of £1·25/GJ (1987 prices) (at 1·40$/£).

(d) The effect on BC's prices would be determined by the outcome of current negotiations with the ESI as to its post-privatization commercial relationship.

(e) The 1987 Area Business Plans, while moving in the right direction, projected operating costs of production which would be insufficient to achieve the Corporation's objectives even if the negotiations with the ESI successfully established the long-term contracts BC preferred. Average operating costs would need to be reduced to around £1·20/£1·25 per GJ by the early 1990s.

(f) The present BC cost parameter guidelines relating to closure action and the allocation of capital investment required strengthening, and rigidly enforcing, to achieve the levels of operating costs called for in the early 1990s.

The paper recommended the adoption of the instructions to Areas described in paragraph 4.6.

4.5. The Strategic Planning Exercise follows the Strategic Planning Conference. In June the Areas are asked to prepare their five-year business strategies. The instructions reflect the discussion on the Technical Director's paper to the Executive Committee.

4.6. In 1988, the instructions to Areas expressed satisfaction with the progress made towards achieving objectives, confirmed the policy direction, and the need to continue the drive to maximize output from low-cost collieries and to reduce costs. Areas and other formations were required to prepare possible business strategies for the five years to 1993–94 plus further spot years. The paper reaffirmed commitment to the BC objectives (see paragraph 3.8); it looked for cost reductions over and above those in the 1987 Area Business Plans. The following guidelines were provided:

(a) *Associated with colliery viability*
    (i) £1·50/GJ should be regarded as the upper limit of acceptable operating cost for long-life collieries;

    (ii) all collieries (with the exception of anthracite collieries) should plan to achieve operating costs of no more than £1·50/GJ within the next two years (ie this level of cost should be achieved in 1990–91 or earlier);

    (iii) if any colliery was unable to achieve the criteria at (ii), after consideration of all means of reducing costs, reasons should be given for the colliery's inability to meet this requirement; and

    (iv) all collieries should plan to achieve year on year cost reductions per GJ of *at least* 2 per cent in the planning period up to 1993–94 (inclusive).

(b) *Associated with capital investment*
Except for projects which were essential for safety reasons:
    (v) no capital should be allocated to collieries (other than anthracite mines) unable to achieve operating costs of no more than £1·50/GJ within the next two years;

    (vi) at collieries likely to exhaust before 1995, capital spending should be restricted to that required to maintain efficient operations until closure;

    (vii) new major investment should be directed only to those long-life collieries clearly capable of producing at or below £1·50/GJ bottom-line (ie after capital charges, including interest) after taking account of the benefits and the additional costs associated with this new investment; and

(viii) where assets were not directly associated with the efficient extraction of coal, eg commercial road transport vehicles or surface mobile plant, Areas should evaluate the option of buying in the services on contract, or by some alternative means, and pursue that option where this would be economically attractive to BC.

Areas were particularly asked to consider, as means of reducing unit costs, maximizing output to spread fixed costs, extension of retreat working, increased shield support/heavy duty equipment, reducing Area overheads and looking for opportunities for demanning. Areas were recommended to adopt a 'top-down' planning approach in assessing the prospects of individual collieries as follows:

(a) calculating how much income (expressed as saleable proceeds) would be obtained if all the production were sold and there were a 'real' reduction in prices of 2 per cent per annum;

(b) from this, calculating how much could be spent on production, ensuring that all essential commitments (including capital charges) were met and the mine still be at least viable;

(c) Areas were asked to draw up a plan to do this; and then to consider how it could be improved to generate surplus revenue to make the mine increasingly self-financing.

The Areas were also asked to explore for each colliery alternative ways, employing major capital projects or major changes in shifting or working patterns, which might achieve substantial additional low-cost output or significant cost reductions, and which should then, if appropriate, form the basis for alternative plans for the colliery.

4.7. After these business strategies have been prepared, special meetings of the CIC are held with each Area. These deal with the Area submissions pit by pit. The plans for each individual colliery, including those for investment, are discussed. Discussion may include approval of items which would be within the Area Director's delegated authority but for the £1·50/GJ rule or the requirement to provide 500,000 tonnes per annum from a heavy duty project (see paragraph 5.30 for details of delegated authority). Following these meetings, Headquarters issues a Headquarters Strategic Plan which shows the planned capital investment programme for the next five years. Adjustments made to Area submissions by Headquarters staff tend to change the time profile of investment by reducing the investment programme in earlier years and increasing it in later years.

4.8. This analysis of forward investment forms the basis of the paper on Business Strategy by the Technical Director to the Executive Committee in October. This, in 1987, discussed the approach to capital investment and coal-producing capacity and, in particular, raised the question of how the proposed privatization of the ESI might affect future revenues.

4.9. In October the Areas are informed of their provisional capital allocations for the following year, and asked to submit their five-year business plans, comprising Area profit and loss accounts, colliery projections (operating costs, operating profit, operating costs per GJ, sales output, overall OMS, average manpower, overall man-shifts), and revised capital expenditure requirements. These are aggregated at Headquarters, and this forms the basis for a paper, normally by the Finance and Technical Directors, in November to the Executive Committee on the Corporation's business plan. This paper looks at financial prospects, comparisons with the previous IFR, and considers the External Financing Limit (EFL).

4.10. In December, Areas are asked to prepare their budgets for the following year, with projections for the year after that. The request to Areas to prepare their budgets indicates how these should vary from (eg by showing better performance than) the first two years of the business plan. The minimum objective for each Area for the following year is specified in terms of (for deep mining) minimum colliery profit, maximum operating cost/GJ, maximum end-year manpower, minimum

OMS, and (for opencast) minimum mining profit and licensed mine royalties, at current pay and price levels. Other management units also prepare similar documents. Discussions follow between the Operations Director and each of the Area Directors in which improvements and other changes are identified and agreed. This normally forms the basis for a paper to the Corporation by the Operations and Finance Directors, seeking agreement for the budget for the forthcoming year, and for the final budgets notified to Areas.

4.11. On the basis of the budgets and business plans, the Finance Director and the Technical Director prepare a paper to the Board, proposing the IFR to be submitted to the Secretary of State. In 1987, this paper set out BC's five-year Business Plan to 1991–92, which formed the basis of the IFR submission, and the principles of corporate strategy lying behind the business plan. It outlined: progress since the strike; the way in which the shortcomings of the Area Business Plans submitted the previous autumn were to be remedied, so that BC achieved the targets it had set itself; an assessment of the risks affecting the plan, notably in respect of the market for steam coal and in respect of manpower productivity; and the principles of the cost parameters applying to collieries. Subsequently the IFR is prepared and presented to the Secretary of State, for his agreement.

The function of the planning cycle

4.12. The planning system thus provides a means of dialogue between Headquarters and Areas about what action to take at each colliery, placed in a five-year context. We were told that collieries are essentially cost centres (although profit and loss accounts are prepared, in which operating profit and profit after depreciation and capital charges are computed for each colliery; we describe the construction of the profit and loss accounts in more detail in paragraphs 7.30 and 7.31) and that Areas are an administratively convenient way of aggregating them. Areas' organizations can take care of regional aspects, and be aware of local issues; Areas have a 'team building' function. BC told us that the organizational tension in the planning process between Areas and Headquarters favours critical examination of plans, and encourages proposals for new investment.

Colliery plans

4.13. The business plans prepared for each colliery are consistent with, and based on, the plans for physical progress at each colliery. These plans include:

(a) action programmes for the next at least six and usually eight quarters, reviewed quarterly on a rolling basis;

(b) medium-term plans covering five years, reviewed annually, involving face layouts and the resources required; and

(c) long-term plans (up to 20 years) which are reviewed annually, and cover physical factors and reserves.

4.14. These plans are prepared for the colliery managers by Area planners, reporting to the Area Chief Mining Engineer. The colliery action programmes set out the colliery managers' short-term physical objectives. In the longer term, plans are needed to replace current faces, as they are exhausted, with new faces, and thereafter to develop new districts of the mine. This requires capital investment, for example to develop new drivages, and install new transport systems. These decisions are the subject of five-year and long-term plans. In this process, one of the key decisions is how to access a complete new seam of coal. Usually a number of alternative means of doing this will be assessed, and the chosen scheme will become the subject of a capital investment project.

Manpower planning

4.15. Whether in relation to normal manning requirements or a specific investment project manpower planning is a required element in the overall planning process. BC's 'preferred' system of manpower planning, dating from 1981, was designed as a manual system but has been adapted for use with personal computers.

4.16. Standard job plans are produced for each colliery which take into account any proposed manpower savings and efficiency schemes. After making allowances for projected non-attendance effects, estimates of manpower requirements by skills are derived from these standard job plans. Having identified the needs of individual collieries by skill, Area plans for recruitment, wastage and other action are produced to ensure that the manpower needed, by skills, is provided. Computer models have been produced in conjunction with the ORE to assist particularly in the production of recruitment and training programmes.

4.17. We understand that work study techniques are not universally employed in determining standards for each new face or operations planned, although projected manning standards are derived from method study investigations and/or synthetic data, taking into account the current best practice in similar installations or operations.

Assessing the business environment

4.18. The planning cycle described above does not call upon Areas to make any assessment of the external business environment. Areas are advised to assume that all the collieries' output can be sold, and are informed by Headquarters of the price they should assume they will get for their products. The various phases of the planning cycle at Area level are concerned only with the relationship of costs, revenue and capital investment, and the ability to achieve profitability targets, on a colliery-by-colliery basis.

4.19. Headquarters departments are responsible for aspects of planning to do with the examination of the future business environment. This includes consideration of such things as international coal price, United Kingdom coal consumption in the long term, the internationalization of the energy market, interchangeability between fuels and between suppliers, and the relationship between competing prices and BC's cost structure. Studies relating to the business environment in a longer time-scale (eg up to and beyond five years) are carried out as and when required. We were told that the review of the external environment was a continuous process, with the emphasis changing as circumstances dictate; but that the position was formally reviewed at the beginning of the annual planning round.

4.20. Formal statements on these matters are prepared from time to time. The results of work of this kind are presented in different ways. Public statements, such as a presentation on coal consumption to the Select Committee on Energy, are an example of this. Such statements are discussed by the Commercial Director and the Deputy Chairman prior to publication. In other cases papers on particular subjects are provided to the Executive Committee, or sometimes to one Director.

Headquarters organization of planning

4.21. A number of Headquarters departments are involved in the corporate planning process:

(a) The Commercial Director, the Finance Director and the Technical Director are the directors principally involved in the preparation of formal business plans. The Deputy Chairman and Operations Director is also involved, but primarily in that part of the planning process (notably budgets) which has a time-scale of up to two years. We were told that the Technical Director has the main responsibility for strategy formulation.

(b) The Economics and Statistics Unit and the Marketing Department jointly have responsibility for instigating and carrying out work on the medium/long-term business environment. Within the Technical Department, the Environment and Planning Branch is responsible to the Technical Director for the business planning cycle, and for working out aspects of policy related to deep mine operations.

(c) The Finance Department has responsibility for financial evaluation including estimates of profitability and cash requirements of the overall industry plans.

(d) Other departments such as the Coal Research Establishment, the ORE, and the Industrial Relations Department also provide inputs as required.

Contribution to strategy

4.22. BC told us that the business planning cycle was the main means by which the investment programme was made to follow the strategy. It was also one of the means by which BC was changing the culture at mine manager level and above. We were told that the members of the Board were dedicated to making BC a business. Certainly the most senior management were dedicated in the same way. We were told:

> It would be foolish to pretend that we had converted everybody. On the other hand, I think we have everybody working towards it, which is perhaps more important. You may not be able to get them all to believe in it, but as long as they are all doing it that perhaps is a bit more important than belief.

The strategy conferences provide opportunities for ways of cutting costs and increasing productivity to be brought forward by Headquarters or Areas for discussion. Such methods currently include retreat mining, the use of heavy duty equipment, and increasing the number of shifts worked. The strategy conferences' messages are reinforced by conferences held at the staff college for Technical and Operations staff. For example, during the period of our inquiry, each colliery manager attended one of a series on the subject of 'breaking even'.

4.23. We asked BC how it expected its junior managers to be aware of the BC strategy. We were told:

> I want the colliery manager, when he is planning the next face or the next series of faces, to be aware of the planning environment in which he is working, but once he is working on his faces there is only one way for him to go and that is to run those machines as hard as he can.

BC also told us:

> I would not want the under-manager of the colliery to be concerned about strategy at all. As far as I am concerned he is there to operate the suite of machines we pay him to operate. I do not want him arguing he wants a different suite of machines, arguing we should be doing different things strategically. I want him just to be driving those machines as hard as he can drive them, with the minimum of resources.

Organizational changes

4.24. In the course of our inquiry, BC decided that for the four smaller Areas, the remaining productive capacity could no longer justify an Area administrative structure like that of the larger Areas. BC was therefore transferring two collieries to a larger Area and placing the remaining collieries into four groups: Scottish, North-East, North-West, and South Wales. Although there are to be small group staffs, increased self-sufficiency in services is to be sought at the larger collieries, and, to the extent that additional services are required, collieries are to rely directly on Headquarters services. The four groups and Betteshanger Colliery in Kent are to report to a Director of Group Operations, himself reporting, as do Area Directors, to the Deputy Chairman and Operations Director. This new arrangement will come into force on 1 January 1989. The exact arrangements in respect of corporate planning are still being worked out but, broadly, the Director of Group Operations and his four groups will be expected to play the part the Area organization has done up to now, but with the collieries playing a bigger part in preparing their strategy plans, business planning proposals and budgets.

The Capital Investment Programme

4.25. Recent capital expenditure by BC together with its future planned expenditure is summarized in Figure 4.1. BC's capital expenditure over the last six years is given in Table 4.2, which shows it broken down into the main categories.

TABLE 4.2 **BC: capital expenditure by category, 1982–83 to 1987–88**

£ million in constant 1987–88 prices*

	New mines	*Major projects†*	*Heavy duty‡*	*Other§*	*Open-cast*	*Total*	*Non-mining expen-diture*	*Deferred interest*	*Total fixed assets*	*Total fixed assets: out-turn prices*
		Mining expenditure								
1982–83	204	292	53	390	13	952	14	106	1,072	857
1983–84	165	228	40	331	11	775	7	75	857	717
1984–85	64	61	67	222	9	423	10	7	440	387
1985–86	109	143	74	297	17	640	9	59	708	659
1986–87	149	143	58	229	19	598	7	71	676	650
1987–88	184	133	91	155	8	571	8	68	647	647
Total	875	1,000	383	1,624	77	3,959	55	386	4,400	3,917
Percentage of total	22·1	25·3	9·7	41·0	1·9	100				

Source: MMC, based on data from BC.

* Deflated using the Retail Prices Index.

† Projects costing over £0·5 million (other than new mines and heavy duty) and requiring Headquarters approval.

‡ Heavy duty powered roof supports and other heavy duty equipment.

§ Projects (other than heavy duty projects) requiring Area approval, including drivages (to access new reserves in existing seams), plant and equipment and surface works.

4.26. Capital expenditure on new mine projects has increased as a proportion of the total. In the mid-1970s it was less than 5 per cent, but in the mid-1980s it averaged about 22 per cent (see Figure 4.2). By 1987–88, largely because of spending on the Selby Complex, the figure had risen to 32 per cent and was the largest category of expenditure in that year. Expenditure on the heavy duty programme has also risen in recent years, from less than 6 per cent in 1982–83 to almost 16 per cent in 1987–88.

4.27. Area-approved projects have accounted for the bulk of the capital expenditure programme, though the proportion has declined from over 40 per cent in 1982–83 to 27 per cent by 1987–88. The proportion of the programme accounted for by major projects (other than new mines) declined considerably up to 1984–85 and, while there has been some increase since then, it is still below that seen in the early 1980s.

4.28. BC distinguishes between projects according to whether or not they are required to give a marginal DCF yield (see paragraph 5.31). For example, investment needed to ensure continued safety standards at a mine would not be required to show a financial return. Projects such as these, which are not required to yield certain minimum rates of return, account, we were told, for some 15 to 20 per cent of BC's annual capital investment expenditure. The remainder of its investment programme is required to meet the rates of return standards set by BC (see paragraph 3.25).

4.29. The capital expenditure figures broken down by Area are given in Table 4.3 and shown in Figure 4.3. By far the greatest proportion of BC's capital expenditure by Area is accounted for by the North Yorkshire Area (in which the Selby Complex is located). This Area accounted for over 44 per cent of BC's capital expenditure during 1982–83 and 1983–84, and for 33 per cent in 1987–88 (in 1987–88 the North Yorkshire Area accounted for about 17 per cent of BC's deep-mined saleable output).

FIGURE 4.1

British Coal—Capital Expenditure by Category of Mining Activity, 1982–83 to 1992–93

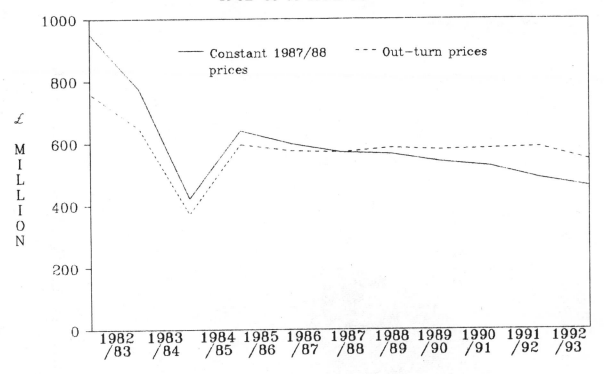

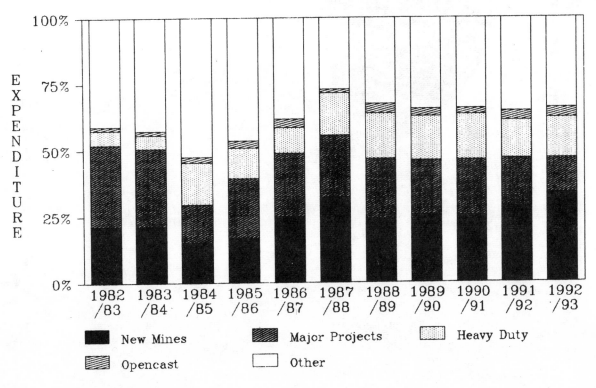

Source: MMC, based on BC data.

182588 D

FIGURE 4.2

British Coal: Mining Activities
Capital Expenditure by Category 1982–83 to 1987–88

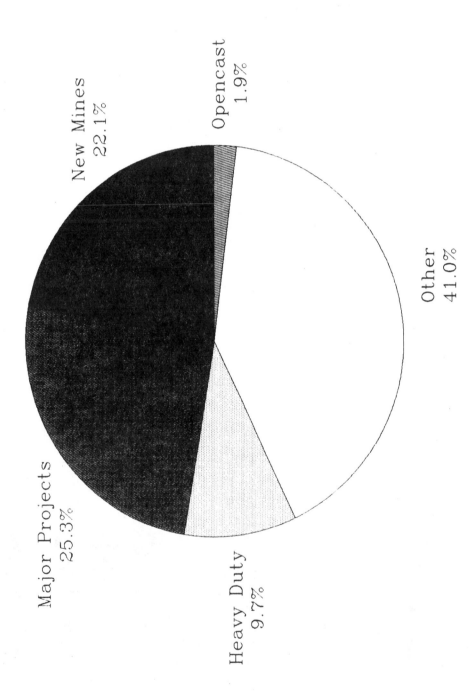

Opencast
1.9%

New Mines
22.1%

Other
41.0%

Major Projects
25.3%

Heavy Duty
9.7%

Total Expenditure at 1987/88 prices:£3959m

Source: MMC, based on BC data.

FIGURE 4.3

British Coal
Capital Expenditure by Area 1982–83 to 1987–88

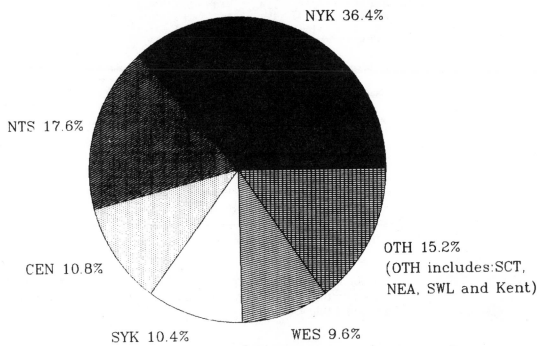

NYK 36.4%

NTS 17.6%

OTH 15.2%
(OTH includes:SCT,
NEA, SWL and Kent)

CEN 10.8%

SYK 10.4%   WES 9.6%

Total Expenditure at 1987/88 prices:£3721.5m

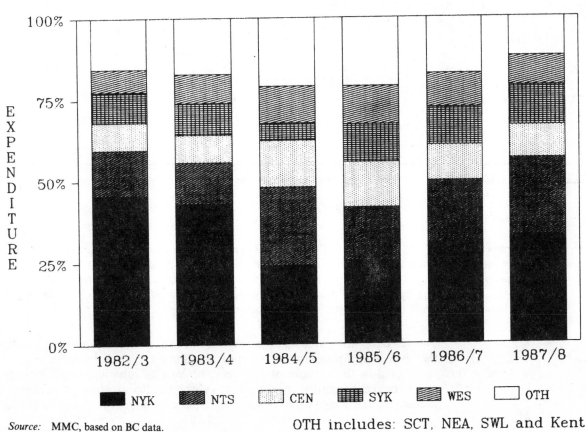

OTH includes: SCT, NEA, SWL and Kent

Table 4.3 BC: capital expenditure by Area

£ million at constant 1987–88 prices*

	SCT	NEA	NYK	SYK	NTS	CEN	WES	SWL	KENT	Total
1982–83	42·3	48·4	415·8	85·7	126·5	76·4	63·2	36·2	—	894·5
1983–84	37·2	45·7	319·6	71·4	93·7	63·2	66·2	28·4	—	725·4
1984–85	28·9	13·4	94·6	20·7	92·5	56·0	44·2	22·0	—	372·3
1985–86	24·9	35·3	158·3	71·2	100·4	86·6	72·6	48·5	2·9	600·7
1986–87	16·1	31·7	182·2	68·3	111·1	63·8	60·7	35·8	3·0	572·7
1987–88	19·6	21·6	183·9	68·1	130·7	55·9	50·3	25·0	0·8	555·9
Total: £m	169·0	196·1	1,354·4	385·4	654·9	401·9	357·2	195·9	6·7	3,721·5
Total: %	4·5	5·3	36·4	10·4	17·6	10·8	9·6	5·2	0·2	

Other than identified to Areas (ie opencast, HQ, non-mining, deferred interest and leasing)	678·5
	4,400·5

Cost of production, 1987–88

£/GJ	2·53	1·48	1·60	1·62	1·49	1·60	1·64	2·31	2·43	1·65

Source: MMC, based on data from BC.

*Deflated by using the Retail Price Index.

4.30. BC's investment plan, revised each year in its business plan, covers a period up to five years ahead. Its latest capital investment expenditure plans are given in Table 4.4.

TABLE 4.4 BC: planned capital expenditure by category, 1988–89 to 1992–93*

£ million at September 1987 prices

Year	Mining expenditure						Non-mining expen-diture	Deferred interest	Total fixed assets	Total fixed assets: estimated out-turn prices
	New mines	Major projects	Heavy duty	Other	Open-cast	Total				
1988–89	136·9	126·0	97·2	184·2	20·1	564·4	24·5	39·1	628·0	650·0
1989–90	138·0	110·0	90·0	186·3	15·4	539·7	21·0	46·1	606·8	650·0
1990–91	133·0	110·0	90·0	180·7	12·1	525·8	20·7	39·8	586·3	650·0
1991–92	138·6	88·0	70·0	172·2	17·0	485·8	18·8	40·0	544·6	624·9
1992–93	155·0	60·0	70·0	157·5	17·0	459·5	18·7	27·0	505·2	600·0
Total: £m	701·5	494·0	417·2	880·9	81·6	2,575·2	103·7	192·0	2,870·9	3,174·9
Total as a per cent:										
1988–93	27·2	19·2	16·2	34·2	3·2	100				
1982–87	22·1	25·3	9·7	41·0	1·9	100				

Source: MMC, based on data from BC.

*Planned expenditure as at October 1987. Categories of expenditure are as explained in the notes to Table 4.2.

The responsiveness of the investment programme to the strategy

4.31. We asked BC for evidence as to the responsiveness of the investment programme to the strategy, notably in respect of the balance as between cost reduction, new capacity at existing mines, and new mines (see paragraph 3.29) and in respect of the allocation of capital investment at collieries according to the operating cost criteria (see paragraph 3.7).

4.32. BC pointed out that the scope for change in the level and composition of the investment programme is relatively limited. When business plans were considered in the autumn of any year, because of inherited commitments and operational expenditure, BC was effectively committed to about 80 per cent of the immediate following year expenditure, 75 per cent of year two, and 70 per cent of year three. In response to our request, BC examined the 18 major projects approved at Headquarters since 1985. Twelve of these projects were within the first priority category, ie to reduce costs and increase productivity at those existing mines able to operate at competitive costs, and to sustain ongoing operations at such collieries. The remaining six projects were within the second priority category, ie to provide new and replacement capacity at the best of existing mines where the marginal cost of such capacity is low; three of these projects involved the expansion of output, as follows:

TABLE 4.5   **Projects approved at Headquarters involving expansion of output 1985–86 to August 1988**

	Project cost £m	Incremental tonnage '000 tonnes	Operating cost of incremental tonnage £/GJ	Total colliery operating cost £/GJ
Harworth	22·2	350	0·65	1·12
Daw Mill	23·0	500	0·72	1·04
Silverdale	32·5	300	0·67	1·17

Source: BC.

These three projects are expected to provide incremental output at well under £1/GJ at collieries with low operating costs. The remaining three projects were for creation of replacement capacity at collieries with operating costs less than £1·50/GJ.

4.33. On major projects approved since the new strategy was introduced, the total approved costs had been as follows:

TABLE 4.6   **Categories of projects approved at Headquarters 1985–86 — August 1988**

	1985–86	1986–87	1987–88	£ million 1988–89 to August
Category 1	29	56	26	—
Category 2	54	—	45	33

Source: BC.

The category 2 projects approved in 1987–88 and 1988–89 are the ones shown in the previous table, producing very low-cost coal.

4.34. BC also pointed to its investment in heavy duty equipment; this had enabled the large reduction in faces to be achieved with the consequential reduction in manpower particularly at the face and increases in output per face. The effect had been to double investment in heavy duty equipment (an average of £35 million per annum in the three years to 1983–84 and £70 million per annum in the three years to 1987–88).

4.35. Of the 18 major projects referred to in paragraph 4.32, 17, to a total project cost of £221·1 million, were at collieries with operating costs of £1·50/GJ and below. The one above £1·50/GJ, Sutton Manor, had been approved prior to the cost criteria becoming policy: the colliery had since improved its operating costs to £1·30/GJ and was planned to remain below £1·50/GJ. BC said it believed this analysis showed the extent to which its overall strategy had been reflected in the decisions on capital expenditure taken since 1985.

Efficient use of manpower

4.36. The balance of investment between new mines and existing mines is affected, *inter alia*, by the efficient use of manpower. In this section we consider general issues: manpower issues relating to specific capital projects are covered in Chapter 5, and manpower planning has already been considered in paragraphs 4.15 to 4.18.

Productivity 4.37. We here consider the recent changes and potential for further improvement in manpower productivity. BC has provided us with information on the large improvements in labour productivity which have been achieved since 1982–83[1]. It states that the main reason for the growth in productivity has been improved performance at the collieries which were in production both in 1982–83 and 1987–88. Between 1982–83 and 1987–88 there was a 48·4 per cent improvement in overall labour productivity. Of this 34·5 per cent was through improvements in productivity at continuing collieries and only 11·9 per cent followed from the change in mix as collieries closed. The change is shown in Table 4.7:

TABLE 4.7 **Labour productivity at continuing collieries** *(average over year)*

	1982–83	1985–86	1986–87	1987–88
OMS (tonnes)	2·71	3·01	3·46	3·69

Source: BC.

4.38. BC told us that the main factors which brought about this improvement were the increase in the provision of new shield support (heavy duty) installations, the concentration on fewer faces and an increase in the proportion of retreat faces. Tables 4.8 and 4.9 illustrate these developments:

TABLE 4.8 **Heavy duty faces** *(at fiscal year end)*

	1982–83	1985–86	1986–87	1987–88
Total faces (number)	574	381	305	246
HD faces (number)	32	87	119	117
% HD to total	6	23	39	48

Daily output per face (tonnes) *(average over year)*

	1982–83	1985–86	1986–87	1987–88
Conventional	711	766	900	1,003
Heavy duty	1,390	1,393	1,459	1,496

Source: BC.

TABLE 4.9 **Faces worked (at fiscal year end)**

	1982–83	1985–86	1986–87	1987–88
Advance	454	278	202	155
Retreat	120	103	103	91
Total	574	381	305	246
% retreat to total	21	27	34	37

Daily output per face (tonnes) (average over year)

	1982–83	1985–86	1986–87	1987–88
Advance	710	809	984	1,106
Retreat	872	1,042	1,260	1,385

Source: BC.

4.39. These developments are also summarized in Appendix 4.1 (Key Supply Indicators). It will be seen that in relative terms output and performance have been maintained or improved with fewer collieries, fewer faces and a greatly reduced manpower.

---

[1] See in paragraphs 7.78 to 7.81 for BC's measurement of capital productivity.

4.40. The reduction in the number of faces has the effect of reducing the supporting manpower requirements EBG and it will be seen that the improvements in face productivity are not fully matched by the improvements in overall productivity (Appendix 4.1). OMS at the face has improved by 61 per cent whereas overall OMS has improved by only 48 per cent. The difference is due to the large number of EBG and surface workers required to support those at the face. Estimates of productivity improvement in the cases we studied showed the same effect.

4.41. Although BC has reduced overall numbers EBG it has not been able to reduce the proportion (said to be 38 per cent but in some of our studies over 50 per cent of man-shifts were EBG). BC told us that the effect of some technical change is to reduce the face manpower proportion; and that health and safety considerations affect the ability to reduce EBG manpower.

4.42. Reducing travelling time by improving transport to remote faces, as in the North-Eastern (undersea) collieries, will increase actual machine working time per shift but only by increasing shift lengths could further improvements in efficiency be achieved.

4.43. Scope for further improvements in productivity exists, notably through further reduction in the number of faces, investment in heavy duty installations and retreat faces, reduced absence levels and reduced EBG manning. BC told us that it has not been able to establish satisfactory relationships with the NUM or with NACODS since the end of the strike. This has inhibited progress in developments such as flexible working and in achieving the full commitment of the workforce. On the other hand BC has nothing but praise for the way the workforce has accepted new technology.

Flexible working   4.44. We were told that new mines would go ahead only on the basis of an agreement with the trade unions on six-day working. BC has concluded that for new mines the most appropriate working pattern identified to date would be on a four-team, four-week roster of six days each week, with three teams working and one off in any week. BC calls this 'classical' flexible working.

4.45. 'Classical' flexible working is based on the following principles:

(*a*) the yearly contracted hours/man will remain the same;

(*b*) changes in shift times for individuals should be kept to a minimum;

(*c*) 'teams' should be kept together as much as possible;

(*d*) no man should normally work more than six consecutive shifts in any one week; and

(*e*) roster systems should be as simple as possible, and the 'roster cycle' should be as short as possible.

4.46. The four-team system would require up to a third more men. The benefits of 'classical' flexible working would come, BC argues, not from increases in manpower productivity, but from spreading the fixed revenue costs over a higher tonnage and from increased capital productivity. The greatest benefit would therefore be in new mine situations where the capital costs are very high.

4.47. BC told us that 'classical' flexible working at about 10 to 15 existing pits would also be worthwhile. Some seven mtpa might be produced in this way at low operating cost, thus reducing BC's average unit costs and improving its competitiveness, enabling it to sell more into the United Kingdom market. If, after exploiting all the practical opportunities to expand its United Kingdom market, BC found it still had available a significant tonnage, it would explore the scope to sell profitably into the European steam coal market. [

Details omitted. See note on page iv.   ]

4.48. We asked BC to provide us with details of how much coal, at what incremental cost and with what additional employment, would be achieved through 'classical' flexible working at these 10 to 15 mines. BC told us that its initial drive was aimed at securing agreement to 'classical' flexible working for new mines only, and in all the circumstances, did not regard any other approach as practical at present. [

Details omitted. See note on page iv.

]

4.49. BC stated that major constraints to the application of various forms of flexible working have been the existing five-day week agreement, legislation (the Coal Mines Regulation Act, 1908, as amended), which limits the underground shift to 7·5 hours plus one winding time, and the requirements for major maintenance (some statutory).

4.50. In the major capital investment projects we studied we found the issue of flexible working formally covered only at Margam and Asfordby, which are new mine situations, as a condition of approval, and at Harworth in the initial submissions. In other cases we were told that the issue was not relevant at the time of project submission and approval.

Sources of coal other than from deep mines

4.51. We examined the potential for supplying additional tonnage to the United Kingdom market from opencast mines and from imports.

Opencast

4.52. In England and Wales, the Opencast Executive is responsible for exploration, site selection and development, land acquisition, and supervision of mining activities and site restoration. In Scotland, this is the responsibility of the Scottish Area. They contract civil engineering firms to carry out the mining operations. BC also licenses other companies (licensed operators) to develop smaller sites. The total output of these licensed opencast operators in 1987–88 was just over two million tonnes. BC's opencast production for the past four years has been as follows:

TABLE 4.10. **BC opencast output, 1984–85 to 1987–88**

	1984–85	1985–86	1986–87	1987–88
Output (million tonnes)	13·6	14·1	13·3	15·1

Source: BC.

In the United Kingdom, most of the mines are to be found in a number of relatively populous areas. Many opencast sites are of relatively small annual output (about 0·25 million tonnes) and of short duration (about four to five years' production life). Approximately 50 sites are needed to maintain production at the present level of 15 million tonnes, and a fifth to a quarter of all sites have to be replaced every year.

4.53. BC told us that the constraints on expansion of opencast capacity lie in a mixture of logistic and environmental difficulties and that recently even the maintenance of existing output levels has proved very difficult because of the problems involved in obtaining planning permission. During 1987–88, the Housing and Planning Act 1986 came into force and removed the need to obtain an authorization for new sites from the Secretary of State for Energy. New sites require approval from either the county council, the district council or the borough council (known as the Mineral Planning Authorities), depending on where they are. During 1987–88, 19 sites were applied for, five of which, together with three applied for in earlier years, were approved by the Mineral Planning Authorities. Of the remaining 14, three had gone to appeal, and at the year-end the remaining 11 were still with the Mineral Planning Authorities. If the Mineral Planning Authorities turn down an application, BC can seek a public inquiry. Following public inquiries (all relating to applications originally made to planning authorities in previous years) in 1987–88, the Secretary of State for the Environment granted permission for six sites but in the same period refused permission for seven. If this situation were to continue BC thinks it likely that opencast output would decline. The Department of the Environment issued in May 1988 new guidance to local authorities on opencast coal mining which may, by providing for a different balance to be struck between environmental considerations and opencast output's economic advantages, assist BC's applications for new sites. BC told us that it was still too early to say whether this will in fact be the case.

4.54. BC told us that it continues to press for new opencast sites as a vital element in its strategy of increasing profitability through an increased proportion of output of low cost coal. In 1987–88 the average cost of opencast production was £1·02/GJ and in BC's view there is no reason to think that this will not be representative of new sites for some time to come.

4.55. We asked BC what increase in opencast output it thought might be possible if the constraint imposed by the difficulties in obtaining planning permission were significantly relaxed. BC thought that in those circumstances it would be possible to increase opencast output to around 20 mtpa, ie an additional five mtpa. Most of the additional coal would be steam coal. Both replacement and additional sites would be in the areas where opencast mining already takes place.

4.56. The investment by the contractors in opencast mining equipment is substantial. The private sector employs plant of an estimated cost of £600 million. If output were to increase to 20 million tonnes, there would be a need for the private sector to invest in additional plant to the order of £200 million. In contrast, the investment necessary by BC would be relatively modest and would be associated with the cost of acquiring land and the upgrading of certain disposal point facilities.

Imports   4.57. The CEGB told us that it believed that it could, if necessary, obtain up to 30 mtpa of its total requirement from imports, building up to this figure over five years. It could obtain up to 10 mtpa within a year, a further 10 mtpa within two years and another 10 mtpa within five years (involving some investment in port facilities). The CEGB also told us that it had current contracts for coal at between $33/tonne to $39/tonne ARA [1] at a net calorific value (NCV) of 25·5 GJ/tonne. Transshipment charges to a United Kingdom port would be about £5 per tonne but these would be avoided if there were a facility for directly discharging from large bulk carriers. Table 4.11 shows a range of costs of imported steam coal in £/GJ, for sample values of ARA prices and £/$ exchange rates.

TABLE 4.11   **Sample values of prices of imported coal**

ARA price $/tonne	Exchange rate $/£	Cost* £/GJ
33	1·7†	0·75
39	1·7†	0·90
42‡	1·75‡	0·95‡
55‡	1·45‡	1·50‡

Source: MMC from CEGB material.

* Evaluated at NCV of 25·5 GJ/tonne. Rounded to nearest 0·05.

† Approximate value in August 1988.

‡ Range in the year 2000 suggested by CEGB.

[1] See glossary.

4.58. The remainder of the delivered cost is the cost of transporting the coal from the port or mine to where it is to be used. The balance of cost advantage between imports and locally mined coal would be determined by the relative costs of transportation as between port and mine, as well as the cost of imported coal at the port compared with the pithead cost of deep-mined coal.

4.59. The CEGB told us that the typical cost of transporting ARA coal to Thameside station is close to £5 a tonne (about 17 pence/GJ). The further costs of getting coal to the centre of the country would average out at around £9 a tonne (about 31 pence/GJ). That average covers a very wide spectrum, between deliveries to Didcot and deliveries to the Upper Trent, where stations are rather less accessible for imports.

4.60. We were told that, at present prices, the cost of building a two-berth jetty capable of handling up to 15 mtpa would be of the order of £45 million. Including the cost of rail connections and the site, the total could be expected to cost under £80 million.

Operational research

4.61. BC's ORE provides a management science and mathematical modelling service to the rest of BC. Client departments are free to contract work from ORE as required (subject to the necessary authorization of the expense) and ORE charges its clients for the work, at an economic rate. ORE has made a number of contributions to the effectiveness of BC's capital investment programme. ORE has had a longstanding involvement in developing methods of project control, and in the past three years it has been involved in developing the ARTEMIS system, which is the one introduced at Asfordby, for general use in BC, and promoting and supporting its application, including for small-scale projects where the computer system can now be run on desk-top computers. ORE has also been involved in developing techniques for use in risk analysis, in equipment assessment, in underground material handling system design, in the design of ventilation equipment and in subsidence analysis. It would generally expect to be involved from an early stage in a major project; for example, in a new mine project, in site selections.

Research and development

4.62. We asked BC if it did not consider that the recent cut-back in its mining machinery research and development might prejudice the long-term future of the industry. BC told us that the main work now required in its field was development of existing technology, and this, BC thought, was the responsibility of the manufacturers who were willing and capable of undertaking the necessary work. The United Kingdom mining machinery industry was servicing orders world-wide. BC's main research effort was more directed at developing control technology, such as the MINOS system.

4.63. BC took the view that its own research department, in the event of its own privatization, should not be broken up, but should continue, supported by levy or Government grant. Nevertheless, BC felt that other countries, where this was the arrangement, had been less successful than BC in technology transfer.

Evidence from trade unions

4.64. We invited all major trade unions involved in the industry to give evidence, but, in the event, we received evidence only from APEX, BACM and NACODS; we held hearings with the latter two. NACODS told us that the morale of those employed in the industry was at a low ebb, of which the eagerness of many miners to accept redundancy was taken as symptomatic. The low incidence of appeals against pit closures (10 per cent) was also felt to be significant. This was due partly to a view that appeal was a waste of time and partly to a desire to get out of the industry. Whilst BC was not entirely to blame for the situation, being forced into it by Government guidelines, it had adopted a ruthless and short-term approach which was damaging to morale.

4.65. Examples were cited of pit closures which served only to meet BC's short-term objectives (eg South Kirby and Wooley) giving rise to further insecurity and lower morale. In the past a high performing pit might have a bad year but work through the problem. Now it seemed likely that it could be doomed to closure or at the least to no investment.

4.66. The increasing employment of contractors underground and suggested changes to legislation were perceived by NACODS as likely to lower safety standards. The same was true of other changes such as the use of roof bolting as an alternative to arched roof supports and the attempts to introduce longer shifts and a longer working week. Part of the problem was the lack of consultation resulting from BC's unilateral decision to terminate the existing national agreements and arrangements. Although consultation still occurred at colliery level, it was informal and given less importance than formerly, frequently no longer involving the colliery manager.

4.67. The apparent contradiction between declining morale and improving productivity was, it was felt, explained by new technology and techniques. The increasing use of heavy duty shield supports on faces, retreat mining, reducing the number of faces worked, and improved transport to faces (thus increasing machine available time (MAT)) were all contributing to this improvement. Miners had shown a readiness to accept change and to adapt.

4.68. New techniques, however, brought their own risks. A single face mine lacked flexibility and was in greater danger of closure if insurmountable problems were encountered on that face.

4.69. BACM gave us its views on the uncertainties facing the industry, the current restructuring process and the reasons for the impressive improvements in productivity. It was its view that these improvements could not have been accurately predicted. Although in large part due to investment in new technology and reorganization, there was also a substantial change in attitudes, particularly since the strike. Much of the improvement had resulted from more effective management.

4.70. BACM believed that six-day working was by no means a panacea. It could be appropriate in some pits, and in others some alternative form of flexible working would be more appropriate. The publicity about six-day working had made it harder for a pit manager to get agreement to any form of flexible working. Misunderstandings had resulted from misrepresentation of the proposals.

4.71. BACM's view was that morale in the pits was to a large degree determined by uncertainty about the future which now seemed to rest upon the performance of the pit in terms of the objective of £1·50/GJ. Even managers were affected by the long-term uncertainty about their future.

4.72. It was difficult to convince men that by greater efficiency and flexible working hours their future could be assured when their pit could be closed because of a change in the market. This could occur following electricity privatization if there were substantial imports of coal.

4.73. On the question of EBG manning BACM felt that whilst it was obviously sensible to reduce the non-producers where possible its members as managers could never permit a situation where the level of safety was put at risk. Much had been safely achieved in this respect with the introduction of new technology and new systems of monitoring.

Conclusions: Systems and organization

4.74. In Chapter 3 we reviewed BC's strategy, drew conclusions about how it had met the needs of the immediate post-strike period, and how it now has to respond to new circumstances. In Chapter 6 we look at the technical aspects of BC's examination of how its business environment will change. Here we draw conclusions about the systems and organization by which BC formulates its strategy, particularly through its investment programme.

4.75. BC has revised its corporate planning arrangements. Its business planning system is now an effective structure for planning and appraising the Areas' business plans, including those for investment, for each mine. The system provides a vehicle for dialogue between Areas and Headquarters, and is the main means by which BC makes its investment programme follow its strategy. The business planning cycle is also one of the means BC is using to change the culture of management at the level of mine manager and above. The business planning system is thus well constructed to meet the requirements of the main planks of BC's strategy since the strike.

4.76. In BC it is the Chairman who fulfils the function of Chief Executive Officer, and, as is appropriate at a turbulent period for the organization, strategy is an integral part of his role. At present, analyses of different aspects of the external environment are carried out in different parts of the Headquarters organization, and are brought together to permit a corporate view to emerge. The new challenge BC has to meet is the prospect of major discontinuities in its external environment. We think that BC's Board will need to ensure that the systems and organization are conducive to systematic and rigorous review of future prospects in BC's business environment.

4.77. The business planning cycle does not at present call upon the Areas or mines to provide any formal input on the local business environment. This has been appropriate to BC's present circumstances. As these change, and particularly when the ESI is privatized, these arrangements will need to be examined, and if necessary revised.

4.78. In the course of our inquiry BC announced organizational changes, involving a smaller management organization to supervise the collieries in some coalfields. A number of features, including technological changes and rising productivity, have already enabled BC to become a smaller, better controlled organization. We recommend that BC should, as we assume it will, continue to examine the prospects of further simplifying its organizational structure to enable it better to respond flexibly to a more rapidly changing business environment.

4.79. BC's system for selecting investment projects relies on colliery unit cost criteria, expressed in £/GJ, to act as a first hurdle. For investments at existing collieries where the increments are small compared with the capital already sunk, the assessment is expressed in operating costs[1]. For major investments in new capacity, total colliery unit costs, incorporating capital charges, are used. Projects surviving these tests are subjected to DCF analysis, and are expected to meet BC's rate of return criteria. This is satisfactory as a system.

4.80. The £/GJ criteria have been progressively tightened in two ways. First, they have not been indexed for inflation, Secondly, greater emphasis is now being given to an upper limit of £1·50/GJ, rather than £1·65/GJ which was the upper limit when the policy was introduced. This reflects BC's objective to reduce its operating costs by at least 20 per cent between 1985–86 and 1989–90. We think that any further tightening should be linked to the kinds of assessments of the future economic environment we refer to in Chapter 6 and clearly related to a view of BC's future market situation. The total cost cut-off for large projects in new capacity is now the same as the operating cost cut-off for small projects, at £1·50/GJ. Acknowledging that these both approximate to avoidable costs, [1] BC should consider making the former lower than the latter, to reflect the greater uncertainty attached to the longer pay-back periods of such projects.

---

[1] See glossary.

4.81. We accept BC's argument that six-day working at new mines would be commercially advantageous, and we note that this has now been agreed in principle with the UDM.

4.82. BC fully recognizes the commercial importance of maximum utilization of capital plant. To achieve this there are a variety of forms of flexible working which could be employed at existing mines. We commend BC in continuing to explore all options.

4.83. BC has met considerable resistance to its proposals for more flexible working arrangements, particularly from the NUM at national level; but we have been told that there has been considerable misunderstanding of the proposals. It is clearly important that the need for flexible working, in its various forms, is properly discussed and understood by the workforce. We therefore recommend that the unions should be fully consulted at the appropriate level, and that the objectives, options and proposals should be explained clearly to the workforce at colliery level.

4.84. Another obstacle to flexible working is the limitation of underground shift length to 7·5 hours plus one winding time in the 1908 Coal Mines Regulation Act (as amended). BC should seek early consultations with the trade unions, preparatory to making further representations to the Government on this matter.

5 The appraisal of investment projects

5.1. BC's Capital Investment Manual (the Manual) sets out the procedures to be followed and the information to be provided when seeking approval for capital expenditure. The Manual sets out in considerable detail, the information, appendices and plans which should normally be prepared for all 'major' capital projects whether approved by Headquarters, or under Area Directors' delegated authority.

5.2. All projects over £0·5 million are 'major'; abbreviated procedures are available for projects of £0·5 million to £1 million. Some major capital projects costing up to £5 million can be approved by Area Directors under delegated authority, providing they meet the return on investment criteria, and are included in the agreed list of approved projects in the Business Plan. Projects costing below £5 million which are not in the approved list and all projects costing more than £5 million must be submitted to Headquarters for approval.

5.3. Sponsors of capital projects are held responsible by BC for ensuring that all information relevant to the project is included in the project's submission document, even where it is not specifically referred to in the Manual. Major projects at existing mines and those for the construction of new mines are considered within the general framework of the annual Area and national business planning cycle (as described in Chapter 4). Investment priority is determined for major projects after taking into account, principally, the financial return and the markets to be served. A list of projects in the Business Plan is then agreed by the Board.

5.4. The Manual states that all related capital investment to be incurred simultaneously and consecutively at a colliery should, generally, be considered as parts of the same project. 'Piecemeal' investment is to be avoided, unless an investment is self-contained and can be justified in its own right. The Manual accepts, though, that control over projects can be improved by keeping them more compact and reducing the lead times.

5.5. We understand from BC that the aim of the appraisal procedures set out in the Manual is to establish that for all of BC's individual investment decisions:

(a) all the available options have been examined and the best choices made;

(b) the project is necessary and financially attractive;

(c) the decision is made within the right time-scale (ie that sufficient time is allowed at the various planning stages of the project through to completion to ensure the achievement of Business Plan objectives); and

(d) the decision is wholly consistent with the overall Business Plan.

The stages of project appraisal

5.6. The main stages to be followed in the preparation of a project are outlined below.

(a) *Existing mines:*

Stage I—Agreement to proceed to Stage II. For projects costing £5 million or more, a Stage I submission has to be made to Headquarters which sets out in broad terms all the practical options. The evaluation of the technical, commercial and financial implications in it should be adequate to enable a choice to be made as to which option should be proceeded with to Stage II. The aim at Stage I, the Manual states, is to select the best option to enable the colliery's performance to be consistent with the Board's plans and objectives.

Stage II—Approval. This is required for *all* projects. For projects costing £5 million or more, the Stage II submissions will generally be based on the option agreed at Stage I. For all other major projects for which there has been no Stage I, the Stage II submission must include details of the options considered and the reasons for selecting the option on which the Stage II submission is based. The Manual states that the aim of the Stage II submission and paper is to provide to the decision-taking level a prospectus if approved which sets out the objectives of the investment and to which if approved the individual responsible will be held accountable.

Stage III—Authorization. This is required for all sections of major projects approved at Stage II. Commitments (such as orders placed or contracts let) may only be entered into after the Stage II proposals have been given Stage III Authorization. (There is a variation to this in exceptional circumstances, Interim Stage III Authorization, which is explained below.)

(b) *New mines*

Strategy Report. This is usually the first report called for in considering any new mine, or new mine complex, or, exceptionally, any other substantial change of a major technical or commercial nature. The aim is to establish whether to proceed with the next stage. The Manual states that as there may be only limited factual information available, the Strategy Report may be largely based on interpretation of the limited information and on informed opinions based on experience.

Feasibility Report and Stage I Agreement. This stage follows on from acceptance of a satisfactory Strategy Report. Incorporated in the Feasibility Report and Stage I submission will be the same kind of considerations for a new mine and substantial complex as are normally included in a Stage I submission for an existing mine. In addition, though, a wider examination will be given to markets and demand, geology and reserves and mining parameters, infrastructure and environmental matters, recruitment and training and the broader financial effects of implementing the various alternatives. The aim at this stage is to produce a broad prospectus for each of the various options, indicating the risks involved in pursuing each so that the decision-taking level can judge what the next move should be.

Stage II—Approval is as for existing mines.

5.7. The following stages are applicable both to *existing mines* and to *new mines:*

Interim Stage III Authority. In order to obtain services, or to provide essential supplies or information, or acquire some essential asset in limited supply, eg land, prior to obtaining Stage I agreement or Stage II approval, an application for the authorization of expenditure, known as an Interim Stage III Authorization, may be submitted. The Manual states that it is important that commitments entered into by this means should not in any way prejudice the future decisions regarding the Stage II submission. Authorization is not to be seen as giving tacit agreement/approval to any subsequent related Stage I and Stage II submissions.

Supplementary Stage III Authorization. This authorizes additional expenditure on the sections of a project previously authorized at Stage III, provided that the latest estimated cost of the project, including the supplementary authorization, is within the total approved out-turn cost and does not constitute a Technical Change (see below).

Technical Change. After Stage II approval, any significant technical change in the objectives or plans contained in the prospectus must be notified to Headquarters and approved before there is any further commitment.

Revised Stage II. If, after a project has been approved at Stage II and is in progress, it becomes apparent that a substantial change is needed from what was originally approved (technically, commercially, or financially), the Manual requires that the project has to be revised and re-submitted, and the need for the continuation of the project demonstrated.

5.8. We now consider in more detail some aspects of this staged project appraisal process.

Consideration of options

5.9 In the case of projects costing over £5 million the Manual requires that all the feasible options should be identified at Stage I. Indeed, it also requires that even those options not considered feasible or obviously worth while should be listed together with a brief explanation for not giving them further consideration.

5.10. The options to be considered are always to include the 'do nothing' option. In the case of collieries whose operating costs (either before or after investment) are in excess of BC's guidelines for investment, the options should also include the 'closure' option.

5.11. The Manual requires that for each option in Stage I brief details and comments include: information on the markets to be served (including coal quality and proceeds); the reserves; output and productivity; manpower requirements; technical and commercial proposals; time and cost estimates; and financial appraisal. In the case of proposed new mines the options considered should include the relative merits of different locations, and of operating at varying levels of output.

5.12. The options are to be compared and the preferred option selected (together with reason for the choice). The Area Director is required to make specific recommendations in the Stage I submission.

5.13. The Manual does not require a re-statement at Stage II of the options rejected in Stage I, provided that the comparisons made at Stage I remain valid and the Stage II submission is based on the previously determined best option. If a Stage I submission was not required (ie for projects costing less than £5 million) all the feasible options including 'doing nothing' and 'closure' are to be briefly set out in the Stage II submission. The 'best option' chosen then forms the basis for the Stage II submission.

5.14. The Manual provides that, where the options are not considered in the Stage I or Stage II papers to Headquarters, assurances are to be given that the Area has fully considered all realistic options. It also requires that for a composite project, where it is clear that certain components of the project can 'stand alone' and can be financially assessed and justified independently of the whole project, the financial effects of such components should be separately evaluated and shown.

Market assessment

5.15. In setting out investment options at Stage I the Manual requires that consideration of each option includes brief details and comments on the markets to be served. This information should include the method and means of coal preparation, the sizes and approximate analysis of each quality of coal needed, together with other key physical or chemical properties of relevance to the target market, outloading arrangements, stock or reclaim facilities, and saleable proceeds valued at list price less the appropriate Market Adjustment Fund (MAF) contribution (see paragraphs 7.2 to 7.27).

5.16. Stage II should include further more detailed analysis of the anticipated proceeds. The Manual includes an example of a *pro forma* table for this purpose which enables the colliery's future proceeds to be set down, contrasting the with and without project expectations. The Area Director's Stage II paper is expected to specify the colliery's present markets, and how these are expected to be changed by the proposed project, including tonnages and percentages of total saleable output intended for each market sector.

5.17. In July 1987 Areas were instructed that, in the preparation of the projected cash flows in all subsequent project submissions, saleable proceeds should be reduced by 1 per cent a year. This figure was subsequently increased to 2 per cent as from April 1988 to be applied for each of the years 1988–89 to 1992–93 inclusive (see paragraph 3.27). The resulting proceeds figures are intended to establish base cases for projects, and this procedure is not intended to preclude the assessment of other projected levels of proceeds as part of the usual risk assessment of projects.

Financial appraisal

5.18. At Stage I the Manual requires that financial appraisal be based on the physical features of each option, reflecting such factors as the effects of variations in project cost and time to complete, productivity, working patterns, and quality of product. The estimates are to take account of any perceived disadvantages one option may have compared with another. Any adverse effects one or more of the options may have on other aspects of the Area's operations are also to be evaluated. Revenue results are to be calculated on the basis of saleable proceeds assuming all output is sold. Income from sundry sales and services are also taken into account, but shown separately from saleable proceeds.

5.19. In the Stage II submission the aim of the financial appraisal is to enable the decision-taking level:

(*a*) to judge whether the proposed investment will be financially successful (or, if the investment is not being made for financial reasons what the financial effect will be);

(*b*) to compare the financial effects of the various options, including 'do nothing' and 'closure', in very brief summary form; and

(*c*) to assess why the investment should be made at the time proposed.

All the evaluations of costs, proceeds, cash flows and so on in this section are to be made at current price levels.[1] The evaluations should be regarded by the Area Director as being achievable, ie as likely to be exceeded as to fall short. The estimates, which incorporate the adjustments to future proceeds described in paragraph 5.17, are then referred to as the 'base case'. The main differences between the 'base case' and existing results should be explained.

5.20. In addition, the Area Director's Stage II paper should include a completed version of the 'Financial Indicators' *pro forma* table shown in the Manual. For projects submitted to Headquarters for approval, this table is prepared by Headquarters Finance Department and annexed to the paper prepared by the Area. In the case of major projects costing up to £5 million for approval by the Area Director under delegated authority, the table is prepared by the Area, in an abbreviated form, if considered appropriate.

---

[1] BC's definitions of 'current', 'out-turn' and 'real' price levels for this purpose are:

(a) 'current' price level relates to the present time and is not expected to be more than six months out of date;

(b) 'out-turn' price level is that expected in the future incorporating inflation or deflation; and

(c) 'real' price level is that by which the 'current' price level is altered by changes in the value of the various factors for reasons other than general inflation or deflation.

5.21. As mentioned in paragraph 3.25, BC currently applies two discount rates in the financial assessment of its investment projects. These rates are reflected in the 'Financial Indicators' *pro forma* table. In completing it a 10 per cent discount is to be applied to the colliery's cash flows, and a 15 per cent rate is to be applied to the marginal cash flows generated by the proposed project.

Risk assessment

5.22. To enable BC to assess the financial effects of any risks associated with any proposed investment project, risk assessments are undertaken. Projects being prepared for consideration by Headquarters CIC are subject to detailed assessment by individual Headquarters Departments and by the Project Committee. A major element in this assessment is the identification of the risks associated with each project.

5.23. In the case of Area approved projects, the parts of the project which are considered to be sensitive to risk are to be identified and risk-rated. It is up to Areas to judge the extent of the risks and to assess the impact they are likely to have on the results and success of the project. The Area Director is to have this information before reaching a decision on the project.

5.24. Each project is considered in isolation. BC's present management structure depends heavily for its expertise upon the collective knowledge held by members of the team in general of individual collieries and coalfields, but in particular held by members of the Project Committee, which includes staff from Headquarters Marketing, Technical and Finance Departments. BC told us that it is this advice which is used in the first instance in the assessment of the risks associated with individual investment projects, and that it is this assessment which is attached to the project.

5.25. Even so, BC told us, each project is subjected to DCF appraisal based on identified specific risks covering the possibility of: lower output; lower proceeds; delayed project completion; higher operating costs; higher project costs; or combinations of these. This information contributes to an assessment of the 'most likely' and 'pessimistic' prospects for each colliery after project completion.

5.26. For all project submissions to Headquarters, sensitivity tests are undertaken by the Finance Department using a computer software package designed by BC specifically for the purpose. Though parameters are fixed, the package allows for variation in the weights attached to each variable. The package, called 'Appraise', is also available for use by all Areas.

5.27. Project approval is normally granted where, in the 'most likely' case, the project is expected to give a marginal DCF yield of 15 per cent or higher.

Levels of authority for approving capital investment expenditure

5.28. BC's levels of delegated authority to incur capital expenditure on individual projects and to dispose of land and property are as follows:

	Stage I & Stage II	Interim Stage III	Disposal of land & property
Executive Committee	—	No limit	£10m
Capital Investment Committee (CIC)	£30m	£2m	£5m

5.29. The CIC considers all projects whether they fall within its delegated authority or require the approval of the Board. For investment proposals over £30 million, the CIC will, after initial consideration, make recommendations to the Executive Committee, which considers these views and then in turn makes its own recommendations as appropriate to the Board. Board members and senior officials also have delegated authority to approve capital expenditure but this is limited to £1 million in the case of certain departmental heads, and to £5 million in the cases of the Finance and Technical Directors (for projects recommended by the Head of Finance and, in some cases, the Head of Mining).

5.30. The limits of delegated authority for Area Directors are shown in Table 5.1. Before any project costing more than £0·5 million can be approved under this delegated authority, it must have been included in the agreed capital programme as part of the Area Business Plan. If the project is not in the agreed capital programme, it is necessary to obtain clearance from Headquarters before it is approved and before any commitment is entered into. In addition to meeting the criteria in Table 5.1, proposals for expenditure on heavy duty supports have also to meet the criteria detailed in Table 5.2.

TABLE 5.1 **Limits of delegated authority for Areas**

Stage II project approval by Area Directors

	Upper limit of delegated authority
1. *Collieries* with a DCF yield of 10 per cent or over and an operating cost per GJ of £1·50 or less†*	
	£m
A. Projects required to give a marginal DCF yield	
(i) a marginal DCF yield of over 40%	5·0
(ii) a marginal DCF yield of over 30%	3·0
(iii) a marginal DCF yield of over 20%	1·0
B. Projects not required to give a DCF yield	
(i) Specifically in the agreed capital programme	1·0
(ii) Other projects	0·5
2. *All other colliery projects*	
(i) Face installations within action programme	0·5
(ii) Other projects	0·1
3. *Other Area activities*	*£*
Offices (buildings and equipment):	
—at collieries with a DCF yield of 10% and operating cost of £1·50 per GJ or less	250,000
—at other collieries	5,000
—at Area	400,000
Houses—purchase of and improvement to houses (including houses damaged by subsidence)	100,000
Others—including Area training centres, internal railways, central stocking, road transport service, Area laboratories, cars, etc.	250,000
4. *Disposals*	
Disposals of land, buildings and other assets	100,000
5. *Write-offs*	
Of assets (other than land and property) because of obsolescence, loss or surplus to requirements not involving disposal	500,000

Source: BC.

---

* Including face installations and land for operational purposes, but excluding offices.

† Or other cost per GJ as agreed with Headquarters.

TABLE 5.2 **Authorization of heavy duty supports**

Area Directors have delegated authority to approve applications for heavy duty supports* installations providing the undermentioned criteria are met:

    (*a*) the installation is in the capital programme in the agreed Area Business Plan;

    (*b*) the application meets certain financial criteria including:

        (i) that the operating cost of incremental output after installation will not exceed £1·00 per GJ; and

        (ii) that the operating cost of the colliery after installation will not exceed £1·50 per GJ;

    (*c*) an average of 500,000 tonnes per annum can be produced over an eight-year life; and

    (*d*) a detailed programme of re-deployment, preferably without returning the equipment to the surface, demonstrates the ability to achieve the criterion in (c) above.

An application for a heavy duty supports installation, as defined above, which does not meet the above criteria, must be submitted for approval by Headquarters. The submission should be a brief paper by the Area Director, for consideration by the CIC or the Finance and Technical Directors, setting out the reasons why the installation should be made and summarizing the key parameters of the installation.

Source: BC.

---

*Chock shield or shield supports with a yield load of 250 tonnes or more.

5.31. As is indicated in Table 5.1, BC distinguishes between projects according to whether or not they are required to give a marginal DCF yield. The distinction is as follows:

Objectives of projects: examples

1. *Projects required to give a marginal DCF yield:*
To save manpower, energy, staff, or install new plant, and thus to improve efficiency and reduce costs, etc.
To access reserves and/or install new plant, to increase output and reduce costs.
To access reserves, to maintain output and profitability.
To reorganize and refurbish, and thereby to increase proceeds and profitability.

2. *Projects not required to give a marginal DCF yield:*
To secure safety of the mine.
To replace existing facilities (not necessarily like with like), and thus to maintain continuity of necessary operations.
To drive tunnels to ensure normal development of mine and maintain profitability. This is to enable drivages to be driven to ensure continuity of output, and is part of the normal drivage programme and not part of a specific investment project.

Approval procedures

5.32. Apart from the Central Channel, which co-ordinates activities between Headquarters departments and the Areas, the main elements in the investment project approval system are:

(a) the Project Committee (PC); and

(b) the Capital Investment Committee (CIC).

5.33. The PC is a long-standing committee whose main functions are to consider proposals for colliery and related projects and for opencast projects, to review progress on approved projects during construction and to consider results on the completion of projects. The PC consists of representatives of appropriate Headquarters departments, and it meets generally monthly, or more frequently, according to volume of submissions and other business.

5.34. The terms of reference of the PC include:

(a) to examine and appraise all colliery and related projects submitted by Areas to Headquarters thus ensuring an early exchange of inter-departmental views so as to enable consideration to be given to the principal issues involved;

(b) to ensure the expeditious progress of projects until their approval or rejection at Headquarters or their withdrawal by Areas, having regard to overall priorities;

(c) to examine and progress other matters relating to projects received from Areas (technical changes (including approval where appropriate), control to out-turn, and so on), and to bring the issues involved to the attention of the appropriate decision-taking level;

(d) to advise, as requested by Areas, on the content, preparation and submission of projects, and to make available, as appropriate, best information and knowledge gained from contacts with Areas;

(e) to examine all Annual Reviews, Completion Reports and any special reports on projects approved at Headquarters, thus ensuring an early exchange of inter-departmental views thereon and to advise the decision-taking levels of the issues involved;

(f) to co-ordinate departmental comments to be annexed to project papers submitted to the various Headquarters committees; and

(g) to advise and make recommendations to the Technical Director, Accountability Meetings, the CIC, the Executive Committee and the Corporation on all matters relating to the expeditious processing of project submissions, Annual Reviews, and Completion Reports received at Headquarters, and their content and on other matters concerning the use of BC's capital resources.

5.35. The CIC, previously known as the Mining Committee (1971 to April 1984) or the Mining Investment Committee (April 1984 to November 1985), is the decision-making authority for major investment projects. We were told that in contrast to the PC, whose role is to co-ordinate, discuss, advise, inform and comment, the CIC's role is to consider, request and decide or recommend.

5.36. Area Directors now have primary responsibility for the preparation, form and content of all papers containing capital investment proposals, including those which are outside their delegated authority.

5.37. In the case of projects requiring Headquarters approval the Area first submits a formal *project submission,* via the Central Channel, to be considered by Headquarters departments through the PC. After preliminary discussions between Headquarters departments and their Area counterparts as necessary, initial assessments by Headquarters departments will be sent to the sponsoring Area.

5.38. After receipt of Headquarters departments' comments:

(a) the Area Director prepares a *project paper* which takes account of, as he thinks appropriate, Headquarters' comments, for consideration, via the Central Channel, by the CIC;

(b) Headquarters departments prepare formal comments for inclusion in an annex to the Area's paper (if there is a major difference of view remaining between the Area Director and Headquarters departments this is to be stated clearly in the paper's annex); and

(c) the Area Director is then usually expected to attend the CIC personally to present the project.

Department of Energy   5.39. BC told us that it is required to consult the Department of Energy, for its view as to the public interest, on all new mine projects and on any individual capital investment project which is expected to cost more than £5 million and whose DCF return applied to the marginal benefits from the project is less than 10 per cent (after discounting for most likely risks). The requirements apply whether or not the unit or activity is profitable and otherwise meets investment criteria.

Case studies

5.40. We selected ten projects as case studies of how BC has actually conducted the appraisal and monitoring of projects in its investment programme. In addition, we chose two examples of completed projects to establish from the relevant papers how progress on those projects had in practice been monitored. We also looked at two examples of heavy duty supports installations.

5.41. Brief details of the case studies and the other individual project studies that we undertook are given in Table 5.3. Summaries of the case studies are given in Appendices 5.1 to 5.11. Reference is made in various parts of our report to each of the investment projects listed in Table 5.3. In the remainder of this chapter we summarize our main findings from the case studies.

TABLE 5.3 **BC's investment projects: case studies and other projects examined by MMC**

Colliery and Area	Project description	Approved cost £m	Date of Stage II approval	Completion date	Status
Case studies					
Allerton Bywater, NYK	Drift access	0·9	12 Jul 1985*	Dec 1986	Completed
Asfordby, NTS	New mine	471·6	9 Dec 1985	Jun 1993	In progress
Daw Mill, CEN	Capacity extension	23·1	2 Apr 1987	Mar 1990	In progress
Dawdon, NEA	Rail rapid loading station	3·5	16 Jun 1983	Aug 1986	Completed
Harworth, NTS	Capacity extension	22·4	11 Mar 1988	Sep 1989	In progress
Margam, SWL	New mine	89·8	6 Feb 1987‡	§	Planning stage
Markham, CEN	New seam access	13·5	6 Mar 1984	1993–94	In progress
Prince of Wales, NYK	Extension of surface drifts	3·2	3 Feb 1986*	Oct 1987	Completed
Sutton Manor, WES	Reconstruction	17·3	10 Apr 1985	Nov 1987	†
Warsop, CEN	MINOS system, pumps, fans etc	1·2	20 Dec 1985	Dec 1986	Completed
Other projects					
Creswell, NTS	New mine fans	1·4	May 1983	Sep 1985	Completed
Merthyr Vale, SWL	Installation of skip winding	3·4	28 Nov 1985	Sep 1986	Completed
Cynheidre, SWL	Heavy Duty supports, etc	3·8	12 Nov 1986	May 1988	Completed
Daw Mill, CEN	Heavy Duty supports, etc	3·8	Mar 1985	Mar 1988	In progress

Source: MMC, from case studies.

*Approved under Area Director's authority.

†Project terminated on 15 May 1987, before completion.

‡Approved subject to certain conditions being met.

§Initial coal output is expected five years after work on the scheme begins.

Profitability of investment case study collieries, 1985–86 to 1987–88

5.42. We looked at the profitability, based on colliery profit and loss accounts for each of the three years 1985–86 to 1987–88, of the collieries listed in Table 5.3.

5.43. From this information we noted, briefly, that: (a) Dawdon, Daw Mill, Warsop and Harworth Collieries had saleable proceeds in excess of total costs in 1987–88; (b) Allerton Bywater Colliery showed a trend over the three years of reducing saleable proceeds and increasing costs, running into loss in 1987–88; (c) Creswell Colliery showed a steady improvement over the period but remained in loss in 1987–88; (d) Sutton Manor, Merthyr Vale and Prince of Wales Colleries have remained in loss over the period (the percentage of operating costs covered by net saleable proceeds in 1987–88 being 72·2 per cent, 77·4 per cent and 85·7 per cent respectively); and (e) the percentage of operating costs covered by net saleable proceeds at Cynheidre Colliery deteriorated over the period from 84·9 per cent to 76·8 per cent.

Identification of need

5.44. BC's Manual makes it clear that each project must be individually justified and be compatible with the Area's Business Plan. In particular, papers proposing projects for Headquarters approval must include a section which details the project's justification. We found that in all the case studies the need for the project had been identified and that objectives for the project had been set.

Consideration of options

5.45. As outlined in paragraphs 5.7 to 5.12 consideration of options is undertaken before the Stage II submission is prepared. We found in a number of the case studies that the chosen option, appraised at Stage II, was not in the event fully implemented as the final project (see Table 5.4).

TABLE 5.4 **Case Studies: choice and appraisal of options**

| Case | Stage II submission included DCF appraisal of: | | | | Did final project consist of option chosen at Stage I and appraised at Stage II? | |
| | Colliery* | | | Other | | |
	with	without	closure			
Allerton Bywater	✓	✓			Yes	
Asfordby	✓			Colliery DCF based on CEGB rebate as well as usual MAF discount.	No	Subsequent revisions to proposals. These included the introduction of 6-day production, which was assessed in the enhanced Stage II.
Daw Mill	✓	✓			Yes	Project expenditure re-phased.
Dawdon	✓	✓			No	Technical Change necessary to substitute 2000 tonne bunker etc, for approved 1000 tonne bunker.
Harworth	✓	✓			No	Project in progress.
Margam	✓				No	Major revisions to proposals, including introduction of 6-day production.
Markham	✓	✓			No	Changes made to pit bottom layout. Proposed diesel locomotives changed to battery operated ones.
Prince of Wales	✓	✓			Yes	
Sutton Manor	✓	✓	✓	1. MINOS alone. 2. Scheme without skip winder.	No	Project terminated. Full scheme benefits subsequently obtained, though further investment is necessary if the colliery is to remain in production.
Warsop	✓	✓			Yes	

Source: MMC from case studies.

*Projected colliery cash flow with or without proposed project, or with colliery closure.

5.46. In the Dawdon scheme for example, the approved 1,000 tonne bunker was subsequently up-graded to 2,000 tonnes. This was a result of a lower tender price than envisaged, and of expected added benefits from the virtual elimination of a coal stock and reclaim process (with consequent savings in operating costs of some £2 per tonne of coal stocked). In the Margam case, the Stage II proposals (of September 1984) have been revised three times subsequently, and now encompass retreat face mining and six-day working.

5.47. In the Harworth scheme, the option chosen at Stage I—to expand the mine to 3·3 mtpa—eventually became one of three options considered at Stage II, but was not the preferred option chosen for expanding capacity at the mine because its costs had increased substantially since Stage I and the financial return had fallen. The option actually chosen at Stage II—to expand capacity to 1·7 mpta and build a new winding tower over the existing one—was not considered at Stage I.

5.48. In the Sutton Manor case, we found that the Area's initial proposal (of January 1983) was put forward without feasible alternatives. However, even after alternatives had been subsequently looked at and presented in a revised Stage I submission requested by Headquarters, the final proposal was for a project not much different from the initial proposal. We also found that the project's main objectives had been achieved even though the project was terminated with only slightly half of the approved budget having been spent. BC told us that the colliery could only maintain output at the current level for a limited period without further capital expenditure, and that consideration will be given to implementing the remaining elements in the project.

5.49. We put it to BC that the consideration of options prior to the Stage II submission appeared to be not only incomplete in the light of the Manual's guidelines, but also inadequate in that the chosen option had, in some cases, to be significantly modified subsequently. BC said that for all its individual investment projects, it wants all the alternatives to be set out. This is the basis for deciding which option to examine in detail at Stage II. BC told us that it is satisfied that this is what in fact happens.

Composite projects

5.50. BC's Manual says that the piecemealing of projects is to be avoided (see paragraph 5.4). This is because it does not wish to find itself committed to a particular project without knowing what other investment requirements would then follow as a consequence. BC said that 'piecemealing' describes a process in which an Area might seek to engineer the implementation of a large project by gaining approval for its various constituent elements piece by piece over a period of time. This, it said, is particularly inappropriate if the composite project, submitted for approval as a whole, would not meet BC's investment criteria. As the case studies showed, individual projects usually do consist of several inter-related elements which are appraised together. The Sutton Manor case is a clear example of this.

5.51. We found in one case study, Prince of Wales, that a form of piecemealing was the chosen method for seeking approval for the project. In this case the Area felt that the need for the project had become urgent (after the loss of workable reserves as a result of subsidence and geological problems), and that some three or so months delay in obtaining approval would be avoided by splitting the project into two clearly defined parts which could, individually, be approved by the Area Director and implemented more rapidly. This was done with the approval of the Chairman of the CIC.

5.52. We noted in our 1983 report (paragraph 9.67) that composite projects need to be carefully appraised. In the Sutton Manor case, for example, the financial appraisal in the Stage II submission (of August 1984) recognized that the project consisted of a number of elements which could be constructed independently and improve efficiency without committing BC to the full proposals. In this case a DCF appraisal of the colliery's results for all elements of the project except the skip-winding element showed a very poor result, and further limitations on the project's scope were expected to reduce the resulting performance. In addition, the MINOS[1] element in the project was individually assessed by BC as likely to produce a marginal DCF yield of 31·5 per cent. BC did not think it appropriate to undertake any other partial DCF analyses for this scheme.

5.53. In our report (published some 12 months earlier) we had stated the view that in composite projects:

> each component should be appraised separately and the most profitable taken as the base case for appraising successive combinations of the components. (Paragraph 9.67.)

BC does not appear to have followed this approach in the Sutton Manor case (approved in April 1985).

5.54. In contrast, the recent investment programme at Harworth Colliery emphasizes the need for discrete projects which offer a quick pay-back and are in themselves entirely justifiable on a stand-alone basis. Each individual investment project has been required to contribute to colliery profitability and justify itself within those terms, as part of a broader long-term strategy to develop the colliery.

---

[1] See glossary.

Financial appraisal   5.55. We found that DCF analysis of projected colliery cash flows was included in all the Stage II submissions that we examined. The DCF analyses show the colliery's projected cash flows both with and without the effects of the proposed projects.

5.56. The discount rate used in each case was 10 per cent. In most cases the internal rate of return (IRR) was also calculated. This was done on the colliery's results including the effects of the project, and on the marginal cash flows which arose when comparing the 'with project' results with the 'without project' results. In one case such a comparison was also done against the projected cash flows (including cash out-flows) which would result if the colliery was closed (see Table 5.4).

5.57. We questioned BC about how it viewed the 'without project' results. It told us that in its appraisals both the closure option, which is the likely result if the proposed project does not proceed, and the minimum feasible alternative have to be compared with the preferred option. It pointed out that the marginal DCF yields for many of its projects can appear very large because in an extractive industry such as coal, the 'do nothing' option usually means a significant deterioration in performance compared with the present.

5.58. BC said that at Stage I it was looking for the minimum feasible option. It does not assess 'doing nothing' at this stage. At Stage II, it told us, the preferred option is appraised in detail, and on the basis of this assessment a decision is made as to whether or not to proceed with the proposed project.

5.59. The colliery cash flow projections used in the DCF analyses, include projections of revenues. We found that in all the case studies except one these revenue projections were based on 'saleable proceeds'. These are derived from the list prices of individual qualities of coal by deducting a percentage amount representing the average rebate allowed to customers against the list prices of all coals of those types sold nationally. A fuller description of saleable proceeds is given in paragraphs 7.2 to 7.27. The exception is the Margam new mine project where, since the second revision (of May 1986) to the Stage II prospectus for the mine, BC has adopted forecasts of the market price for coking coal as the basis for its projections of proceeds rather than continuing to use saleable proceeds.

Project interdependence   5.60. As we note in the previous paragraph, the revenue projections used in the preparation of projects are normally based on saleable proceeds. This method of estimating future revenue emphasizes the point that the proceeds for the base case assessment at each colliery depend to some extent on the output of other collieries, and that for the bulk of its sales the output from BC's collieries is interdependent. We noted, for example, that even in the Margam case study, where a new coking coal mine is planned, the project papers show that BC considers that Margam would be a source of low cost general purpose steam coal if its output could not be sold as coking coal as planned.

5.61. We questioned BC about the implications of this colliery interdependence, or 'system effect', for its investment planning and appraisal. BC confirmed that all its investment projects are considered on a stand-alone basis. It pointed out that the output effect of the vast majority of its investment projects was very small in relation to BC's total output. Headquarters departments' comments, however, can provide, it said, an appropriate wider perspective on major investment projects.

5.62. BC acknowledged, however, that it did on occasion look at its pits as part of a system when this was considered appropriate. It said that the system effect of investment projects is more clearly seen when the investment programme is looked at as a whole. Then, the extent to which supplies of lower cost coal arising from new investment might displace existing higher cost supplies can be assessed in relation to market forecasts. Thus, BC sees its business planning system as the appropriate means by which the system effect of new investment should be assessed and taken account of.

Cost per Gigajoule criteria

5.63. As explained in Chapter 3, BC's strategy sets out clear financial criteria as the basis for investment in capital projects. These are not over-riding guidelines for determining whether or not new investment shall take place, but are intended to provide a guide to the prevailing financial environment. The guidelines were established in October 1985, though instructions to include details of cost per GJ in project submissions were not issued until 26 June 1986. Thus only three of the case study projects were approved after they were introduced (see Table 5.5).

TABLE 5.5 **Case studies: DCF yields and cost per GJ**

| Case | Date of Stage II approval | Marginal DCF yields % | | | | | Operating Cost per GJ £ | | |
| | | Area | | Headquarters | | | | Expected, after investment | |
		Base case	Worst case	Base case	Most likely	Worst case	Actual 1987–88	(1)	(2)
Allerton Bywater	Jul 1985	85·1	49·6	—	—	—	1·78	Na	
Asfordby	Dec 1985	11·5*	1·3*	14·1*	9·1*	2·0*	—	Na	
Daw Mill	Apr 1987	46	30	46	35	2	1·24	1·04	1·20
Dawdon	Jun 1983	–ve	Nc	–ve	Nc	Nc	1·41	Na	
Harworth	Mar 1988	37·0	22·5	37	35	28	1·23	1·12	1·34
Margam	Feb 1987	23·1	7·9	16·9	12·2	6·4	—	0·87	1·11
Markham	Mar 1984	22·5	17	22	21	17	1·80	Na	
Prince of Wales	Feb 1986	51·0	45·6	—	—	—	1·76	Na	
Sutton Manor	Apr 1985	35·5	Nc	35·8	34·4	11·1	2·18	Na	
Warsop	Dec 1985	40	Nc	—	—	—	1·44	Na	

Source: MMC, from case studies.

* Assuming six-day working.

Notes: Na: Project approved before guidelines introduced.
Nc: Not assessed.
(1) Before capital charges.
(2) Including capital charges.

Risk and sensitivity assessment

5.64. We found that a standard range of sensitivity tests had been applied in the Area approved projects. BC told us that the smaller schemes approved under Area Directors' authority have to be of relatively low capital cost with very high DCF returns. In such cases, it said, an across the board deflation of proceeds and limited risk assessment is justified. Formal risk analysis is not considered by BC to be appropriate for heavy duty projects.

5.65. Headquarters approved projects are, we were told, subject to project-specific risk tests as identified by Headquarters departments. We noted, however, that while the Sutton Manor project was subject to risk assessment, this did not include a specific analysis of the risks attached to the anticipated market for industrial and domestic coal in SW Lancashire (and for which production was planned). This market has not yet materialized to the extent envisaged by BC in 1984 because of the subsequent slump in oil prices.

5.66. In the Margam new mine case, though, two particular risks were identified and examined in detail by Headquarters Marketing Department. These were the future price of coking coal, and the prospects for the United Kingdom coking coal market.

Geological assessment

5.67. In examining the case studies we came across examples of projects having to be changed as a result of geological problems. In the Asfordby case for example, boreholes drilled to provide data for engineering design revealed further details of igneous rocks which resulted in an alteration of the pit-bottom design.

5.68. In the Markham case identification of hard strata and faulting resulted in the redesign of pit-bottom roadways and the proposed bunker, and caused delays. Geological problems also caused delays to the installation of the heavy duty equipment at Daw Mill.

5.69. Although we mention these geological risks, it is in the nature of mining that underground conditions cannot be predicted with total accuracy before project development begins. We note BC's view that it is a world leader in the use of technology to minimize geological risks in underground operations.

Efficient use of manpower

5.70. We considered utilization of manpower resources in the context of the investment process as a whole in Chapter 4 (paragraphs 4.36 to 4.50). We now examine manpower planning, the assessment of manpower requirements, and the coverage of manpower and industrial relations issues in individual capital projects, with special reference to the case studies.

5.71. In relation to capital investment projects the first stage of the manpower planning process involves the Planning Department and Methods Study (see also paragraphs 4.15 to 4.17). At this stage it is assumed that manpower, like any other resource will be available as required. In preparing the project proposal, estimates are produced of the main categories of labour required and of the wages costs and productivity expected by comparison with current or recent data from the same or similar faces or pits.

5.72. The next stage of the process concerns the Industrial Relations (Manpower) Department. It is responsible for determining how the required manpower is to be supplied, eg by transfers, recruitment, training or (in the case of reduced manpower requirements) redundancy.

5.73. For the Daw Mill and Markham projects we were told that face manning was determined by calculation, by requirement or by standard manning. The expected level of performance of machines could be calculated from studies and from this standard performance the work content of the various operations could be determined. This in turn made it possible to determine the number of men required to ensure that the machine was not delayed. This technique was said to be particularly relevant to advancing support and face-end operations.

5.74. We were told that some jobs have to be filled throughout the shift. Examples are the machine driver, who must always be by the machine and ready to work at every opportunity, and the fitter or electrician, who must be readily available in the event of a breakdown.

5.75. BC told us that unless there is a significant change in the method of work the most common way of determining manpower needs is by standard manning. The majority of faces and developments are similar to earlier installations and the standard manning would then be used against standard performance.

5.76. We were also told in relation to the Daw Mill and Markham projects that manning EBG was based on 'what is normal for the colliery'. This evolves at each mine as the result of normal practice coupled with the results of investigations as appropriate. These investigations could be in the form of comparisons with similar operations at the same or other collieries, *ad hoc* studies, or as part of a general evaluation of new schemes.

5.77. Manning for surface activities is in general decided in a similar fashion to manning EBG, though with more emphasis on comparisons with similar operations at other collieries, particularly where these jobs are of a more permanent nature and have been the subject of detailed studies in past years. Area teams were said to be currently reviewing surface manpower with particular reference to job combinations [*   ]

5.78. By way of example, the proportional manning levels of the main categories of labour at Markham and Daw Mill Collieries by man shifts worked are shown in Table 5.6.

TABLE 5.6 **Man shifts worked***

	Daw Mill Colliery				Markham Colliery			
	1982–83		1987–88		1982–83		1987–88	
	No.	*%*	*No.*	*%*	*No.*	*%*	*No.*	*%*
Face	51,455	21	60,567	23	127,609	30	113,079	29
EBG	143,798	59	148,588	56	216,704	51	206,192	53
Surface	49,313	20	56,528	21	79,426	19	71,367	18
Total	244,566	100	265,683	100	423,739	100	390,638	100

Source: MMC, from BC information.

* Based on 'revenue shifts' (ie shifts for which costs are charged to the revenue account) and excluding 'capital shifts'.

5.79. Our 1983 report (paragraph 7.129) laid particular emphasis on the need to reduce levels of manpower employed EBG (ie not at the face) but, with one or two exceptions, this did not feature prominently amongst the objectives, set out for the projects we have studied. Markham project did make provision for a reduction of 60 jobs in the transport category underground. The Asfordby project submission stated that EBG requirements would be minimized by improved pit layout and remote monitoring and control in roadways and face lines.

5.80. BC told us that since the MMC last reported on the industry, the control and reduction of EBG manning levels, and the associated improvements in productivity, has been the subject of a major drive; a target of reduction of 5 per cent a year has been set, and exceeded.

5.81. EBG manshifts per thousand tonnes have been reduced by 28·3 per cent and OMS increased by 39·5 per cent. EBG men on books (MOB) have been reduced by nearly 40,000 (55 per cent) since 1982–83, accounting for about 35 per cent of the total manpower reduction achieved in this period. The fact that the EBG reduction is proportionately not significantly different to that of other categories is said to be due to the large reductions in face manpower as a result of new techniques (such as the use of shield support installations). With retreat working, for example, the face team is about half that on a conventional face and proportionately more men are employed on development and other roadway work, thus effectively transferring numbers from face to EBG.

5.82. In BC's view the fact that continuous action had been taken and was still being taken on EBG manning at every colliery meant that it had no special or separate relevance to individual investment projects.

5.83. An aspect of the manpower planning process is the use of a non-attendance percentage (representing absences for all reasons) in determining the number of men required to carry out any job plan. The non-attendance percentage includes absence due to sickness, accidents, training, voluntary absence, trade union business, jury service, individual holidays and rest days for each labour category for a preceding period.

*Details omitted. See note on page iv.

5.84. The formula for calculating the MOB required to cover a number of essential jobs is:

$$\text{Number of men required} = \frac{\text{Number of essential jobs} \times 100}{100 - \text{non-attendance percentage}}$$

Thus, in the case of Markham project the proposed saving of 60 jobs represented an actual saving of 72 MOB.

5.85. It is clear that there has been significant improvement in the national absence trend since 1979–80 (see Table 5.7). BC told us that it would expect non-attendance cover to be no more than about 10 per cent, although the figure varies from colliery to colliery.

TABLE 5.7 **BC: National absence trends**

The absence percentage is a measure of non-attendance obtained by expressing the number of non-deployment due to:

   (a) certified sickness, industrial disease or injury;
   (b) absence authorized by management, eg jury service, local authority services, death of a near relative, individual holidays and rest days; and
   (c) absence for no known reason.

Year	Absence percentage
1972–73	16·4
1973–74	17·9*
1974–75	16·0
1975–76	16·7
1976–77	17·3
1977–78	17·6
1978–79	17·1
1979–80	14·8
1980–81	12·4
1981–82	11·4
1982–83	10·4
1983–84	10·6
1984–85	6·8†
1985–86	12·1
1986–87	11·0
1987–88	9·7

Source: MMC from BC information.

* 48-week absence percentage due to national strike.

† Figures affected by NUM dispute.

Project submissions   5.86. The coverage of manpower and industrial relations issues in the project papers was limited compared with that of the financial, technical, and geological aspects. In more than half the case studies a required appendix, which should show the basis of computation of estimates of manpower, shifts, productivity and wages costs in connection with the project was missing or incomplete. In general we noted that in the case papers there was no attempt to justify the stated manpower requirements and productivity estimates for each category of labour. In the text of submissions the focus was generally on manpower availability. Manpower reductions arising from particular aspects of a project were however usually described in some detail.

5.87. BC pointed out to us that the Manual requires only relevant information to be included in project submissions. It argued that all manpower aspects were anyway fully covered and discussed in the planning of projects and preparation of submissions.

Conclusions

5.88. BC now has a comprehensive Capital Investment Manual which gives full guidance on the preparation, and submission for approval of capital investment projects. We also found, in the case studies of investment projects that we undertook (the approval dates of which ranged from mid-1983 to March 1988), that the most recent cases showed noticeable improvements in the preparation of investment projects over the earlier cases. Even so, we think that there is scope for further improvement in BC's procedure.

5.89. We found it difficult to form a clear picture of the extent to which BC believes that its mines form a coal supply system—that is, the extent to which the output of one mine is affected by, and in turn has an effect on, the output of other mines. BC told us that for some purposes the mines should not be thought of as forming a supply system. Thus its smaller investment projects, each of which would in itself have a minor impact on BC's total supplies, at particular mines are appraised on a 'stand alone' basis. For other purposes, however, BC does manage its mines as a coal supply system. For example, the procedure by which BC averages the proceeds for individual collieries is a clear indication to each colliery that its financial performance is not independent of the activities at other collieries. This interdependence is also recognised, for investment purposes, in BC's annual business planning cycle.

5.90. In our view BC's output-related investment projects are not mutually exclusive in that each project will have some effect on the cash flows projected in connection with other projects. Indeed, with the present emphasis on investment only in low cost collieries, each investment project will in principle have implications for the continued viability of higher cost sources unless BC can increase its sales. For many projects this effect will be minimal. In some cases the output effect may be more significant but only in relation to a discrete market (eg coking coal). But for almost all of BC's major output related projects, this interdependence of projects should be explicitly recognized in the appraisal. This interdependence becomes increasingly significant as the number of collieries declines.

5.91. We therefore recommend that BC incorporates into the Manual practical guidance on how to ensure that the relevant 'system effect' of all projects for new or replacement capacity which require Headquarters approval is taken account of in the appraisals of those projects.

5.92. We recommend that BC gives close consideration to how options are assessed in the first stages of project preparation. There are three matters to which BC should pay particular attention:

(a) The Manual requires that a 'sufficiently adequate' evaluation of *all* (our italics) practical options be made in the preparation of the Stage I submission. We found that in a number of the case studies the assessment and choice of options at Stage I was inadequate, and this led to sometimes protracted discussions at Stage II or to significant modifications to the project after approval.

(b) We found that the detailed analysis in Stage II normally relates only to the option which has been chosen prior to the preparation of the Stage II submission and to the 'do nothing' option. We think that the important comparison is with the minimum feasible alternative and that, as BC acknowledged, this is not necessarily 'doing nothing'. BC should set out clearly in its Manual the basis for establishing what the minimum feasible alternative is for the purpose of its investment appraisal.

(c) We think that for appraisal purposes a more thorough analysis of the individual elements of composite projects should be undertaken at Stage II. The combination of elements showing the highest net present value (NPV) should form the base case for assessing the merits of alternative combinations of the scheme's proposed components.

| Manpower, productivity and industrial relations | 5.93. Our examination of the case studies and the procedures for the approval of capital investment projects leads us to conclude that potential opportunities to make the most efficient use of manpower resources may be missed. In those projects we studied there was in most cases only a limited formal coverage of manpower and industrial relations issues. |

5.94. While accepting that these issues would be discussed between Headquarters and Area staff, and that not all projects have on the face of it significant manpower implications, we expect that every major capital investment project provides the opportunity for a critical examination of the utilisation of manpower resources. The procedures for the submission and approval of capital investment projects, whilst requiring that these issues are covered where relevant, do not ensure that estimates of manpower requirements and productivity for the various categories of labour are fully discussed and justified in project documentation.

5.95. We recommend that those submitting capital investment project applications be required in every case to cover fully all manpower and industrial relations issues and to justify estimates of manpower requirements and performance. We also consider that those responsible for approving projects should critically examine these aspects of submissions to ensure that no opportunity has been missed to maximize the efficient use of manpower resources.

5.96. We were further concerned that the manpower planning system itself could in some circumstances lead to initial overmanning or inflated estimates of manpower requirements. This could arise from the use of the 'non-attendance percentage' in the formula employed for the calculation of essential manpower requirements. We recommend that the use of this formula for calculating manpower is critically examined in those project submissions where the non-attendance percentage of any category of labour is higher than current target levels. BC told us that its aim is to reduce the non-attendance percentage to a minimum: implementation of this recommendation may assist in the achievement of that aim.

5.97. Our 1983 report attached considerable importance to the control and reduction of EBG manning levels. We were therefore surprised to note that this had not become a feature in most of the capital investment projects we studied. In most cases this category of manpower as a proportion of the total remained virtually unaffected. We note that BC has been making a continuing effort in this respect and that targets have been set and met. We accept that retreat working and other forms of modern mining technology at the face will (with lower face manning levels) initially lead to an increase in the proportion of indirect labour.

5.98. Whilst fully accepting this, and welcoming the efforts which are already being made by BC, we feel that in the context of major capital investment projects it would be appropriate fully to demonstrate this effort. We therefore recommend that the EBG issue should be covered in all project submissions, and where appropriate the required levels of EBG manpower should be demonstrably justified.

5.99. In the closing stages of our inquiry we were pleased to learn that BC had issued instructions to Areas which went a considerable way towards addressing the concerns expressed in paragraphs 5.97 to 5.98.

| Asfordby | 5.100. The Asfordby project has a long history. It originally formed part of a three mine project developed in line with the 1974 Plan for Coal. The planning application for this was rejected by the (then) Secretary of State for the Environment in 1982 following a Public Inquiry. A revised application for Asfordby alone was approved in 1984. The decision, in December 1985, to grant Stage II approval for the new mine at Asfordby followed support for the project from the (then) Secretary of State for Energy and an announcement by the then National Coal Board during the 1984–85 miners' strike that Asfordby would be the site for a new mine. Wider considerations of the importance of Asfordby for |

the industry appear to have played a significant part in decision taking in addition to the commercial assessment of the mine in isolation. Approval for contracts to sink the shaft and for other expenditure totalling £50 million were agreed before the project had received Stage II approval.

5.101. The granting of Stage II approval in 1986 was conditional upon the search for an improved financial prospectus and the introduction of six-day working. The project has been reviewed a number of times as a result but none of the financial appraisals we have seen show an improvement in financial prospects adequate to meet BC's criteria even if an agreement is successfully reached on six-day working. During this period work at Asfordby has continued and expenditure incurred or committed now amounts to £120 million.

5.102. In our view Asfordby has always been marginal in financial terms. After allowing for risks associated with the project, the financial appraisals have at no time shown a return which meets the minimum DCF yield which BC has set for collieries. The most recent estimates of total unit costs including capital charges fall well outside the Corporation's present criteria for investment both in replacement and incremental capacity.

5.103. BC has taken a different view and has argued that although initial contracts were let prior to Stage II, approval for further contracts was always conditional on the achievement of improved performance and six-day working. BC told us that the decisions to go ahead have been solely on the basis of the financial prospectus for the project. The results of the latest review were not available during our inquiry but BC told us that it was likely that this would show that Asfordby would satisfy its DCF criteria.

5.104. We are concerned that so much expenditure has been committed to a project over three years during which time it has not been possible to show a strong financial case. This concern is increased by the uncertainty about the revenue that can be earned from Asfordby coal, which is reported to be of a low quality and whose ash characteristics are now of concern to CEGB. ESI privatization may add to the uncertainty surrounding revenue. We understand the reasons why BC embarked on the project in 1984 but we cannot accept the view that the project has been shown to be financially attractive. To suggest so can only undermine the value of the DCF and cost per GJ criteria as instruments of management control.

5.105. We accept that the project now has sunk costs and that this, combined with an agreement on six-day working, may mean that the remainder of the project can be shown to be a worthwhile investment. We accept that it would be right for BC to continue with the project if it now meets BC's financial criteria. However we would regard this as a bad precedent for BC to set if the project can, in effect, only be justified by disregarding a significant part of its capital cost. BC has itself told us that it seeks to avoid the 'piecemealing' of projects which can lead to unjustified expenditures. We consider the history of Asfordby may illustrate a problem of 'piecemealing through time', that is spending money on a marginal project and subsequently treating the money already spent as a 'sunk cost'. Using this approach almost any project could at some stage become financially attractive. In future the sort of conditional approval which was given for expenditure on Asfordby, in advance of its showing a sound financial prospectus, should not be allowed by the Board, except when other factors are explicitly judged to be of sufficient weight.

5.106. BC agreed with us in principle that the achievement of a wider corporate objective could make worthwhile going ahead with a project which would otherwise be rejected on strict financial grounds. Where this is the case, the wider benefits should be clearly laid out in the project appraisal, and, for a significant project, the responsibility for making such an important judgement should lie with BC's Board.

6 Forecasting

6.1. In developing its strategy for achieving the Board's overall objectives BC prepares forecasts of future coal supply, demand and price within both the domestic and international coal markets. These form part of the Board's assessment of the risks and uncertainties facing the business.

6.2. Within BC, forecasts are prepared both by the Economics Unit (formerly the Central Planning Unit) and the Marketing Department. The Marketing Department prepares its forecasts annually, as part of a continuous process in parallel with BC's five-year business plans (see paragraphs 4.1 to 4.21). It gathers information on movements in the variables affecting United Kingdom demand from its commercial branches and sales regions, the Economics Unit and a wide variety of external sources. It also employs the ORE to provide calculations based on this information. Short-term forecasts prepared in this way are the major source of advice to the Board for the five-year planning period.

6.3. Medium- to long-term forecasts of supply, demand and price within domestic and international coal markets are prepared by the Economics Unit in consultation with Marketing and ORE. These forecasts are prepared on a rather more *ad hoc* basis and are a major source of advice to the Corporation, Select Committees and other external agencies.

The BC energy model
6.4. A primary input to both Economics Unit and Marketing Department forecasts are the outputs from BC's energy model prepared by ORE. The model considers the energy economy as 'a complex system of interactions between the supply, demand and price of the various competing fuels and the rest of the economy'. To prepare short- and medium-term forecasts of United Kingdom coal demand, the energy model maps movements in specified exogenous variables to obtain a range of estimates of changes within BC's business environment over varying time horizons.

Structure of the model
6.5. The overall structure of the United Kingdom energy model is shown in Figure 6.1. The principal external factors put into the model and about which assumptions are made are economic growth, fossil fuel prices, and determinants of demand affecting the electricity supply industry.

Economic growth
6.6. BC forecasts of gross domestic product (GDP) growth are based on the long-run averages of past growth, Treasury projections, and estimates from various independent agencies. From that range of forecasts, BC derives ranges for growth in industrial and commercial output and consumer expenditure. The effect of this analysis is to produce projections of electricity growth which are rather less than those for growth in GDP but with electricity taking a rising share in final energy demand. BC told us that this was in line with trends in Western Europe.

Competing fossil fuel prices
6.7. Future crude oil prices are forecast because the oil price tends to influence the price of all other fossil fuels, and because the ESI is able to switch easily between oil and coal in response to changes in relative prices. BC's forecasts of crude oil prices are based on an examination of published projections and on regular discussions with oil companies and academics. Its view that the current low crude oil price is unsustainable in the long term, together with the nature of the OPEC cartel, results in a forecast range for crude oil prices of $12 to $25 per barrel in 1990, rising to $20 to $40 per barrel in the year 2000.

FIGURE 6.1

Overall structure of the BC energy model

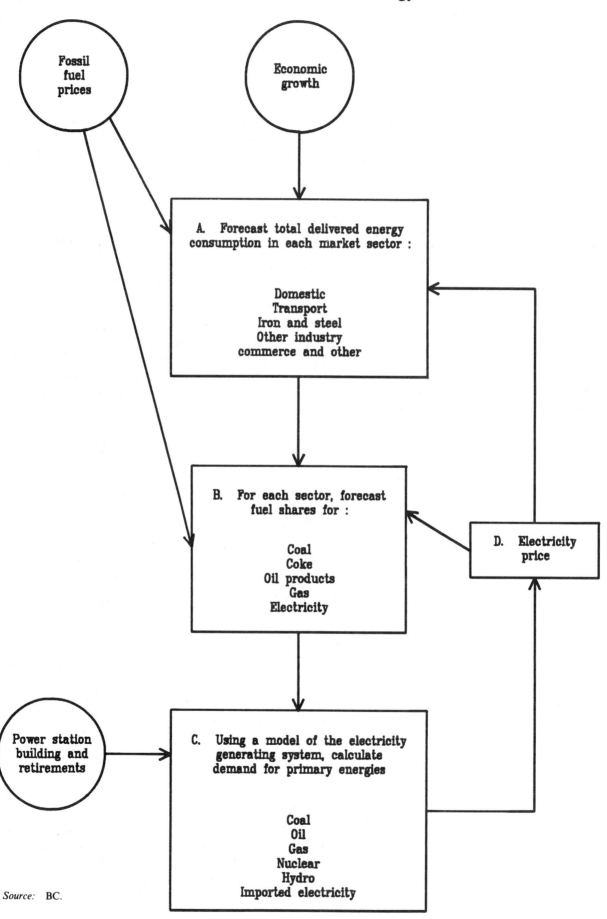

Fossil
fuel
prices

Economic
growth

A. Forecast total delivered energy
consumption in each market sector :

Domestic
Transport
Iron and steel
Other industry
commerce and other

B. For each sector, forecast
fuel shares for :

Coal
Coke
Oil products
Gas
Electricity

D. Electricity
price

Power station
building and
retirements

C. Using a model of the electricity
generating system, calculate
demand for primary energies

Coal
Oil
Gas
Nuclear
Hydro
Imported electricity

Source: BC.

64

6.8. Gas prices are also an important influence on the outlook for coal and affect the extent to which existing oil and gas-fired plant will be used. In the case of gas, price will also determine the extent to which new plant is built and the take-up rate of improvements in technology. With the collapse of both oil and gas prices in 1986, forecasts of future United Kingdom gas prices took on a new significance as gas moved out of the position of being regarded as a premium fuel. BC forecasts beach-head prices of 13 to 21 pence per therm for 1990 and 20 to 36 pence per therm in the year 2000.

United Kingdom energy consumption

6.9. For each main market sector total delivered energy consumption is forecast five years ahead on the basis of past consumption, economic growth and energy conservation (which is related to fuel prices). The sectoral forecasts of total energy consumption for particular years are then split into the market shares for each secondary fuel based on a historical analysis of past shares, the relative prices of these fuels and their suitability for particular uses.

6.10. The forecast demand for each secondary fuel is summed across sectors as the basis for calculating the demand for primary energy. The main feature of this calculation is BC's model of the electricity generating system which uses information on the power stations available and simulates the operation of the merit order to calculate the 'burn' of primary fuels required to meet the forecast levels of electricity demand. The price of electricity is calculated from the forecast use of primary fuels and other power station costs. This price is then fed back into the model and forecasts are re-estimated in an iterative process. The estimates obtained are then used in the model as the basis for a further set of forecasts another five years ahead using the same procedure.

6.11. The research required to provide updated values for the variables contained within the model is undertaken annually in line with the model's annual forecasting run.

Forecasts of United Kingdom coal demand

6.12. BC's forecasts do not estimate a single figure 'best estimate' of domestic coal demand, but cover a forecast range. For all variables, the range is a broad one and BC considers that it is very likely that the actual outcomes will fall inside the forecast range.

6.13. The dominant influence on the forecast is the fact that 75 per cent (79 million tonnes) of coal produced within the United Kingdom market is consumed by power stations. The merit order system of operation is such that the coal burn is predetermined by the demand for electricity, the number and type of power stations available and the price of competing fuels. BC has identified three exogenous variables as major causes of uncertainty in forecasting future United Kingdom ESI coal demand: levels of economic growth, future fossil fuel prices and the future mix of power stations. A remaining area of uncertainty for BC is the extent to which these variables will in turn affect both the demand for electricity and the direct use of coal in industry, commerce and the domestic sector. BC told us that it had not changed its estimates of demand in these last three sectors from those it had presented to the House of Commons Select Committee on Energy in November 1986.

6.14. In addition to the uncertainty surrounding the privatization of the ESI, and the proposed break-up of the CEGB, BC faces the possible increased use of gas for electricity generation. Improvements in gas turbine technology, increased gas supplies and de-regulation may make a significant impact upon energy markets and the demand for steam coal. BC told us that it was incorporating these factors within its forecasting approach but no revised estimates were available during our inquiry. BC's current estimates of total United Kingdom coal demand are set out in Table 6.1.

65

TABLE 6.1 **BC estimates of total United Kingdom coal demand, 1995 and 2000**

Market sector	*Million tonnes coal equivalent/(mtce)*	
	1995	*2000*
Power generation	75–90	75–95
Industry/commerce	9–12	10–15
Commerce/public services	1–2	2–4
Coke ovens	9–10	9–10
Domestic	7–8	6–7
Total UK coal consumption (inc colliery own use)	105–120	105–130
Minimum imports/non-vested supplies	15–10	20–10
Potential BC sales in UK	90–110	85–120

Source: BC.

Note: These projections are before allowing for possible additional power station coal imports following ESI privatization. No allowance is made for the limited tonnages of BC exports.

United Kingdom supply

6.15. BC told us that it has discontinued the publication of forecasts of future supply although it continued to analyse future potential output of all collieries as part of the Business Planning system.

The international market for sea-borne steam coal

6.16. There has been a significant rise in the international sea-borne steam coal trade in the past 15 years. Whilst the volume of world imports is very small by comparison with world consumption its significance for domestic production is considerable. Although world prices for steam coal vary depending on country of origin and quality, the dollar price available at Amsterdam, Rotterdam and Antwerp (ARA) is the price against which BC understands it has to compete.

6.17. In 1986 and 1987 BC undertook a major study of each of the significant variables determining international price and import levels to North-West Europe in order to forecast the likely range of prices against which BC would be required to compete to the year 2000. To enable BC to examine the potential evolution of world steam coal prices 'in the absence of additional imports into the UK' BC excluded the United Kingdom from its analysis.

6.18. To obtain estimates of future international price levels, BC first projected future world demand for imported steam coal. This, it judged, would be overwhelmingly concentrated in the power generation sector. Estimates were based on forecasts of growth in electricity demand in the coal importing countries, nuclear-generation capacity, coal-fired capacity, and international oil and gas prices. The effect of these projections, carried out in 1987, and the assumptions contained within them give the figures for hard coal consumption at power stations in the importing countries set out in Table 6.2.

TABLE 6.2 **Hard coal consumption at power stations**

	1985	1995		2000	*mtce*
		Low	*High*	*Low*	*High*
EEC (excl UK)	105	81	136	79	146
Other Western Europe	5	8	16	8	21
Pacific Rim	38	58	81	73	101
Others	3	7	19	13	25
Total coal importing countries	151	154	252	173	293

Source: BC.

Note: Estimates are in millions of tonnes of coal equivalent at 29·3 GJ per tonne. To convert to average actual traded quality tonnages would need to be increased by about 10 per cent.

6.19. Having obtained projections for power station markets, BC then calculated steam coal use in markets other than electricity supply. On the basis of its assumptions about the competitive nature of the fossil fuel market in the 1990s and the view that coal's competitive advantage outside the power station market is less marked, BC forecasts only a modest increase in international steam coal consumption in other markets.

6.20. Combining these two components of international demand and subtracting projections of indigenous coal production levels within the importing countries (excluding the United Kingdom) BC arrived at estimates of total sea-borne steam coal imports. These are set out in Table 6.3.

TABLE 6.3 **Projected levels of sea-borne steam coal imports**

| | 1985 | 1995 | | 2000 | *mtce* |
		Low	High	Low	High
EEC (excl UK)	58	63	105	69	120
Other Western Europe	10	12	22	12	28
Pacific Rim	41	71	98	88	121
Others	11	14	30	21	36
Total	120	160	255	190	305

Source: BC.

Note: See note to Table 6.2.

6.21. Based on its estimates of an average 2 to 3 per cent per annum growth in electricity demand across most importing countries, BC projects a doubling of demand for international steam coal by 2000. The range of uncertainty depends principally upon assumptions relating to the commissioning of nuclear plant and the rate of contraction of high cost indigenous coal production in the importing countries.

6.22. In estimating international levels of supply, BC differentiates between Communist and non-Communist exporting countries, and between the US and other non-Communist exporters. The US is singled out in this way because US exports are deemed to be 'marginal' in the sense that most exports come from mines that primarily supply the US domestic market. The relatively high prices available on the home market, and reluctance of foreign importers to pay prices which match US prices, despite the high quality of the coal, makes supply to the domestic market more attractive than exporting. However, BC estimates that in consequence of guaranteed levels of profitability arising from domestic markets, the price of US exports need cover only operating costs. There is over 150 mtce of US coal potentially available for export in 1995.

6.23. BC estimates that the combined potential availability of coal from Communist and non-Communist exporting countries could total some 350 mtce in 1995, and 450 mtce in 2000. However, BC estimates that a large proportion of these exports would not be forthcoming unless prices were 'very high'. It calculates that significant tonnages of US steam coal would be unlikely to be placed on world markets at c.i.f. prices of less than $45 per tonne, but that at prices at or above $50 per tonne supplies would be considerably increased.

6.24. It is this analysis of variables determining international supply and demand which has led BC to adopt projections of ARA prices of internationally traded steam coal (at a quality of 24·5 GJ per tonne) within the range of $35 to $50 in 1995 and $40 to $55 in the year 2000.

Exchange rates
6.25. The significance of estimating the ARA coal price for the United Kingdom market arises from the use of that price as the benchmark for United Kingdom competitiveness. However, as all international coal prices are denominated in US dollars, the exchange rate is a significant variable affecting BC's ability to compete. In consequence, BC has sought to plot long-term trends in the dollar/sterling exchange rate with reference to purchasing power parity, using the producer price index to convert from nominal to real exchange rates.

6.26. BC's analysis both of purchasing power parity and historical trends leads to an estimate that the current weakness of the dollar is unlikely to persist much beyond 1990 with the central value for the real sterling exchange rate settling around $1·40 (plus or minus 10 per cent).

Use of forecasts   6.27. During the first half of 1988 average ARA prices for internationally traded steam coal were in the range $33 to $38 per tonne. The sterling exchange rate against the US dollar averaged approximately $1·85 during the first six months of the year. BC's forecasts suggest that current international price levels are unsustainable in the long term and will rise. Its analysis of past trends in the sterling exchange rate suggests that the rate against the dollar will fall but that there will still be considerable fluctuation about a lower level.

6.28. In order to achieve a competitive position under these forecast conditions, BC has instructed Areas to reduce all future calculations of 'real' proceeds by two per cent per GJ over each of the next five years. This results in proceeds of around £1·50 per GJ in 1992–93—the same level identified by BC as the upper limit of acceptable cost for continuing collieries receiving new capital investment. The use of this level of projected proceeds in the 'base case' is intended to ensure that projected future costs, including return on new capital of 10 per cent 'real', are less than £1·50 per GJ across the industry. This level relates to BC's view of sustainable international coal prices in the late 1990s equivalent to £1·40 per GJ and a real exchange rate of £1 = $1·40. After allowing for transport costs, BC calculates that these rates will result in an average pithead 'netback' of £1·50 per GJ. BC considers that at these levels of cost and prices, it is more likely than not to be competitive with international coal on an ongoing basis. This conclusion is, however, very sensitive to the exchange rate assumption.

6.29. BC projects broadly stable demand within the power generation sector and stable or marginally increased demand within the industrial sector to the year 2000. Whilst it has not yet produced estimates of changes in consumption potentially arising from privatization of the electricity supply industry, or increased use of gas in electricity, it has altered certain of the assumptions underlying its projections published in 1986. It considers that electricity demand in 1990 may be 'somewhat higher' than originally assumed; that significant growth in the nuclear contribution to electricity generation is doubtful; and that the use of natural gas, particularly in small, purpose-built combined cycle plant, may increase. However, BC's provisional view is that the net effect of these changes may not materially alter its 1986 estimates.

6.30. BC's emphasis upon estimates of future prices reaffirms its rejection of supply targets and its commitment to operating cost targets with the attendant closure of high-cost collieries. In consequence, investment and production are becoming increasingly concentrated at existing and new collieries located within the central coalfields. This is mainly because it is here that economic reserves are concentrated but also because BC considers that demand for indigenous coal will remain concentrated upon those power stations located within that region, away from the coast, where BC has an advantage over imported coal by reason of transport costs.

Conclusions and recommendations

6.31. As part of the process of assessing risk and uncertainty, BC maintains systems for modelling United Kingdom energy demand and international trade in steam coal. We consider that these are useful systems which can make a valuable contribution to BC's strategic planning and to the assessment of its competitive position. However, we are concerned at the limited use which BC at present makes of these facilities.

6.32. BC's United Kingdom energy model is updated and forecasts prepared only once a year and other forecasts are prepared to meet particular requirements on an *ad hoc* basis. We were surprised that BC had not made more use of its models to carry out 'what if?' analyses of, for example, possible outcomes from ESI privatization. We consider that a more frequent systematic use of the forecasting models would help BC management in its assessment of the many uncertain factors affecting the industry.

6.33. In its 1987 study of world coal trade BC excluded the United Kingdom from its world trade model. While that may have been appropriate at the time we think that as a general practice United Kingdom coal production and demand should form part of the world trade model.

6.34. We recommend that BC should:

—create a system for more frequently updating and running its forecasting models and should incorporate the United Kingdom coal market into its world model;

—broaden the use made of its models to allow it to consider the effect of a wide range of possible developments, both in the United Kingdom and elsewhere, on the industry; and

—plan a regular programme of 'what if?' analyses to examine the effect on the industry of specific developments, for example ESI privatization, exchange rate movements, competition from alternative fuels and possible rapid growth in world trade in coal.

7   Management Systems

7.1. We review here a number of BC's management information and control systems, notably those determining and reporting on colliery costs and profitability, and those for reporting on and controlling capital projects. These are: the system for allocating sales proceeds to business units, including the price structure; the accounting system for reporting colliery and higher formations' results against budgets; the organization and control of capital projects, and monitoring of the costs of the capital programme; and Annual Reviews and Completion Reports. We then consider BC's project control performance, the monitoring of the Heavy Duty Programme, and indicators of capital performance.

Attribution of sales proceeds to production units for the purpose of investment and business decisions

7.2. BC told us that its accounting system sought to accommodate the following facts:

(a) The key figure for BC on revenue is what the customer actually pays.

(b) In the highly competitive environment in which BC is now operating, most customer prices are negotiated individually according to the degree of competition in each particular case.

(c) Within individual contracts there are provisions for prices to vary according to external factors, so price levels to individual customers can fluctuate throughout the year.

(d) Coal is a natural product with a wide range of chemical and physical properties, some of which are valued more by some buyers than by others. No two coals are exactly the same and their differences have to be reflected in the price which customers pay, in a way which is meaningful to them.

(e) The quality of individual named coals can also vary according to method of mining, preparation, seam proportions, and variations in inherent quality within different parts of the same seam. Larger customers monitor quality very carefully and expect the variations to be reflected in the price they pay.

(f) Despite this wide diversity of quality between and within individual coals, BC can usually offer a choice of suitable coals to individual customers. Many customers take a variety of coals and many coals are supplied to a number of different customers. The pattern of coal flows is constantly altering, and it is only exceptionally that individual coals are linked necessarily to individual customers with one or both of the parties having no realistic alternative available to it.

(g) Many price arrangements with individual buyers are not specific to named qualities or collieries, eg the CEGB 'tranching' system and quantity discounts.

7.3. BC believes it to be necessary to rationalize this complexity within the management accounting system in such a way as to enable true comparisons to be made between the performance of individual production units. This it sees as an essential prerequisite for sound management decision-making on matters such as investment and closure.

7.4. In the profit and loss account the same value is assigned to all coal of the same quality standard (with one or two minor exceptions). This value equates to the true income BC actually obtains for that quality of coal on average over the year as a whole.

7.5. In BC's view this system:

(*a*) avoids individual colliery profit and loss accounts showing wide month-to-month income variances which would obscure underlying trends and distort comparisons between units;

(*b*) enables local managements to concentrate on reducing costs, over which thay have a substantial degree of direct control;

(*c*) avoids situations in which high-cost collieries could be shown to be more profitable than low-cost collieries producing similar types of coal which are fully interchangeable in the market place; and

(*d*) thereby facilitates sound management decisions on investment and closure.

7.6. The system depends on two principal mechanisms:

(*a*) *price structures*—which assign appropriate relative values to coals of different quality standards; and

(*b*) *Market Adjustment Fund (MAF)*—a suspense account which has the effect of collecting income from customers and allocating it in an equitable way to individual units according to the tonnage and quality of coal that they produce.

Price structure   7.7. About 95 per cent of the volume of BC coal is priced according to its price list for industrial coals; the remaining 5 per cent is domestic bituminous and naturally smokeless fuels for which a separate price list applies. In this context 'domestic' means coal sold for use in household appliances. Small tonnages of low grade fuel such as slurry are sold at prices unrelated to the two main pricing systems, ie by commercial negotiation.

7.8. BC's normal quotation is for prices ex-pithead or opencast disposal point, but coal despatched by sea is quoted f.o.b. Occasionally coal is sold on a delivered price basis by agreement with the customer.

7.9. Under European Coal and Steel Community (ECSC) rules, every coal producer within the European Community is obliged to publish price lists setting out certain information and to lodge copies with the European Commission in Brussels.

Industrial coals   7.10. The list price of individual industrial coals is determined according to the Industrial Coal Price Structure, as set out in the price list. This price structure recognizes that the most important feature of a coal is its heat content. The primary price component is therefore calorific value expressed in terms of kilojoules per kilogram (kJ/kg); a secondary adjustment is made in respect of ash; and final adjustments are made in respect of sulphur content and degree of preparation (washing and sorting by size).

7.11. The Industrial Coal Price Structure ensures that within a given coalfield, coals of comparable quality carry the same price; and that coals of different quality bear a commercially meaningful price relationship to each other. However, between coalfields the price of comparable coals differs, and these price relationships have varied through time.

Domestic fuels   7.12. Bituminous house coals are not priced on the same basis as industrial coals, but are assigned to a particular group according to their commercial value in practical use, taking account of such factors as free-burning propensity, amount and nature of ash, size, friability, and general appearance. Assignments are made by a Regional Quality Monitoring Committee consisting of experienced representatives of the wholesale and distributive coal trade. These representatives individually test the coal in their own appliances and submit formal reports to the

Committee, which then decides a group assignment on a consensus basis. Efforts have been made from time to time by BC and others to find a workable scientific formula for use in pricing house coals, but although most coals can be made to fit sensibly within any given formula, there are always exceptional cases which simply do not conform in practical tests with the scientific prediction.

7.13. The number of house coal groups has varied through time and currently there are four. As with industrial coals, prices for a given house coal group vary according to coalfield.

7.14. Naturally smokeless domestic fuels (anthracite and dry steam coal) are produced only in the South Wales coalfield, in the western and central parts respectively. These are highly specialized fuels. Qualities are classified by size range, and there are two groups in the larger size range. Significant tonnages of domestic grade anthracite are also sold on the industrial or quasi-industrial (commercial, local authority establishments etc) markets, but there is a common price list.

7.15. For all domestic fuels, supplementary charges may be raised in respect of special services rendered, eg use of mechanical baggers.

Manufactured fuels

7.16. BC's wholly-owned subsidiary National Smokeless Fuels Ltd is responsible for producing and selling coke and manufactured fuels.

Purpose of the price structures

7.17. The price structures seek to achieve the following objectives:

(a) enabling the list price to be calculated for individual coals;

(b) determining price relationships between coals of differing quality specification which are meaningful to the customer;

(c) providing a methodology for retrospective price adjustment should the quality of a coal as actually supplied vary from the standard specification upon which the invoice price is based;

(d) providing a base from which to determine revenue for collieries and opencast disposal points; and

(e) providing a base against which to judge any price negotiations with individual customers.

Allocation of net revenue to collieries

7.18. Up to 1979, the total value of rebate was relatively small. The accounting practice was to credit individual collieries with list price, and (with minor exceptions) to allocate rebates to the coalfield in which they arose. These coalfield rebates were debited back to individual Areas/opencast regions within the coalfield, but they remained on Area account and were not allocated to collieries.

7.19. When in 1979 rebates had to be extended for the first time to the coking market, and it became evident that steam coal rebates would also have to be offered on a wide scale in 1980 (including to power stations, again for the first time), BC decided that the time had come to debit individual collieries with the rebates. This change was made at the start of the 1980–81 financial year. In BC's view, continuation of the previous system would have unduly exaggerated the profitability of production units and given wrong messages for investment.

7.20. In deciding the method of allocation, BC concluded that it was impractical simply to allocate rebates to the unit at which they arose. An alternative system was devised which attributes the same value to all coals of equivalent quality standard; this works by means of a suspense account known as the Market Adjustment Fund (MAF). Before the start of each financial year, the monetary value of rebates expected during the year ahead is estimated and expressed as a percentage of the value of sales at full list price. Subsequently, when coal is sold (or used internally), the profit and loss account of the unit concerned is credited with list price for the coal less this percentage amount; this credit is known as *saleable proceeds*. Within the accounts, the term 'saleable proceeds' applies to total output, irrespective of whether or not the coal is sold immediately. The difference between saleable proceeds and list price (ie the predetermined percentage amount, known as the 'contribution rate'), is credited to MAF. Any rebates arising from the sale (or any other rebates which are not specific to individual sales transactions) become a debit to MAF; such rebates are the difference between the list price and the actual customer price. If the forecasts at the start of the year were to be precisely accurate, the MAF suspense account would be in balance at the year end (though not necessarily at any point during the year, since some rebates are seasonal). In practice, there are inevitable variations from forecast in tonnages sold and rebates given, and often there is a list price change during the course of the year. If it becomes evident during the course of the year that the MAF account will be out of balance (either credit or debit) at the end of the year, a revised MAF contribution rate is introduced during the course of the year to correct the imbalance.

7.21. The detailed working of the MAF system has been modified in various ways since its inception in 1980. Current arrangements are that there are four separate MAF suspense accounts which reflect the main coal types and markets served, viz:

Bituminous coals:	Graded coals
	Non-graded coals
Anthracite:	Graded coals
	Non-graded coals

The two anthracite accounts are specific to South Wales, and were introduced at the start of the 1985–86 fiscal year, on the recommendation of external consultants, to reflect the largely discrete nature of this coal. (Nevertheless, there is, in fact, considerable interface with bituminous coal, in that the greater part of small anthracite is blended with higher volatile bituminous coals for use in power stations. For this reason such sales are deemed to be bituminous coal for accounting purposes.)

7.22. The division of each main coal type into 'graded' and 'non-graded' reflects the fact that the net price paid by most customers for graded coals (irrespective of market) is much higher both in terms of £ per tonne and £ per GJ. BC told us that the division helps to underline the true value to BC of preparing coals to a high standard, and enables investment decisions on coal preparation to be taken against an accurate yardstick.

Stock coal and sundry items

7.23. Saleable proceeds are not the final determinant of revenue attributed to collieries for the purpose of compiling the profit and loss account. They need to be further adjusted for:

(*a*) stocking provisions; and

(*b*) income from sundry sales and services (eg sales of colliery methane, payments for special services such as mechanical bagging etc).

These items are shown as separate line entries on the profit and loss statement. The bottom line proceeds figure (ie saleable proceeds adjusted for the creation or release of stocking provisions and sundry items) is known as *net proceeds*. Net proceeds are set against operating costs to determine operating profit/loss.

7.24. When coal is put to stock, it is valued in the accounts at the lower of 'net realizable value' or 'cost of production', within the following broad meaning of these terms:

Net Realizable Value (NRV)

—saleable proceeds less such stocking provisions as are judged to be needed to cover costs incurred while the coal remains in stock, plus the expected future costs of lifting and marketing; and

Cost of Production (COP)

—the annually calculated average cost, excluding Area and Headquarters overheads, of producing a tonne of coal in that coalfield (rather than at the individual colliery which produced the coal).

This credit is to a revenue account known as 'Changes in Stock'.

7.25. Where NRV exceeds COP at the time of stocking, a further provision (known as the general provision) is raised to reduce the book value to COP. The book value of the stock is adjusted whenever list prices and MAF rates are changed, but not so as to increase it above COP.

7.26. No credit to the MAF account is made at the time coal is stocked; this credit only arises when the coal is actually lifted and sold (or used internally). At the time of sale, the colliery is credited with the value of the coal as if it were current output (ie list price ruling at the time of sale less the contribution into the MAF suspense account). At the same time, the book value of the stock, ie NRV or COP (as the case may be), is debited to the 'Changes in Stock' account referred to in paragraph 7.24. The difference between these two amounts represents BC's gross profit on the particular sale. The arrangements described in this and the preceding paragraph satisfy the accounting requirement that profits are not brought to account ahead of sales, but losses are.

7.27. There are detailed mandatory standing instructions governing the accounting treatment for stocks and for the MAF system, issued by the Finance and Marketing Departments after agreement with the Audit Department.

BC's accounting and related systems for reporting operating and 'bottom line' results against budgets

7.28. BC operates an integrated accounting system which, in addition to keeping the books of account, provides the management accounting information. All the management information used for reporting financial performance originates from this system, or from one of the linked sub-systems. The integrated system has facilities for detailed breakdowns of costs by function, by location within a colliery and by spending officer. Such analyses support the standard performance documents.

7.29. At production unit level, a great deal of management information for day-to-day control and monitoring is derived from locally developed manual or partly computerized systems.

Basis of the profit and loss accounts for production units

7.30. Profit and loss accounts are prepared on a 'full cost' basis. Overheads at Area and Headquarters level are apportioned to units on equitable bases. Saleable proceeds are established in accordance with the arrangements described in paragraphs 7.20 to 7.22.

7.31. Since 1985, results have been calculated at the operating level and on a 'bottom line' basis after capital charges. Capital charges are calculated on a percentage (currently 11 per cent) of the written down value of the fixed assets employed at the colliery, or in support of the colliery.

Profit and loss accounts

7.32. Profit and loss accounts are produced each month on a 4.4.5-weekly basis. The format is standard for all collieries. For opencast disposal points a slightly different standard form is used. A disposal point is a washery/coal treatment plant, serving up to four opencast sites. It is the lowest level at which opencast profit is calculated.

7.33. These reports compare the current month and cumulative result with budget and the cumulative result with that for the same period in the previous year.

7.34. In addition to the profit and loss accounts, trend statements are produced each month for all deep mines, with aggregations to Area level. Trend statements give summary information, both statistical and financial, and relate to profit and loss performance over a period of five completed years, together with budget, forward projections and actual results for the current year.

Organization of capital investment projects

7.35. Every capital investment project is the responsibility of the appropriate Area (or other formation as appropriate). Under the control of the Area Deputy Director (Mining) (DDM), who is responsible to the Area Director for capital investment, are the Area's Planning Department, mechanical, electrical and civil engineers, and the collieries, which report through a Production Manager or Managers. In the small Areas (SCT, NEA, WES, SWL)[1] the DDM's role in Investment is the responsibility of the Head of Technical Services. The Planning Department is generally responsible for co-ordinating the preparation of all capital projects, which includes liaison with other departments (notably Finance, IR, Marketing, Staff) to ensure all relevant documentation and comments are completed and included in the Stage I, Stage II (see paragraph 5.6), Annual Reviews and Completion Reports (see paragraphs 7.50 to 7.54). Once Stage II approval has been given progressing of capital projects is again co-ordinated by the Planning Department, although, once nominated, the Project Manager takes specific responsibility for the project.

7.36. On major projects it is now customary for the Project Manager to be nominated by the time the Stage II prospectus is submitted. The level of the appointment is required to be stated in the submission. Staffing proposals by number, grade, discipline and calibre for each stage, the basis for control of the duration and cost, and the system for monitoring and control of the project are all agreed at Stage II.

7.37. The Project Manager may be full- or part-time, and his level of seniority is determined by the complexity and cost of the project or projects for which he is responsible. Ideally, he should be involved in the development of the project from its conception through to commissioning.

7.38. The Project Manager is responsible for the overall monitoring and control of the project. He is responsible for ensuring that:

(a) there is a forward looking, responsive project control system capable of producing out-turn forecasts (physical/financial: time/cost) against plan;

(b) specific facilities are provided for planning and controlling the issue and approval of drawings and specifications;

(c) specific facilities are provided for the planning of material and services procurement and letting of contracts;

(d) project contracts are controlled;

(e) BC labour is adequately controlled; and

(f) there is a means of evaluating rapidly the effects on the project programme of any decisions or actual events affecting the project.

If the achievement of the prospectus' goals is at risk, these arrangements should enable the Project Manager to be aware of the effect of the shortfall/overrun and enable remedial action to be taken.

7.39. Each individual contract within the project is supervised by a BC staff member, reporting to the Project Manager, nominated as engineer, architect, or supervising officer to the contract. The duties of supervising officers and a schedule of meetings typically found in large project organization is laid out in our previous report (paragraphs 10.10 to 10.17). In addition to the monitoring arrangements shown there, capital projects are the subject of regular meetings (usually monthly) held by Area Directors with their staff.

---

[1] See glossary.

7.40. The Stage II document is expected to incorporate estimates of costs and time sufficient to allow effective control of physical progress and expenditure. Estimates are built up with regard to the nature and order in which the work is to be done, how it is to be contracted out and how services are to be provisioned, grouping the project into sections, sub-sections and items. Planned rates of progress for the important aspects of the project, eg shaft sinking, drivage of drifts and underground roadways, are provided, and a schedule showing the planned physical programme of construction on sections and sub-sections is prepared.

7.41. A contract plan, covering all items which will be contracted out, is also provided. Time-critical contract works are identified and an assessment of the consequences a delay in any of these critical items would have on the completion time of the project is required. Where appropriate, a Critical Path Analysis is prepared for inclusion in the submission.

7.42. Because the most usual reason for cost overruns is delay in physical progress, the arrangements stress physical control of the project, although there are the normal arrangements for confirming contractors' claims for payment and controlling variation orders.

Control of project costs

7.43. Project costs are recorded within the Fixed Asset System, which comprises a Project Ledger and an Asset File. The Project Ledger is a database for the collection of costs relevant to each project. The Asset File records the creation of assets, specifically in the case of identifiable assets and collectively by category for other capital expenditure such as expenses of a general nature encountered on major projects.

7.44. BC's Investment Manual requires all expenditure included in submissions of capital projects for approval to be sectionalized under 14 main headings (the first of which, relating to exploration for reserves, being recorded, when relevant, as a memorandum item only). Each of the main sections is further divided into sub-sections covering major categories of works within each main heading. Comprehensive lists are provided of the items which fall to be included under each sub-section. Each section and sub-section has its own numeric reference for use when entering data in the Fixed Asset System.

7.45. As soon as a project has received Stage II approval, full details are entered in the Project Ledger, items being identified by their section and sub-section reference numbers and given the status of approved expenditure.

7.46. As the various works included in the Stage II approval are given Stage III authorization, appropriate entries are made in the Project Ledger to record the extent to which expenditure has been authorized against each sub-section. Commitments entered into, eg orders placed, contracts let, are likewise recorded, as is expenditure as incurred. Expenditure incurred on each specific asset or category of asset is identified by reference number and additionally recorded in the Asset File.

7.47. A detailed report for each project is prepared by the system for each accounting period. This gives for each sub-section the total approved expenditure, the total authorized, the total committed and the total spent in the year to date, the relevant totals for previous years and the aggregated totals to date.

7.48. The reports derived from the Fixed Assets System are supported by returns reporting progress on related contracts (including the effect of variations orders issued or anticipated, contractual pricing adjustments, and contractual claims outstanding or anticipated) and actual expenditure compared with phased allocation.

Monitoring the capital investment programme

7.49. Detailed summaries of individual project cost statements are prepared for each colliery within an Area and much less detailed summaries of an Area's capital expenditure for the accounting period and cumulative to date are prepared, which include comparisons with budgeted capital allocations. These latter Area summaries are aggregated to provide a report to the Board, in which each Area's performance against budgeted allocations is set out.

7.50. As part of the formal monitoring of all projects over £0·5 million, BC has a system of Annual Reviews and Completion Reports. Projects with a completion time of less than 12 months or less than £1 million in cost require only a Completion Report, in abbreviated form. Over £1 million, Completion Reports and Annual Reviews are both required, and provide:

(a) a brief description of the project, its costs and objectives, and the expected results compared with the prospectus:

(b) progress achieved; difficulties encountered; action taken; and actual expenditure;

(c) marginal benefits, in terms of manpower, cost savings, increased output; changes from those put forward in the prospectus and the reasons for these changes;

(d) overall colliery results on project completion, in physical and financial terms, expected now compared with those expected at Stage II;

(e) other factors of importance; and

(f) conclusion and recommendations for approval or otherwise, including action to be taken, eg stopping the project.

7.51. Annual reviews should be prepared as at the anniversary of the project's approval at Stage II and the first review becomes due no later than 15 months from project approval; Completion Reports are due within 15 months of completion. Annual Reviews and Completion Reports are made to the decision-taking level where Stage II approval was given. The decision-taking level is responsible for seeing that any remedial actions necessary during the progress of the project and on completion to achieve the prospectus' results are taken and reported upon in the appropriate Annual Reviews and Completion Report.

7.52. Since November 1985 the procedure has been established whereby Annual Reviews and Completion Reports are subject to review by the Accountability Meetings, an arrangement incorporated into the Capital Investment manual issued in May 1987. We were told that these procedures were taken very seriously indeed. Annual Reviews were previously dealt with by a sub-committee of the Project Committee. The Project Committee now deals with them itself, providing advice to Accountability Meetings.

7.53. The Annual Reviews do not include current pit profitability, although we were assured that this is on hand when they are reviewed by the Project Committee, in the form of the Financial Trend Statements.

7.54. Annual reviews and Completion Reports use, as the standard against which expenditure is measured, the Stage II estimate, not the Stage III committed sum. In our 1983 report we said (paragraph 10.59):

> We remain concerned that in circumstances where tender sums are different from Stage II estimates, monitoring may be against an inappropriate amount. We consider that there should be an automatic formal notification to Headquarters in all cases where the tender sums differ from the Stage II estimates by an amount greater than some fixed percentage or amount. We recommend that the NCB institute such a formal system of notification and, whether or not a revised Stage II submission is required, that monitoring of progress is measured against a sum that reflects the tender price.

We put it to BC that these arguments still stood, and that once the contract was let, the key reference point was the contract price: the changes we had suggested would improve control of capital investment in respect of annual expenditure; monitoring against commitment; and monitoring against approval. BC pointed out that BC's Capital Investment Manual made provision for the circumstances in which a project is likely to exceed the approved out-turn total cost. BC took the view that there was a need to safeguard the Stage II approval as the contract between those responsible for managing the project and those responsible for approving it. There would be difficulties in frequently changing that contract, since this would call into question the original approval and so weaken accountability. For this reason, the project management monitored progress against Stage III authorization, and the approving body did so against the Stage II approval, expressed at out-turn prices. BC told us, however, that our arguments were being considered by the Working Party on Project Management which BC has established to see how best they could be accommodated.

Post-investment appraisal

7.55. We distinguish between the post-investment audit which BC carries out for every capital investment project for the Completion Reports, and full scale post-project appraisal which sets out to examine wide issues—the thinking behind the investments as well as the project management, and close comparison of all the outcomes, including those outside the control of local management, with objectives and expectations—by an independent team on a few, selected projects. Amongst the evidence we received, Professor Atkinson, head of the Mining Department at Nottingham University, told us that few British mining houses carry out such studies. He told us that such appraisals have three major benefits: the opportunity to initiate corrective action on current projects; managers know their claims will be compared with performance; and the quality of future proposals and control over them is invariably improved. We were told that BC was in a unique position to carry out such studies, since it did not, as do other mining houses, have to contend with the problems of having to deal with units in a number of different countries, exposure to the effects of unpredictable changes in metal prices, and movements in exchange rates.

7.56. We put this to BC, which told us that the Headquarters organization which monitored project performance and advised Areas and other formations on technical and other matters provided a means of transferring experience from one part of BC to another. BC gave as examples of changes arising from lessons learnt through the project monitoring arrangements: changes in the Capital Investment Manual, the introduction of a new project control procedures, the use of externally contracted quantity surveyors, and the accumulated experience gained from the development of successive new mines—for example, the reduction in the number of faces planned for Asfordby in the light of experience with heavy duty equipment at Selby. BC also drew attention to symposia organized for BC by the professional institutions, whereby delegates might learn of ways in which others had improved their capital productivity.

Project management and control

7.57. The amount of detail used in the control system varies according to the complexity and total cost of the project. The system is expected to provide:

(a) Clearly defined plans in both physical and financial terms;

(b) records of actual performance, both physical and financial, at regular intervals;

(c) the means of comparing the actual and planned performance, with the facility to highlight significant differences by main resources, eg contractor, BC labour, materials issue, and so on;

(d) a facility to assess the likely effect of variations and knowledge to date on future events, the completion date and out-turn costs; and

(e) reports on progress and completion, based on the 'exception' principle, to various levels of management, as appropriate, including the decision-taking level.

Optimum use of computers is expected to assist in managing and controlling the project.

7.58. This was the subject of recommendations in our 1983 report. At that time BC made some changes and improvements to its system of project control. In 1983 the Department of Energy commissioned management consultants to carry out an appraisal of the proposed Asfordby coal mine, including reviewing the financial appraisal, key assumptions, critical factors affecting the project which might have been omitted, and identification of any other factors. In their report (July 1983) the consultants expressed concern about the organization and control of the project. In 1985 BC commissioned a study of project management at Asfordby, from the same consultants, who reported in October 1985. This report recommended: organizational changes, notably that there should be a full-time project leader; that the project team should all be situated on site; that the project control function should be strengthened (from 9 to 15); and that an up-to-date computer system be employed. BC accepted this report, and, furthermore, commissioned the consultants to implement the project control system, including providing project control staff whilst BC staff were trained to take on these new roles. The system is now in full use at Asfordby, and, we were told, also in use elsewhere. The consultants' staff are being phased out as BC staff develop expertise. Asfordby, so far, is running to time.

7.59. At the time the consultants' proposals for implementation of the project management system were accepted, the CIC asked the Head of Environment and Planning to promulgate project management methodology, and the lessons from Asfordby, within BC. A project management manual is to be issued as soon as possible. BC told us that it would cover the consequences of differences between operational and project management; the objectives of project management; team structure; the relationship of the project team with line and departmental management; relationships with outside bodies (other than consultants and contractors); project management and control; information systems; accountability and review; and training and career development. We were told that the lessons being learned at Asfordby and elsewhere were being absorbed and would continue to be so, and that the computer information systems were now being used for smaller projects with the aid of desktop computers.

7.60. We asked BC whether there was enough major project control work to sustain in-house development of project management skills. At present there is no traditional career path through project management. On the contrary, colliery management is still the recognized route to senior positions. In the course of our inquiry, as preparations were being made to replace four smaller Areas with four Groups, it had been agreed in principle that there will be a project management function under central Headquarters control, although the details had still to be settled. This will provide a core of experienced Project Managers and staff for projects in certain locations and of a certain size (still to be determined), including some larger projects in operational mines in the new Groups.

Project control performance   7.61. In our 1983 report we examined the results of 77 large major projects completed by December 1981. Analysis of the time taken to complete these projects compared with the time estimated at the Stage II submission revealed that all but six of the projects were completed late. The details are as follows:

Number of projects
(table taken from MMC 1983 report)

Early or on time	6
Up to 12 months late	35
13–24 months late	26
25–36 months late	5
37–48 months late	3
Over 48 months late	2
Total	77

7.62. At the time of that report the NCB (as it was then) had just issued new instructions on project planning, appraisal and management, with the aim of improving the progressing of major projects from the planning to the commissioning stage. These instructions had come into force in April 1982. The main changes were the introduction of:

(a) changes in project sectionalization;

(b) the extension of the Contract Plan;

(c) the changes in the arrangements for technical changes;

(*d*) changes in the arrangements for contract administration;

(*e*) changes in the appointment of management resources;

(*f*) changes in the use of consultants; and

(*g*) changes in the design and construction of coal preparation plants.

These revised arrangements were described in Chapter 10 of our earlier report. In December 1982 BC introduced monitoring against out-turn prices. From January 1983 onwards the following changes were also introduced:

(*a*) risk assessments by Headquarters departments;

(*b*) the requirement for Stage I submissions for all projects costing over £5 million;

(*c*) the preparation and presentation of papers by Area Directors; and

(*d*) the submission of all Completion Reports and, where necessary, Annual Reviews to quarterly accountability meetings.

7.63. In February 1988 BC's CIC considered a paper on major project performance against Stage II prospectus. This examined performance on the 37 major projects (excluding Asfordby) approved at Headquarters since 1 January 1983, of which:

(*a*) 17 had been completed;

(*b*) 17 were still in progress; and

(*c*) three had been aborted or the colliery concerned closed.

Asfordby new mine was not included in the review because of the size of the project, which it was thought would distort the information. The latest Annual Review indicated that this project would be completed within the time and cost approved at Stage II.

7.64. In order to establish the project performance it was necessary for appropriate adjustments to be made to eliminate the effects of the major industrial dispute (1984 to 1985) on the actual project cost and duration. After making these adjustments the analysis showed that, for those 17 projects which had been completed:

Number of projects, 1983–88	
On time or early	12
Up to 12 months late	4
13–24 months late	1
Total	17

Of the 17 which had not been completed, the estimated durations gave the following results:

Number of projects, 1983–88	
Early or on time	12
Up to 12 months late	4
13–24 months late	1
Total	17

7.65. Appendix 7.1(i) and (ii) shows these data in graphical form. However, the need to make adjustments to allow for the effects of the 1984–85 strike has meant that an element of judgment has been applied, making conclusions drawn from this analysis less certain than they might otherwise be. Three of the completed projects analysed by BC were amongst those we selected as our case studies. BC's calculations in the analysis of project performance do not correspond with calculations made by our staff based on the information provided to us, on two out of three of these projects (in one case less favourably, in the other more favourably). BC agreed that the data would bear alternative interpretations, but considered its to be the more reasonable.

7.66. The analysis also showed the estimated and actual cost of the 17 completed projects, and the 17 uncompleted projects. None of the completed projects had cost more than its Stage II estimate. Whilst most were within 15 per cent of the Stage II estimate, two were more than 30 per cent under the estimate. This is shown in graphical form in Appendix 7.1(iii). Of the incomplete projects, all are expected to come in at or under their Stage II estimates, although only one at more than 15 per cent under.

7.67. Until recently (end 1984/early 1985) the Stage II cost estimates prepared by the quantity surveyors were intended to reflect a situation where supply and demand in the construction industry were in normal balance. At the time many of the projects we examined went out to tender, market conditions were such that prices obtained for civil works on contracts let were exceptionally low. This explains why so many of the contracts were let at markedly below the Stage II estimate. BC has changed its instructions to those preparing Stage II estimates, and they are now required to make the estimate on the basis of the market prices currently being tendered.

7.68. BC concluded from the analysis referred to in paragraphs 7.63 to 7.66 that actual and expected project durations compared with Stage II showed a marked improvement over projects approved before January 1983, and that actual project costs on completed projects were some 12 per cent less than that approved at Stage II, on average. Ongoing projects were estimated to be going to cost, on average, 4 per cent less than the Stage II estimate. BC also noted that the average estimated cost of projects approved after January 1983 was some £12 million, about a third of that for those approved pre-January 1983; this reflected the policy of developing a strategy for a colliery and then undertaking a series of separate smaller and more easily managed projects rather than undertaking a single large composite project with much longer duration. BC concluded from this analysis that projects approved since January 1983 were generally being completed on time and within estimated costs and that results on completion were better than those of Stage II, and that these improvements could be attributed to the preparation of more robust Stage II plans and estimates and better project control following the introduction of revised procedures.

Monitoring the heavy duty investment programme

7.69. Table 7.1 shows, by colliery, the investment in heavy duty equipment from 1982–83 to 1987–88:

TABLE 7.1 **Investment in heavy duty in collieries in production as at March 1988**

							£ million
Colliery	1982–83	1983–84	1984–85	1985–86	1986–87	1987–88	Total
Scottish Area							
Barony	—	—	—	—	—	—	—
Bilston Glen	1·331	(0·012)	3.347	—	2·119	—	6·785
Longannet Complex (including Castlehill and Solsgirth)	—	2·106	4·376	—	—	—	6·482
Monktonhall	—	—	—	1·900	—	—	1·900
Others	—	—	—	—	0·352	—	0·352
North-East Area							
Dawdon	—	—	—	—	—	—	—
Easington	—	—	—	1·800	—	—	1·800
Ellington Combine	—	2·210	1·389	—	—	—	3·599
Murton	—	—	—	—	—	—	—
Vane Tempest/Seaham	—	—	—	—	—	—	—
Wearmouth	—	—	—	—	—	—	—
Westoe	—	—	—	—	—	—	—
Others	—	—	—	—	—	—	—

Colliery	1982–83	1983–84	1984–85	1985–86	1986–87	1987–88	£ million Total
North Yorkshire Area							
Allerton Bywater	—	—	—	—	0·136	1·636	1·772
Barnsley Main (Barrow)	2·731	—	—	—	—	—	2·731
Dearne Valley	—	—	—	—	—	—	—
Denby Grange	—	—	—	—	1·793	2·258	4·051
Grimethorpe	2·795	1·964	(0·054)	2·500	—	1·034	8·239
Houghton/Darfield	0·414	0·028	—	—	2·532	—	2·974
Kellingley	2·859	(0·029)	3·405	—	—	—	6·235
Park Mill	—	—	3·262	—	—	—	3·262
Prince of Wales	—	—	—	—	—	—	—
Riccall	—	—	—	—	—	—	—
Royston	—	—	—	—	—	2·035	2·035
Sharlston	—	—	—	—	—	—	—
Stillingfleet	—	—	—	—	—	—	—
Whitemoor	—	—	—	—	—	—	—
Wistow	—	—	—	—	—	—	—
Others	—	—	—	—	—	0·237	0·237
South Yorkshire Area							
Askern	—	—	—	—	—	4·103	4·103
Barnburgh	—	—	—	—	—	—	—
Bentley	—	—	—	—	0·979	1·729	2·708
Brodsworth	—	—	—	—	—	—	—
Dinnington	—	—	—	—	—	—	—
Frickley/South Elmsall	—	—	—	—	0·932	—	0·932
Goldthorpe/Hickleton	—	—	—	—	—	—	—
Hatfield/Thorne	—	—	—	—	2·523	—	2·523
High Moor	—	—	—	—	—	—	—
Kiveton Park	—	—	—	—	—	—	—
Maltby	—	—	—	5·800	—	—	5·800
Manton	—	—	—	2·500	3·096	2·952	8·548
Markham Main	—	—	—	—	—	—	—
Rossington	—	—	—	—	0·806	3·753	4·559
Shireoaks/Steetley	—	—	—	—	—	—	—
Silverwood	—	2·644	—	—	3·289	3·532	9·465
Thurcroft	1·965	—	—	—	—	—	1·965
Treeton	—	—	—	2·700	—	—	2·700
Others	—	—	—	—	0·125	3·531	3·656
Nottinghamshire Area							
Annesley/Bentinck	—	—	—	2·600	—	—	2·600
Bevercotes	—	—	6·829	—	2·289	3·643	12·761
Bilsthorpe	—	0·083	—	—	—	2·313	2·396
Blidworth	—	—	—	—	—	—	—
Calverton	—	—	—	—	—	1·695	1·695
Clipstone	—	—	1·789	—	2·439	2·259	6·487
Cotgrave	3·031	2·075	2·930	—	—	2·062	10·098
Creswell	—	—	—	—	—	—	—
Gedling	—	—	1·783	—	—	2·212	3·995
Harworth	2·772	(0·058)	3·004	—	—	—	5·718
Allerton	—	—	2·693	—	2·766	3·323	8·782
Rufford	—	1·969	—	5·200	2·886	—	10·055
Sherwood	—	1·585	—	3·000	—	2·375	6·960
Silverhill	—	—	—	—	—	4·362	4·362
Sutton	—	—	—	—	—	—	—
Thoresby	5·446	(0·015)	—	2·800	—	3·568	11·799
Welbeck	—	3·033	5·456	—	—	2·516	11·005
Others	(0·014)	—	0·055	—	0·731	11·772	12·544
Central Area							
Baddesley	—	—	—	—	—	—	—
Bagworth/Ellistown	2·674	3·172	3·018	0·400	—	—	9·264
Bolsover	—	—	—	—	—	—	—
Coventry	3·863	—	3·286	—	—	7·639	14·788
Daw Mill	4·111	4·012	(0·277)	9·000	2·851	—	19·697
Donisthorpe/Rawdon	—	—	—	—	—	—	—
Markham	—	—	—	3·100	—	2·508	5·608
Renishaw Park	—	—	—	—	—	—	—
Shirebrook	—	—	2·288	—	—	1·614	3·902
Warsop	—	—	2·868	2·600	—	—	5·468
Others	—	—	—	—	(0·006)	—	(0·006)

							£ million
Colliery	1982–83	1983–84	1984–85	1985–86	1986–87	1987–88	Total
Western Area							
Agecroft	2·930	—	—	—	—	—	2·930
Bickershaw Complex	—	—	—	—	—	3·705	3·705
Florence	—	1·872	—	—	—	—	1·872
Hem Heath	0·160	3·404	—	2·900	1·912	—	8·376
Holditch	—	—	—	—	2·377	—	2·377
Lea Hall	—	—	—	—	—	2·556	2·556
Littleton	—	—	—	3·000	2·598	—	5·598
Parkside	—	—	—	2·000	—	—	2·000
Point of Ayr	—	—	—	—	—	—	—
Silverdale	—	—	—	—	—	—	—
Sutton Manor	—	—	—	—	2·322	—	2·322
South Wales Area							
Betws	—	—	—	—	2·088	—	2·088
Blaenant	—	—	—	—	1·987	—	1·987
Cynheidre	—	—	—	—	2·370	—	2·370
Deep Navigation	—	2·018	—	—	—	—	2·018
Marine/Six Bells	—	—	—	2·600	—	—	2·600
Merthyr Vale	—	—	—	—	—	—	—
Oakdale	—	—	—	—	—	—	—
Penallta	—	—	—	2·200	—	—	2·200
Taff Merthyr	—	—	2·015	—	—	—	2·015
Tower/Mardy	—	—	—	—	2·094	1·300	3·394
Trelewis	—	—	—	—	—	—	—
Others	—	—	—	—	0·253	0·700	0·953
Kent Area							
Betteshanger	—	—	—	—	2·323	—	2·323
Others	—	—	—	—	0·525	—	0·525
Adjustment to previous years (all Areas)	—	—	—	0·800	—	—	0·800
Sub-total	37·068	32·061	53·462	59·400	53·487	88·922	324·400
Investment at closed collieries	4·541	2·538	5·158	11·700	2·495	—	26·432
Total	41·609	34·599	58·620	71·100	55·982	88·922	350·832

Source: BC.

7.70. The installation of heavy duty equipment has become an integral feature of modern longwall mining. Most of the investment in heavy duty equipment has been in the provision of roof supports of the chock shield or shield support category. (Heavy duty shields are those with a yield load in excess of 250 tonnes per chock.) The supports are moved forward hydraulically in conjunction with the armoured face conveyor after the passage of the coal-cutting machine. The unsupported roof behind the advanced chocks is then allowed to collapse.

7.71. BC's investment in heavy duty face equipment began in 1977 with the installation of the first set at Kellingley Colliery, North Yorkshire, although it was 1982–83 before the current levels of investment were committed to heavy duty installations. By 1985 BC regarded heavy duty investment as of sufficient importance to be given priority status within the capital expenditure programme.

7.72. In the BC capital investment manual, the procedure for investment in heavy duty supports is listed as 'mandatory'. Area Directors have delegated authority to approve installation applications provided that they meet the financial criteria established for capital expenditure as a whole, and that an average of 500,000 tonnes per year can be produced from the faces on which the equipment will be successively deployed over an eight-year equipment life. Where applications do not meet these criteria, they can still be approved by Headquarters. Over the period 1986–87 and 1987–88, 54 heavy duty installations were approved and 22 were rejected during the Business Planning Cycle. Others would also have been rejected as part of the planning process at Area, prior to submission of the formal Business Plan. The benefits from an investment in heavy duty equipment depend on the geology of the colliery, the size of the face to be worked, machine available time and machine operating time. These variables can differ from face to face.

7.73. Capital expenditure attributed to the Heavy Duty Programme from 1982–83 to 1987–88 amounted to £351 million, some 9·2 per cent of total deep mining capital expenditure for that period. For the years 1986–87 and 1987–88 this includes expenditure for the purchase of other heavy duty equipment (ie roadheaders, shearers, gate end boxes etc), and price/accrual adjustments from previous years. However, data obtained from the case studies, for example Cynheidre, show that expenditure on other face equipment (non-heavy duty)— necessarily part of investment in heavy duty supports—is excluded from BC's total.

7.74. BC told us that the biggest single contributor to the 48·4 per cent increase in productivity since 1982–83 'is the increasing proportion of heavy duty shield support installations and the associated higher performances achieved'. By 1987–88 the proportion of heavy duty faces had risen from the 1982 figure of 5·6 per cent to 48·0 per cent.

7.75. However, a number of other changes have occurred over this period (1982–83 to 1987–88) which had an equally significant impact upon productivity:

(a) the 57 per cent reduction in the number of faces currently worked;

(b) the 51 per cent reduction in colliery numbers from 191 to 94;

(c) the 56 per cent (end-year) manpower reductions;

(d) the widespread investment in the computerised Mine Operating System (MINOS), totalling some £13 million, is intended to give rise to substantial productivity increases via the monitoring and automation of significant activities underground, and contributing to increased safety underground;

(e) the increased reliance upon retreat mining;

(f) improvements in machine available time; and

(g) increases in overtime working, with the proportion of overtime shifts more than doubling since the 1984–85 dispute.

BC told us that many of these changes have, however, in whole or part, been made possible by the introduction of heavy duty equipment. Its installation at a colliery may permit the number of faces at that pit to be reduced, or make possible an increase of low cost output. Heavy duty equipment had also contributed to increased manpower productivity, permitting reductions in the labour force, and to better reliability, giving rise to higher machine available time.

7.76. Of the £351 million capital expenditure on heavy duty equipment since 1982–83, £26·4 million was incurred at 12 pits which have since closed. While many of these pits were within the 'high cost tail', not all of them had been consistently within that category. Where they had been, however, production increases associated with heavy duty equipment elsewhere did not occur.

7.77. The reason BC gave for there having been heavy duty equipment investment at collieries which it was subsequently decided to close was that the introduction of heavy duty shield supports at almost all of those collieries was, in effect, a last management effort to improve the collieries' relatively low performance. In the main, because of intrinsic operational difficulties of the mining environment at these collieries, productivity levels remained markedly below the national average, and this failure to realize significantly better results was a major factor towards their eventual closure. Much of the heavy duty equipment installed in collieries later closed was subsequently salvaged and redeployed. We also noted that some collieries had greatly increased productivity without heavy duty equipment. BC told us that the reasons for the improvements in these cases (where the geology was not always suitable for the use of heavy duty equipment) included more retreat mining and increases in the number of shifts wherever possible, together with significant reductions in manpower reflecting the general restructuring of the industry.

Indicators of capital performance

7.78. BC told us that it calculated returns on capital employed for each of its main activities at corporate level only. The calculation is made by expressing the operating profit for the year as a percentage of the simple average of opening and closing fixed and current assets, less creditors due for payment within one year (all at balance sheet values). The return for BC as a whole for 1986–87 was 6·6 per cent.

7.79. Returns are not calculated on capital employed at individual collieries, Areas or regions. BC told us that much of the working capital (debts, creditors, stocks, stores and so on) was managed on a regional or even a national basis, and that some collieries still showed operating losses. Under these circumstances BC had decided that the introduction of a capital charge for each colliery would best bring home to Area and colliery management the need to achieve a return on capital. The capital charge was calculated by applying a rate, approximating to the rate payable by BC on its borrowings, to the written down value of the fixed assets employed at or in support of each colliery.

7.80. BC told us that both Area and colliery management clearly understood that the objective is to achieve (at least) breakeven after capital charges at each colliery. Every accounting period, a cost per GJ after capital charge and a profit/(loss) after capital charge were ascertained and included on the profit and loss statement for each colliery. In BC's view, the system of capital charges enables management to estimate the effect of alternative plans, involving different levels of capital expenditure, on the bottom-line profitability of a colliery and of the Area as a whole.

7.81. We asked BC what indicators of capital performance it used to assess the actual performance of completed projects. Except where there are clearly measurable marginal benefits arising from the project, eg manpower savings or improved machine available time, the financial assessment was related to the performance of the colliery after completion of a project and reflected the effect of a combination of factors at that time, only one of which was the completion of the project. BC told us that while it could establish that a project had achieved its objective(s) in physical terms, changes in other circumstances could obscure the benefit obtained in financial terms. BC accepted, however, that, as a general rule, the financial contribution of a project should be assessed as part of the Completion Report procedure.

Conclusions and recommendations

Proceeds

7.82. The discounts which BC allows, other than those which are quality-related, are averaged over collieries by reference to two main categories of coal, bituminous graded and bituminous non-graded. Three other categories exist, viz anthracite graded, anthracite non-graded and South Wales bituminous, but these all relate to South Wales only.

7.83. As long as the bulk of the coal produced is supplied to some 30 national customers from whichever collieries are best placed to meet the customers' needs most economically, it would make no sense to do other than credit each colliery with proceeds established after deduction of the company-wide average discounts.

7.84. We do not believe that the same considerations will necessarily apply in the future when the ESI is privatized and there may be a significant increase in the number of power generating companies seeking supplies of coal from local sources. We believe that the present policy would result in the insulation of individual collieries from their markets, protecting them from the consequences of their geographic position and the nature and grade of their products. Crediting each colliery with its own net proceeds would enable the true profitability of each colliery to be established, by linking it to its own markets.

Monitoring results

7.85. Within the present framework BC has satisfactory arrangements for measuring cost, output and quality against targets for individual collieries, and for monitoring capital expenditure on individual projects and in aggregate.

Annual Reviews and Completion Reports

7.86. The Annual Review provides a formal means by which the decision-taking level can monitor project progress. BC has, since 1985, improved its procedures, and we are satisfied that adequate attention is now given to this task.

7.87. Completion Reports provide a formal means of holding managers responsible for overall project performance (in terms of adhering to time and cost), and for initiating sanctions if this is unsatisfactory. This is an effective way of encouraging well-run projects.

7.88. At the time when many of the projects we examined went out to tender, market conditions were such that prices for the contracts were exceptionally low because of excess capacity in the construction industry. This explains why so many of the contracts were let at markedly below Stage II estimates. BC has now changed its instructions to those preparing Stage II estimates, and they are now required to make their estimates on the basis of the price expected at the time the contract is expected to be let. The previous practice could, in some circumstances, be misleading, and we think this is a welcome change.

7.89. In our 1983 report we commented unfavourably on the way project costs were monitored at Headquarters against Stage II estimates rather than against sums which reflect the prices contracted at Stage III. BC agreed with us that Headquarters monitoring should be against both figures, and we recommend that this should be implemented. This will improve control of capital investment in respect of annual expenditure; monitoring against commitment; and monitoring against approval.

Post-project appraisal

7.90. BC's Annual Reviews and Completion Reports currently fulfil a specific and rather narrow role. We therefore recommend that, in addition, BC establishes a procedure to choose some four or five completed projects each year and subjects them to detailed Headquarters post-project appraisal. We believe that BC is well placed to conduct such reviews and to ensure that the lessons, both favourable and unfavourable, are disseminated widely among its staff. One suitable area for early review would be recent heavy duty installations. This should provide a solid basis for ensuring that the future of the remaining Heavy Duty Programme continues to be soundly based.

Project management

7.91. We note that BC is shortly to issue a manual on project management; this, which we recommended in our previous report, is to be welcomed.

7.92. There is to be a project management function under central, Headquarters control. BC should ensure that thereby expertise once developed is retained and used, and that there is a career path through project management in BC. BC will, nevertheless, continue to need to purchase specialist help in project management and control from outside from time to time, both to refresh its in-house team with new ideas, and to deal with 'lumpiness' in the construction programme.

7.93. The changes BC has made, and continues to make, to its project management improve planning, and financial and programme control. However, we think that BC still has some way to go fully to absorb the lessons recently learned about project control, and may be able to take further advantage of advice from consultants. BC's cost estimating which we commented on in our previous report is still inaccurate, but the errors have been of overestimation.

Indicators of capital performance

7.94. BC does not think it worthwhile to attempt to calculate the actual return on capital of an individual capital investment project after the project is complete. We think that, since the justification for expenditure is ultimately expressed in money terms, the post-completion analysis of the project should always include a financial assessment of the project, including a calculation of the return on capital, and a statement of the contribution to the actual change in colliery performance since the project was approved.

7.95. We believe that the absence of proper calculations of returns on capital employed for individual collieries is of little consequence at the present time with BC treating its mines collectively as a coal supply system. In these circumstances we regard the inclusion in a colliery's profit and loss account of a capital charge, calculated by reference to BC's average rate of interest payable and the written-down value of the colliery's tangible fixed assets (plus other capital assets used at or in support of the colliery), as a useful reminder to the colliery management that a satisfactory return should be achieved on assets employed.

7.96. However, we believe that this procedure may well be inadequate in the likely circumstances following privatization of the ESI; and the more so in the event of privatization of BC. We believe that BC should now be giving thought to ways in which it could fully attribute fixed and working capital to individual collieries or groups of collieries.

R G SMETHURST (*Chairman*)

JAMES ACKERS

F E BONNER

M B BUNTING

ROBERT CLAYTON

A FERRY

S N BURBRIDGE (*Secretary*)

13 September 1988

(referred to in paragraphs 1.1 and 1.36)

Terms of reference

1. On 14 March 1988 the Department of Trade and Industry sent to the Commission the following reference:

The Secretary of State, in exercise of his powers under section 11(1)(a) of the Competition Act 1980, hereby refers to the Monopolies and Mergers Commission ('the Commission') the questions set out below relating to the efficiency and costs of the British Coal Corporation ('the Corporation').

The Commission shall, upon this reference, investigate and report on the following questions:

(1) Whether the Corporation could improve its performance with regard to:

  (*a*) the selection and appraisal of investment projects, with particular regard to future coal demand and prices, market risk, and the achievement of the required rate of return;

  (*b*) the efficient use of manpower in achieving the required rate of return on investment projects;

  (*c*) the contribution of the Corporation's investment programme to its business strategy and objectives, including achieving cost competitiveness; and the responsiveness of the Corporation's investment programme to changes in the Corporation's business strategy;

  (*d*) the post-completion review of capital purchases and investment projects;

  (*e*) the Corporation's management systems, in so far as these relate to the matters specified in sub paragraphs (*a*) to (*d*) above, including the attribution of sales proceeds to production units for the purpose of investment and business decisions, and indicators of capital performance.

(2) Whether, in relation to any matter falling within question 1 above, the Corporation is pursuing a course of conduct which operates against the public interest.

The Commission shall report upon this reference within a period of six months beginning with the date hereof.

(Signed) G C RIGGS
An Assistant Secretary
14 March 1988   *Department of Trade and Industry*

2. On 17 March 1988 the Chairman of the Commission, acting under section 11, sub-section (9) of the Competition Act 1980 and Part II of Schedule 3 of the Fair Trading Act 1973, directed that the functions of the Commission in relation to the reference should be discharged through a group of six members including, as Chairman, Mr R G Smethurst, a Deputy Chairman of the Commission. The composition of the group is indicated in the list of members which prefaces this report.

APPENDIX 2.1
(referred to in paragraph 2.3)

Submission of evidence by third parties

Association of Professional, Executive, Clerical and Computer Staff (APEX)

Professor T Atkinson, Department of Mining Engineering, University of Nottingham

British Association of Colliery Management (BACM)

British Geological Survey

British Longwall Mining Association

British Ropes Limited

Central Electricity Generating Board

Department of the Environment

Domestic Coal Consumers Council

C Ford, Staffordshire

Professor C T Shaw, Department of Mineral Resources Engineering, Imperial College, University of London

Electricity Consumers' Council

Gullick Dobson Limited

Dr Dieter Helm, Centre for Business Strategy, London Business School and Lady Margaret Hall, Oxford

Industry Department for Scotland

International Coal Development Agency

John Kelly Limited

National Association of Colliery Overmen, Deputies and Shotfirers (NACODS)

National Association of Licensed Opencast Operators

Qualter, Hall and Co Limited

South of Scotland Electricity Board

The Chamber of Coal Traders Limited

The Coalfield Communities Campaign

Dr R Richardson and Dr S Wood, The London School of Economics and Political Science, University of London

J Winterton, Lecturer in Industrial Technology, University of Bradford

Welsh Development Agency

The BC/CEGB Understandings—a statement by BC

1. Despite the size of their trading relationship, until 1979 CEGB and British Coal had no medium or long-term trading agreement. They operated on a six-month tonnage programme with two weeks notice of price changes and all coal charged normally at list prices. This relationship had originated after the war, when both industries, with active Government involvement, were concentrating on increasing their capacity to match rising demand. This had been succeeded by more than a decade of low oil prices when the CEGB could rely on oil prices and over-capacity in the coal industry to restrain coal prices and had no interest in any longer-term arrangement. The events of 1979, the second oil rise and two coal price increases, emphasized the advantages of a longer-term arrangement to the CEGB.

2. Both industries saw benefits. The CEGB wanted a guarantee that the price of what had become their cheapest and largest source of fuel could not increase above the rate of general inflation when every expert predicted that all energy prices would do just that and when the oil price increase seemed to give headroom for large coal price increases. British Coal doubted whether the high forecasts for CEGB's coal requirements would be achieved in practice and wanted a guarantee of volume sales.

3. In 1979, British Coal and CEGB entered into a broad Understanding on coal supplies and prices which they intended would run for a period of four and a half years. This provided that CEGB would take 75 million tonnes a year from NCB in return for NCB keeping their coal prices within the rate of UK inflation.

4. Although not an enforceable contract, the arrangement worked satisfactorily and to the benefit of both industries and of electricity consumers over the ensuing years, but the fall in electricity sales caused by the industrial recession, together with the growing contribution of nuclear power, led, despite the big reduction in oil burn, to a fall in CEGB's coal burn. Large coal stocks were built up at power stations, although this was in line with Government policy. A modification was made to the terms of the Understanding in 1982, when international coal prices fell sharply when Poland resumed exports and cut prices to re-enter the market at a time of strong sterling. British Coal agreed to a price concession on three million tonnes to reflect savings that CEGB could make by a switch to other coal suppliers.

5. The Understanding was renegotiated in 1983. The concept of two-tier pricing was further developed based on an analogy with the US practice of differentiating contract and spot coal.

6. It was recognized that the tonnages required would inevitably vary from year to year depending on initial stock levels, economic activity, nuclear contribution and not least the weather. The parties therefore moved away from a fixed tonnage provision to a guaranteed share of the demand available from year to year. They adopted the broad principle that in return for British Coal's willingness to limit price movement on the bulk of its coal to below UK inflation, and to align its prices against internationally traded coal on that tonnage of British Coal that it was practicable for CEGB to replace in the short term, it would be reasonable for British Coal to be able to supply the bulk of CEGB's coal requirements, broadly equivalent to about 95 per cent, although in practice this would be expressed each year as a firm tonnage in the light of the practical conditions as seen at the time. In practice, this allowed ample market share for the small private UK mines but restricted any significant move to imports.

7. The bulk of the tonnage—the 'base tonnage'—supplied by NCB to CEGB (in a typical year some 65 million tonnes out of a total supply of 72–74 million tonnes) was sold at a price which included a small discount on list prices, but with annual price movement limited to 85 per cent to 95 per cent of RPI.

8. The remaining tonnage (the excess over 65mtpa) was supplied at a larger discount, reflecting the fact that for this tonnage NCB coal was in direct competition with imported coal delivered to coastal and estuarial power stations in South-East England. The mechanism for calculating price discounts was that the delivered price of NCB coal shipped to these power stations from normal British Coal sources in North-East England should be aligned to the prices of imported coal from substantial and reliable traders delivered to these stations following transshipment at ARA. The imported prices used for alignment purposes were CEGB's current contract prices for Australian coal together with quotations they had received from other suppliers. These arrangements were made strictly in accordance with the relevant provision of the ECSC Treaty. The alignment discount so calculated, however, was applied to British Coal's supplies on a national basis and not limited to the flow from the North-East to the South-East so as to allow the merit order [of CEGB power stations][1] to be operated without complication.

9. The Revised Understanding worked satisfactorily until the early months of 1986, when the price of oil dropped sharply and suddenly. CEGB then raised with NCB and Government the economic case for reverting to a high oil burn.

10. This was quickly followed by the fall in the international dollar price of steam coal as a result of the determination of South African producers to retain markets and their ability to do so by cutting prices because of the large devaluation of the Rand. Sterling also strengthened against the US dollar and this made the competitive position of British Coal more difficult.

11. The fall in the sterling equivalent price of internationally traded coal had been reflected in a reduction in the aligned price negotiated as part of the Understanding in November 1985, but prices continued to fall sharply and as a result, CEGB argued that the circumstances had changed so much they had a case for importing coal not only to the seaborne stations in South-East England, but also to inland power stations. They submitted a memorandum to the House of Commons Select Committee on Energy, in which they contended that, at the prices they were then paying for United Kingdom coal, it would make large savings if it were to build up coal imports over three to five years to 30 million tonnes a year, and replace the equivalent BC tonnage. BC strongly contested this claim, but acknowledged that there was a case for an increasing tonnage to be supplied at prices aligned to a lower international price.

12. A price reduction was clearly required in the changed market conditions, but in agreeing to renegotiate the Joint Understanding British Coal was concerned that it should be done in such a way as not to jeopardize the programme of orderly modernization and cost reduction on which the industry had embarked. They argued that adjustment needed to be progressive: otherwise, it could have put into jeopardy all that had been achieved in cost reduction, it could lead to the United Kingdom becoming increasingly dependent in the long-term on imported energy just when world prices were rising, as well as causing further major problems for mining communities and incurring massive social costs on top of those already met over the previous two years.

13. The CEGB recognized and accepted that, on grounds of security, it was in their long-term interest that the modernization of the British coal industry should proceed in an orderly way, ensuring the survival of a competitive UK volume coal supplier. They also recognized the advantage of a further long-term agreement with British Coal, in the continuity and predictability in their fuel prices which could not be achieved from large-scale reliance on the international markets for coal and oil.

14. Following negotiation in 1986, a new five-year agreement was reached. For pricing purposes, the tonnage is now divided into three, rather than two, tranches. The base tonnage continues to be priced as before, but was reduced in size and will

---

[1] MMC Comment.

progressively reduce further over the period of the agreement. The price of the second tranche is aligned to reflect both the price of oil and of competitive coal delivered to inland power stations. This tonnage will progressively rise at the expense of the first tranche. The price of the third tranche is aligned to the delivered price of imported coal at coastal power stations (the same principle as with the second tranche in the previous Understandings). The total cost of British Coal's supplies to CEGB was reduced considerably and implicit in the whole deal is a continuing real fall in British Coal's prices in spite of dispensing with State aids, passing on to CEGB the benefits of restructuring the coal industry. This is achieved principally by altering the relative sizes of the three tranches over the period of the agreement, with the first or base tranche decreasing, the second tranche increasing, coupled with a limitation on price escalation for first and second tranche coal to 85–95 per cent of RPI.

15. Arrangements with the SSEB and NIE have reflected the local circumstances, but the concepts have been similar to what have applied to the CEGB Understandings.

16. The Understandings have stood the practical test of major economic and political changes. They have provided both the Electricity Supply Industry and the British coal industry with a degree of stability and continuity on which to base their planning and operations whilst paying proper regard to changes in the energy market, sustainable in the medium term.

APPENDIX 3.1

(referred to in paragraph 3.35)

Select Committee on Energy Inquiry into ESI Privatization

(Memorandum by British Coal)

Introduction

1. Major improvements have been made by British Coal; and to secure continuing progress, it will be important to have a long-term strategy for the coal industry. The most important element will be the relationship with the electricity supply industry. British electricity and British Coal are heavily interdependent. British Coal's present concern is not with the change of ownership as such but that it raises serious questions about the conditions of future coal supplies. The form of British Coal's commercial arrangements with the Generating Boards has reflected the assumption that both parties would remain in common public ownership. These arrangements are not therefore in the form of binding contracts, but mutually-agreed guidelines as to how the two organisations do business together, and as such they have worked well; but the change of ownership now proposed for the ESI requires the negotiation of a new and binding coal supply contract. If a normal commercial relationship already existed, the existing contractual relationship with the coal producer would continue unchanged (as would be the case, for example, if the ownership of a US utility were changed). This transition from a mutually agreed joint understanding to a firm contract would be a major task under any circumstances (given the size of the transactions involved); but what gives rise to such concern for British Coal is that this occurs coincidentally with unprecedentedly low international steam coal prices. We argue that a long-term contractual relationship between British Coal and British electricity should be settled as soon as possible, and well before any formal change of ownership, so that investors as well as suppliers know exactly where they stand on an issue so vital to both.

Interdependence of coal and electricity supply industries

2. The high degree of interdependence between the two industries can be illustrated by the facts that in 1986–87:

  (i) 77 per cent of British Coal sales were at power stations;

  (ii) coal provided over 70 per cent of the power stations' total fuel requirements;

  (iii) 45 per cent of CEGB's total costs and 55 per cent of their operating costs were accounted for by supplies of British coal;

  (iv) British coal sales to power stations represented a quarter of total UK primary energy consumption.

This degree of interdependence is quite normal. Threequarters of all coal mined in the world is burnt in power stations, and power stations in all countries which have a substantial coal industry are predominantly based on coal in a very similar way to the UK.

3. Moreover, this interdependence is an essential component of the ESI's generation system, which has been developed on a fully integrated basis over the past forty years, so that now almost two-thirds of all coal (and half of all the ESI's fuel use) is consumed at ten sites in the central coalfields.

4. This high degree of interdependence will continue through the 1990s as:

  (a) the constraints on the net increase in nuclear capacity (after progressive closure of all the Magnox stations) relative to the growth in electricity sales, will increase the demand for power station coal;

  (b) coal supplies to power stations will continue to represent around three quarters of British Coal's total sales—no other markets can make good any significant loss of power station sales.

Decisions on the future coal supplies to the privately owned ESI will therefore have a crucial impact on the future of the UK coal industry. Because they are so important to the nation, they require a long-term perspective.

International coal competition

5. For the foreseeable future, British Coal expect the major competitor in the power station market to be internationally traded steam coal, and British Coal's strategy is designed to make the industry internationally competitive on an ongoing basis. Coal consumption in British power stations is currently about 85 million tonnes. Only 1 million tonnes of this is imported from abroad. All the remainder comes from mines in Britain. British Coal's current concern arises from the coincidence of two major discontinuities:

(a) The need to establish completely new commercial relationships with the ESI following its change in ownership and possible change in its structure.

(b) International steam coal prices expressed in sterling at an unprecedentedly low level. The mines dedicated to what is still a relatively small steam coal trade (only about 4 per cent of steam coal mined in the world is internationally traded by sea) are in serious oversupply because the investment after 1973, particularly by the oil companies, was based on a very optimistic view of demand in the target markets—those countries which were heavily dependent on oil for power generation. The growth in nuclear generation, greater energy efficiency, economic recession and the relative decline in heavy industry, particularly in Western Europe, all combined to reduce the increase in coal demand well below expectations. The international steam coal trade also failed to break into the biggest coal markets which continue to be dominated by home production, eg the US, where of the 700 million tonnes burnt in power stations less than 1 million tonnes is imported. The low dollar prices for international coal arising from oversupply have been further depressed in sterling terms by the appreciation of sterling against the US $. The Rotterdam steam coal price in sterling recently has been only half in real terms the level of two years ago and half the average value over the past ten years.

British Coal believe that they could handle one or other of the major discontinuities outlined above; but it is the two in combination which create a major strategic problem.

6. Much of the public discussion of this issue assumes that the present low price of international steam coal can continue indefinitely. British Coal firmly believe that it cannot (a view supported by other evidence to the Select Committee's recent inquiry on the Coal Industry) because:

(i) Recent prices are not sufficient to earn profits for the main coal exporting mines. A return on capital has been put off by the biggest of the new mines in an effort to drive out the competition. As a result many of the higher cost mines in international trade are now not covering operating costs and there have been major closures in Australia. A similar effect is now starting to be seen in South Africa, where there are serious doubts about further expansion of export availability.

(ii) On the other hand, demand for seaborne traded steam coal will increase in its main markets of Western Europe and the Pacific Rim in the next few years. Total demand is likely to reach 200 million tonnes in the mid 1990s compared with 133 million tonnes in 1986 (even assuming no increase in UK imports).

(iii) This increase in demand will require investment in new mines once the present spare capacity is taken up. The tonnage can certainly be produced but not at today's prices. The evidence is that very little investment could take place at Rotterdam prices below $45 a tonne (mid 1987 US $) which is half as much again as the recent price levels. On the other hand, if Rotterdam prices moved up towards $60, it would be attractive for the large underutilized underground mining capacity in the Eastern US to re-enter the export market. This effectively puts a ceiling on the sustainable international coal price.

(iv) The recent £/$ exchange rate is not likely to be sustainable in the long-run. Not only is the present rate significantly above the long-term purchasing power parity, but it also reflects the current US deficit position, which cannot be permanent.

7. In fact, despite what has been happening to the short-term price in Rotterdam, the underlying economics of the international steam coal business have remained unchanged. British Coal see no reason to change their view previously submitted to the Committee that the sustainable long-term price (mid 1987 US dollars for coal of 24·5 GJ/tonne) would be in the range of $40–55 per tonne in 2000 (or $45–60 per tonne of average traded quality) associated with a ' real' exchange rate of $1·40 +/− 10 per cent, to give a 'central' view of £34—in line with the average for the last ten years (1987 money values). It is a view of the *sustainable* internationl price which must underlie policy decisions.

8. Indeed, this was clearly the view of the Government in its 'Decision Letter' on Sizewell B of March 1987—which implied a 'central' projection somewhat higher than that adopted by British Coal. Clearly, it would be quite wrong for strategic national decisions on nuclear power to be made on international coal price projections more than twice the recent sterling Rotterdam price, while making strategic decisions on the coal industry based on that depressed Rotterdam price. National policy on coal, just as much as policy on nuclear power, has to be based on a long-term view of the sustainable prices for traded international energy and must be consistent.

Need for long-term contract

9. British Coal regard a long-term contract for coal supply to the privatized CEGB or their successors as essential for both industries for the following reasons:

(i) Short-term international coal prices (as represented by the Rotterdam spot price, expressed in sterling) are far too variable to form the basis of conditions of supply of all coal to the ESI. Over the last ten years, the average year-on-year variation in the Rotterdam $ price (in mid 1987 US dollars) has been $8 per tonne (or 15 per cent) and the average year-on-year variation in the $/£ exchange rate (inflation adjusted) has been 13 per cent. (It was only three years ago that the £ and the $ were almost at parity.) Sometimes these variations offset each other, sometimes they compound, but the net effect is bound to be significant. There are also frequent variations within each year.

(ii) At the same time, coal prices represent by far the greatest proportion of the ESI's future potentially *variable* costs. Thus, if coal prices paid by the ESI were wholly aligned to short-term market price movements, ESI costs would also be very variable and unpredictable, leading to fluctuating profits and/or electricity prices. For example a 10 per cent movement in coal prices would affect electricity prices by 4 per cent, if the profitability of the ESI was to be constant. There is a clear need to reconcile the degree of assurance on electricity price stability acceptable to consumers, with the assurance of profit for investors, without the intervention of a complex and bureaucratic regulatory framework (of a kind which has caused such difficulties in the USA). Only a long-term contract between BC and the ESI covering the greater proportion of coal supplies at stipulated prices can provide the degree of predictability required. A contract for such a large tonnage coupled with broad price stability would not be available on the international market.

(iii) The consumption of coal at UK power stations exceeds the total imports of steam coal into the whole of Western Europe. In practical terms it would be quite impossible to replace 100 per cent of UK coal to power stations by imports; and therefore it would not be commercially right for either party to regulate the price of *all* UK coal according to the changes in the Rotterdam spot market, because the two are just not comparable. Broad alignment with the Rotterdam price should apply (as it does with the present CEGB Understanding) only to that margin of coal supplies to UK power stations which it would be practical to import without upsetting the whole basis of the West European market, and raising coal prices for all consumers within the Community (some of which have no alternative but to be 100 per cent dependent on coal imports, eg Denmark and Italy). It should be pointed out that the largest steam coal importer in the world at the moment is ENEL in Italy and its current purchases are approximately 10 million tonnes. The present arrangements with CEGB allows for the supply of a minimum of 12 million tonnes at world-related prices (including the tonnage dedicated to the QUICs scheme).

(iv) There are severe limits to the extent and speed with which our underground coal industry can adjust its capacity and costs in response to external events. Certainly it is not possible to follow the short-term fluctuations in international prices and exchange rates. Supplies to British Coal's largest market need to be under contract terms which recognize this, as is the case in the USA (the largest market for steam coal in the West) where 89 per cent of the coal supplied to utilities is under long-term contracts with closely determined tonnages and prices.

(v) Given the constraints on the use of alternative fuels, and the logistical limits on imported coal, under any credible scenario the UK coal industry will be not only the major supplier of coal to the ESI, but also their largest single fuel source during the 1990s. Therefore the ESI will have a strong interest in the efficient operation and development of the coal industry. That in turn would be incompatible with major uncertainty on the volume and price of sales to the coal industry's largest market.

Appropriate form of long-term contract between BC and privatized ESI

10. British Coal believe that an appropriate form of contract between BC and the privatized ESI would be along the following lines:

(i) A period of ten years from 1991, when the present Understanding ends and a likely date for the change in the ownership of the ESI. This will enable full weight to be given to longer-term trends, and to provide guidance for investment decisions in both industries.

(ii) BC would contract to supply a base tonnage covering the greater part of ESI coal requirements with prices related primarily to an agreed *sustainable* long-term international price (expressed in sterling), and with escalation limited to general inflation (eg RPI). The Government's own projections of future coal prices used for the Sizewell B Decision could be the starting point for the determination of these contract prices.

(iii) The balance of the ESI's coal requirements, subject to appropriate accommodation for the licensed mine sector, would be open to competition to coal imports, with BC having the first option to bid for these tonnages, but with no obligation to supply, nor for the ESI to accept, unless prices were fully competitive with the delivered price of international coal at the time. These tonnages would be negotiated partly biennially and partly annually.

11. Such an arrangement would have the following advantages:

(i) There would be a high degree of predictability in the cost of coal to the ESI, and hence in electricity prices, with variations being confined to the margin in any one year. This would give a significant degree of assurance to both consumers and investors, and would greatly simplify the problems of regulation of the privatized ESI. Indeed a price regulatory formula for electricity such as exists for the gas industry, and which would need to be incorporated in contracts between the generating and distribution parts of the privatized ESI, would be of no real value unless the coal price element was included. The form of long-term coal contract advocated by British Coal would enable the coal price element to be included in the formula, and for this element to show minimal movements year by year.

(ii) The ESI would be able to take advantage of periods of low international prices to the extent to which they could in practice have the potential to import in the short-term; on the other hand, the ESI would be given a measure of protection against any large upward surge in world prices, whereby the *overall* effect on electricity prices could be kept within manageable proportions. Indeed, such a contract would give the ESI price stability without being deprived of the opportunity to take advantage of movements in the market.

(iii) The coal industry would still be subject to real and continuing price and cost discipline under such an arrangement. The bulk of its supplies would be related in price to the sustainable international coal price and then subject to being kept within UK price inflation. At the margin, it would have to compete directly with the current prices of international coal. Such arrangements would enable the industry to adjust its capacity progressively at a manageable rate.

12. The present Joint Understanding was agreed with CEGB to run for five years from 1986. Because it is an arrangement between two nationalized industries, it has no contractual force. However, a normal commercial relationship between two bodies not in the public sector would have been developed on a contractual basis. British Coal strongly urge that negotiations should begin soon to establish the basis for a new commercial contract with the privatized CEGB (or their successors) and that these negotiations should be settled *prior* to privatization, so as to maintain continuity. Furthermore, the terms and conditions of future coal supply, which will constitute such a large proportion of future ESI costs, will need to be taken into account in the prospectus for sale of the ESI.

13. If the negotiations for a new contract required further adjustment to British Coal's prices, an opportunity could be taken to consider changes to British Coal's existing capital structure, which are clearly necessary. At present, the Corporation's capital is 100 per cent loan based, with historically very high 'real' rates of interest of around 7 per cent. In 1986–87, interest payments were £386 million. Yet British Coal competes with international coal producers who are earning little or no profit, and whose capital structure is quite different. For an organization competing in an international commodity market, at a time when prices are well below the sustainable level, British Coal's capital structure is singularly inappropriate. Recasting the structure to one third debt/two thirds 'equity', in line with more normal commercial practice, would allow some flexibility in determining the prices for the proposed contract with ESI while safeguarding British Coal's financial position.

Potential effect on British Coal of absence of long-term contract with ESI

14. British Coal consider that the case for a long-term contract for coal supplies with a privatized ESI is in the interest of the two parties and in the interests of the nation and the electricity consumer. If the issue is not settled promptly, there is a serious risk that under short-term financial pressures the parties could take up adversarial positions, which, given the availability of very low cost parcels of international coal in the present exceptional market conditions, might lead to a sudden and significant importation of coal. Once decisions to import significant tonnages had been taken, there would be strong pressures to increase imports further. The consumers would want to take steps as quickly as possible to open up the central power stations to large scale imports because without these they would be vulnerable to pressure from the supplier trying to protect revenue/market share. This would require substantial investment in new import facilities. (There are in fact two proposals for discharge terminals suitable for coal scheduled to come before Parliament in this Session). Once such facilities were built, however, there would be a strong economic incentive to maximize their use. This could produce

substantial coal imports in the short-term whilst international prices remain low—at least 15 million tonnes is possible, and this could rise to 20–25 million tonnes. The significant entry of British power stations into the international steam coal market would in due course push up international prices; but a great deal of damage could be done to British Coal in the meantime. British Coal is overwhelmingly a deep mined industry, so that a substantial loss of its power station business to imported coal would mean that there was no alternative but to close equivalent British capacity completely. It could not be kept in suspended animation or the output stocked or the facility mothballed. The practical effects would not only be to reduce British Coal's volume sales, but also to severely affect revenue per tonne across the board.

15. The combined effect of all this would be substantial additional closures and reduction of manpower with effective permanent loss of capacity. The North East coalfield which serves the Thames power stations would be drastically affected, and all coalfields including the central coalfields, and including Nottinghamshire, would be affected to a significant degree. Indeed the most accessible of all the central power stations to imports through the Humber is West Burton. This rapid contraction would be combined with large deficits in British Coal's accounts which would take place at a time when we had just achieved breakeven after immense efforts. This would irretrievably damage the morale of the management and the workforce and would indefinitely postpone the commercial viability of British Coal. It is important to appreciate that in such circumstances, it would not be possible to concentrate losses of capacity on higher cost output. It would be practically impossible to operate the best pits at optimum capacity. Furthermore, opencast sites in the UK are relatively small and short life and rely on a continuing injection of planning permissions. These would be difficult to obtain against the background of loss of markets and rising stocks. In such circumstances, it would also be much more difficult to undertake significant new investment in UK coal. The overall effect might well be to increase, rather than reduce, the industry's average costs.

16. The absence of an appropriate long-term contract with the privatized ESI could therefore lead to the rapid and irreversible decline of the UK coal industry just at a time when the UK economy was having to adjust to the decline in UK North Sea oil. It would not be possible to re-expand the British Coal industry when the sterling price of coal and other fuels increased, or to mitigate the balance of payments problems which arose from additional fuel imports. The UK therefore, from being energy rich, could once again quickly become vulnerable to changes in the prices of internationally traded energy.

European Community Coal Policy

17. A number of the issues in this paper have been covered in a recent British Coal submission to the European Parliament. This draws attention to the way in which rapid contraction in Community coal as a reaction to the present very low international coal prices would increase world coal prices above the level they would otherwise reach, so that Community coal production has an additional value as a restraint on international coal price movements.

Electricity R & D Issues

18. British Coal are concerned that the privatization of ESI might lead to lack of progress with long-term development of new Clean Coal technology for power generation.

Summary

19. It is the view of British Coal that a long-term coal supply contract with the ESI should be negotiated at an early date, and settled prior to privatization, so that it can be taken into account in the prospectus for sale of the ESI. This is most likely to be achievable with continuity of the ESI's present management structure.

British Coal believe that it is possible for British electricity to continue to base its coal requirements on British coal, and for such coal to be supplied at prices which are competitive with the sustainable long-term price of international coal, while giving the electricity consumers the guarantees of long-term price stability that are so important to them for such an essential commodity. At the same time, this would give British Coal the opportunity to achieve financial viability without taxpayers' support. Because British coal burnt in power stations is 25 per cent of all UK primary energy, this is a strategic issue of the greatest importance, not only for British Coal, but for the nation.

27 January 1988

Key Supply Indicators: deep mines

	1982–83	*1985–86*	*1986–87*	*1987–88*	*% change* *1982–83 cf 1987–88*
No. of collieries:					
Start of year	198	160	133	110	−44·4
End of year	191	133	110	94	−50·8
Output ('000 tonnes)	104,051	87,586	86,922	81,576	−21·6
Manpower: average	207,640	154,649	125,362	104,355	−49·7
OMS face (tonnes)	10·09	12·03	14·39	16·20	+60·6
Overall (tonnes)	2·44	2·72	3·29	3·62	+48·4
OMY (tonnes)	504	571	700	788	+56·3
No. of faces:					
Advance	454	278	202	155	−65·9
Retreat	120	103	103	91	−24·2
Total	574	381	305	246	−57·1
No. of faces:					
Conventional	542	294	186	129	−76·2
Shield supports	32	87	119	117	+265·6
Total	574	381	305	246	−57·1
Shifting index	2·13	2·17	2·31	2·38	+11·7
Daily output face:					
Conventional	711	766	900	1,003	+41·1
Shield supports	1,390	1,393	1,459	1,496	+7·6
Overall	730	869	1,067	1,205	+65·1
Operating cost/GJ					
(£) actuals	1·61*	1·78	1·60	1·64	−1·9
Equivalent 1987–88 prices	2·01	1·91	1·66	1·64	−18·4

Source: BC.

*Evaluated using 25·5 GJ/tonne.

APPENDIX 5.1

(referred to in paragraph 5.41)

North Yorkshire Area

Allerton Bywater Colliery

Scheme: Ventilation and man-access drift

Area approval:	12 July 1985
Scheme completed:	December 1986
Approved budget:	£878,631
Final cost:	£886,025

Allerton Bywater Colliery

1. This colliery is a few miles north of Castleford, West Yorkshire. Major reconstruction and modernization at the colliery was completed in 1978 at a cost of £8 million. As part of this reconstruction a new 1,000-metre drift was driven to convey coal to the surface. The colliery employed about 1,200 men and produced some 840,000 tonnes of coal in 1986–87. It has generally been profitable, and it produces high-quality coal mainly for the industrial market.

The scheme

2. This scheme was conceived in January 1984 and consists of driving a new 1 in 4·5 550-metre drift from the existing roadway at the bottom of the upcast shaft down to roadways giving access to new workings.

3. The main elements in the scheme were: driving the new drift to connect with the return roadway to be driven as part of the new development of the Middleton Little seam; construction of a junction with the existing roadway at the top end of the new drift; and the installation of a double-deck man-riding conveyor in the new drift.

Scheme's objectives

4. The two objectives of the project were to provide:

(*a*) a short man-access route to the new working area, and improve the face MAT; and

(*b*) adequate ventilation for production faces and associated drivages in the new area of working.

Identification of need

5. The project was first discussed at a Colliery Action Planning meeting in January 1984. It was noted that such a scheme could save up to 80 minutes per shift in travel time. Later that same month further investigation at the colliery showed that the proposed drift would increase the MAT at the Middleton Little seam by 75 minutes per shift, ie from 265 minutes to 340 minutes. (Average MAT in BC is about 320 minutes, compared with the full shift time of 450 minutes.)

6. The colliery investigation showed further that, at the expected face machine cycle time of 129 minutes, the extra 75 minutes MAT would yield an extra 0·6 machine cycles per shift (equivalent to an extra 258 saleable tonnes per shift). Several more faces were expected to be worked in the seam, giving a total life of about 10 years.

7. The Stage II submission, dated May 1985, stated that the proposed man-riding conveyor would provide an increase in effective MAT of 45 minutes per shift. When applied to the machine cycle times in the Middleton Little seam, such an increase in MAT was estimated to be equivalent to 100 tonnes of saleable output per working shift.

Productivity

8. In estimating future output, existing methods of extraction were assumed to remain, and no allowance was made for future technical advances. The expected increase in productivity from the Middleton Little seam was calculated entirely on the basis of the greater MAT. The extra 45 minutes of MAT expected as a result of the project was estimated by comparing travelling times on the existing route with travelling times resulting from the new drift and man-riding conveyor.

Consideration of options

9. There was no discussion of options in the case papers, except that in the project's financial appraisal a comparison was drawn between the colliery's results with and without the scheme.

Manpower

10. The scheme was not expected to affect manpower requirements at the colliery, and no Appendix XI was provided.

Financial appraisal

11. The estimated cost of the scheme was £1,008,370 (at March 1985 prices), including £172,370 for plant pool equipment.

12. The full benefits of the scheme were expected to be obtained from 1988–89 onwards, when the colliery was expected to achieve an annual output of 840,000 tonnes (some 45,000 tonnes more than would have been the case without the scheme). The value of the extra 45,000 tonnes in 1988–89 was estimated to be £1·677 million, but this was partly offset by higher operating costs and higher interest charges. The net increase on the colliery's profitability (after capital charges) resulting from the scheme in 1988–89 was therefore estimated to be £1·252 million.

13. A DCF analysis of the colliery's cash flow results with and without the scheme from 1985–86 until the end of the colliery's life (1996–97 with the scheme, and 1997–98 without the scheme) showed a marginal return of 85·1 per cent.

14. Four risk factors were assessed:

(a) incremental output reduced by 10 per cent (resulting adjusted yield: 75·2 per cent);

(b) scheme cost increased by 10 per cent (resulting adjusted yield: 79·9 per cent);

(c) scheme takes six months longer to complete (resulting adjusted yield: 58·1 per cent); and

(d) composite of (a), (b) and (c) (resulting adjusted yield: 49·6 per cent).

Marketing assessment

15. The Stage II submission stated that the estimated increase in production resulting from the project would not present any problems at the colliery. Of the additional 45,000 tonnes a year, some 38,840 tonnes were expected to go to the CEGB.

Annual Reviews

16. Annual Reviews are not required for projects of less than £1 million and none were prepared for this project.

Completion Report

17. An interim Completion Report was prepared for the period up to the end of 1987. It reported that the project had been completed on time in December 1986.

18. The first face of the Middleton Little seam began in November 1987. Method study had shown that the new man-riding conveyor had potentially increased the MAT at the face by 57 minutes per shift (compared with the 45 minutes estimated in Stage II).

19. The interim Completion Report did not mention the effect of the project on the colliery's saleable output. We were told that this is because the main purpose of the project was to increase the MAT, and thus the success (or otherwise) of the project was assessed only against this objective.

Cost per GJ

20. This scheme was approved before the present cost per GJ investment criteria were introduced. Operating costs per GJ at the colliery have increased in recent years from £1·47 in 1985–86 to £1·78 in 1987–88. The colliery is targeted to achieve £1·68 per GJ in 1988–89.

APPENDIX 5.2

(referred to in paragraph 5.41)

Nottinghamshire Area

Asfordby New Mine

HQ approval:	9 December 1985
Projected completion date:	June 1993
Latest approved out-turn cost:	£471·6 million

Asfordby new mine

1. The new mine is located on the south-west periphery of the North-East Leicestershire coalfield. The area of reserves assigned to Asfordby covers approximately 60 square kilometres situated to the north-west of Melton Mowbray. The original designs for a new mine at Asfordby were submitted in December 1977. They were based on geological explorations conducted between 1973 and 1976.

The scheme

2. The submission on which planning permission was originally granted projected construction of one deep mine with two shafts and four production faces producing a saleable output of 2·2 million tonnes a year (mtpa) from a total mineral wind of 2·7 mtpa. The 1985 Stage II submission incorporated certain important modifications and outlined the scope of the works. These were summarized in a synopsis of the project included as part of the submission.

3. Hydrogeological boreholes drilled in 1982–83 showed the coal measures to be overlain by water-bearing strata. Various methods for accessing the reserves through the water-bearing strata were examined. A system incorporating a technique to freeze the water was chosen and would be included with shaft sinking.

4. Information obtained from the 1982–83 hydrogeological boreholes on the shaft sites, and five part-engineering boreholes drilled over the proposed pit bottom area, revealed the presence of extrusive igneous rocks which contained water under pressure and indicated that the western side of the proposed pit bottom was within the 45 metre statutory cautionary zone of these rocks. In consequence it was necessary to re-design the pit bottom.

5. The scheme proposed in the Stage II document is set out below:

(a) *Mining and surface works:*

   (i) Two concrete-lined shafts were to provide access to a main arterial roadway network. The upcast and downcast shafts would be 527·0 metres deep. Two winding systems would be installed in the upcast shaft, each to operate with a 26-tonne capacity skip and counterweight giving a shaft capacity of 840 tonnes per hour. The height of the winding towers was limited to comply with the conditions attached to the Planning Consent, and this fact governed the original winding shaft capacity. Work on sinking the shafts began in August 1985, some three months prior to Stage II authorization.

  (ii) Subsidiary roadways would provide access to faces and carry the ventilation system.

 (iii) Face design for four production faces, plus one in reserve, was based on advancing longwall extraction.

(b) *Surface proposals:*

   (i) An integrated plant control system of mineral handling from skip discharge to the coal preparation plant was to be installed. The coal preparation plant was to be of modular design consisting of two independent modules each with a capacity of 500 tonnes per hour. This would match the shaft capacity. The output would be mostly conveyed to a 3,000-tonne rapid loading bunker.

(ii) Dirt would be transported by an automated conveyor and spread by conventional earth-moving equipment across the valley adjacent to the site.

(iii) A two-storey office block would be connected to the two-storey welfare block and pithead baths.

(iv) Boiler plant, explosives store, workshops and stores would be built, with a 25,200 sq metre stockyard.

(v) Facilities for potable water, process water, surface run-off and on-site sewage treatment would be constructed, as would two pipelines bringing water to and from the River Soar.

Manpower

6. The estimated manpower required at full production was set at 1,100 MOB including 299 at the face. Daily output of 2,360 tonnes per face was forecast, with face productivity of 33·8 tonnes per man-shift. Overall productivity of 10·8 tonnes per man-shift was projected.

Marketing

7. After an allowance for small tonnages of nuts (concessionaires) and washed singles (colliery boilers) the main outlet for the product would be CEGB power stations.

Project management

8. A multi-disciplinary team, based at South Midlands Area Headquarters and directed by the Chief Mining Engineer, was appointed to control the project. That team would be assisted by consulting engineers and quantity surveyors for both the surface and mining works. A description of Asfordby project management and the introduction of a project control system is set out in paragraph (7.59).

Technical change

9. Since these proposals were submitted in 1985, they have been subjected to regular review and revision (see Table 1).

TABLE 1   **Proposed levels of output**

Stage I plus	July	1982	2·20 mtpa (5 days)
Stage II	March	1985	2·20 mtpa (5 days)
Amended Stage II	July	1985	2·50 mtpa (5 days)
Enhanced Stage II	Sept	1985	3·02 mtpa (5 days)
2nd Annual Review	Dec	1987	3·78 mtpa (6 days)

Source: MMC, from the case study.

10. Changes to the technical specification since the mine was originally conceived have arisen both as a consequence of the need to reduce costs and to design around geological problems uncovered as the project has progressed. The 1987 second Annual Review contains the most up-to-date project revisions and bases its financial appraisal on a six-day production pattern. Initial output has been brought forward one year to enable 400,000 tonnes to be mined in 1991–92, although the June 1993 completion date for the scheme is unchanged. The small amounts of concessionary and boiler fuel originally planned for would not be produced.

11. The plan for six-day working envisaged a 25 per cent increase in output to 3·78 mtpa, and a 25 per cent overall increase in manpower to 1,588 men.

12. Among the various cost savings made to the original specification were: the decision not to build an office block, but to retain temporary buildings; the institution of an accelerating construction programme, including earlier completion of the coal preparation plant; and a single, on-site, project management team.

13. Boreholes sunk in 1987 provided further detail of the igneous rocks known to be present from previous exploration. This further information led to some redesigning of the pit bottom for the second time.

Scheme's objectives

14. In 1985 the objectives were:

(*a*) to contribute towards the stabilization of the coal industry's capacity by a method that was both efficient and environmentally acceptable;

(*b*) partially to offset the fall in production following exhaustion of other capacity within the South Midlands area;

(*c*) to provide the opportunity for continuation of employment for some of the existing workforce, predominantly from the North-West Leicestershire coalfield, traditionally a moderate and effective labour force; and

(*d*) the enhancement of coal's competitive position in the energy market and continuity of supply to the CEGB.

Identification of need

15. The initial decision to explore the North-East Leicestershire coalfield arose in response to the 1974 Plan for Coal commitment to invest in new capacity. The resulting plans to produce 7·5 mtpa from three mines in the Vale of Belvoir at Hose, Saltby and Asfordby were rejected by the Secretary of State for the Environment in 1982, two years after a full public inquiry. However, indications were given that a planning application for Asfordby new mine alone would be acceptable. In January 1984 the Secretary of State for Energy approved a new mine at Asfordby.

16. Asfordby had not been the preferred site and had always been considered a marginal project in financial terms. However, a number of factors influenced BC's 1985 decision to grant Stage II approval to the project. The original public inquiry had been widely publicized, as had been the Secretary of State's decision to 'call in' the Inspector's decision to approve the planning application and then two years later overturn it. This, BC told us, created pressure for it to 'do something' in that area and during the 1984–85 miners' dispute BC held a press conference at Asfordby and announced that this would be the site for a new mine. By late 1985 Asfordby was considered to be part of BC's new strategy of emphasizing low-cost production, although the very low quality of the coal available and low estimates of DCF yield made it marginal to that strategy.

17. A further consideration in the development of the project has been a wish to support and maintain the local labour force. Asfordby's current prospectus is tied to the introduction of six-day flexible working. The introduction of six-day working at new mines is considered to be of central importance to BC in terms of its ability to meet its current and future financial objectives.

Manpower

18. The proposals for a new mine at Asfordby have altered substantially since the original plans for a mine producing 2·2 mtpa from four faces, operating ten machine shifts per day with five-day working, were conceived. Manning levels estimated in 1985 at full production totalled 1,100 MOB: 299 at the face, 417 EBG, 210 at the surface, and 174 'capital'. The 1985 Enhanced Stage II Prospectus based on five-day working (with 12 machine shifts on five faces) estimated that overall manpower requirements on completion would increase to 1,270.

19. The 1987 second Annual Review was based on the assumption that Asfordby would be worked on a rostered seven and a half hour shift system with three weeks on and one week off and with production on 294 days of the year. On the assumption that such an arrangement would increase manpower requirements by 25 per cent total MOB was set at 1,588.

20. BC regards its trained workforce as a major asset. In consequence, it has sought to retain its trained workforce at pits in the surrounding area. As Bagworth/Ellistown Colliery is due to be exhausted at around the same time as Asfordby is planned to reach full production, it is expected that a large proportion of Asfordby's need for trained labour will be met by transfers from there.

Financial appraisal

21. Appraisal of the financial prospectus for Asfordby has been updated several times since the original Stage I Plus submission in July 1982.

22. In 1985 the Mining Committee said that the project as then specified was not financially attractive. The DCF yield, after an assessment of risks associated with proceeds, project completion delay and project costs, was calculated at only 2·8 per cent and, it thought, might even be worse.

23. In December 1985 the September submission, based upon an Enhanced Stage II prospectus, was authorized contingent on a continuing search for an improved financial prospectus, including further examination of possible shift changes.

24. As Table 2 shows, the financial appraisal has been revised and updated in order to comply with the condition, placed upon Stage II approval, that the Area engages in a continuing search for an improved financial prospectus. The most recent appraisal, conducted as part of the second Annual Review, calculated the DCF yield by excluding sunk costs for both the base case and the most likely case after risk.

TABLE 2

Date	No. days working	Est'd out-turn £'000	Output mtpa	Base case DCF yield %	Base case DCF excl sunk costs* %	Most likely case after risk DCF yield %	Most likely case after risk DCF excl sunk costs* %
Stage I plus							
July 1982	5	518·0	2·2	4·9			
Stage II							
March 1985	5	581·4	2·2	5·0		2·8	
Improved Stage II							
June 1985	5	584·1	2·5	7·0			
Enhanced Stage II							
November 1985	5	579·5	3·0	9·4		4·9	
November 1985	6	579·5	3·6	11·5		6·9	
First Annual Review							
October 1986	5	471·6	3·0	8·8		4·4	
October 1986	6	471·6	3·6	10·9	14·4	6·4	
Second Annual Review							
November 1987	5	470·9	3·8	6·4			
November 1987	6	470·9	3·8	8·9	10·4		6·4

Source: MMC, from the case study.

*DCF yields excluding sunk costs have been calculated by excluding all project expenditure, including land purchases, made prior to the date of the appraisal.

25. Concern over the viability of the project has been consistently expressed by a number of Headquarters departments.

26. In July 1985 BC's Economics Unit considered a re-examination of the project to be essential. It thought that, on the basis of the best assessment that could then be made, the project was barely commercially viable after allowance for risks. In April 1987 the Economics Unit found that even the improved project prospectus, with a DCF yield of 10·9 per cent, was not very robust given the risk factors and optimistic assumptions on proceeds. In April 1988, the Economics Unit questioned whether a satisfactory return on investment could be achieved.

27. In considering likely future proceeds, the Marketing Department noted in July 1985 that the low calorific value and high moisture content of Asfordby coal made the project sensitive financially. Later that year, the Marketing Department expressed concern as to whether the revised output of 3·0 mtpa could be achieved and at the assumptions on proceeds. The anticipated 93 per cent yield from the coal preparation plant, it thought, seemed optimistic. In attaching comments to the 1985 Enhanced Stage II prospectus, the Marketing Department noted that Asfordby coal had no characteristics which made it of special value to the market apart from its geographical location. The coal was described as inherently low grade, with a high moisture content and low calorific value even when fully washed. Whilst the CEGB should be regarded as the sole potential market, it thought that the quality was likely to be at the bottom of the CEGB's normal specification for heat content, and the high moisture content would detract from its general acceptability.

28. In November 1985 the Capital Investment Committee (CIC) decided that Asfordby's importance for the industry as a whole overrode all such considerations, and supported its approval by the Office of the Chief Executive: 'bearing in mind the consequences for the industry as a whole' the CIC 'supported the granting of Stage II approval'.

Annual Reviews

29. Two Annual Reviews have been undertaken. The first Annual Review in 1986 recommended approval of a simplified underground layout, production from three faces rather than four, plus one in reserve, and all faces to be developed for retreat working rather than advance to reduce the degree of geological risk. The surface layout was also amended with the cancellation of proposals for purpose-built offices and concentration upon fast track construction. Modifications to the coal preparation plant were made possible by the decision to produce just one product and to import concessionary coal and boiler fuel from other mines. These modifications permitted the reduction in out-turn costs to £471·6 million, giving a DCF yield of 8·8 per cent. In April 1987, the CIC noted that even the improved prospectus, based upon six-day working with a DCF yield of 10·9 per cent, was not very robust given the risk factors and that the underlying assumption of proceeds of £1·60 per GJ might be difficult to sustain.

30. The second Annual Review, submitted December 1987, presented estimates on the basis of six-day working, 49 weeks of the year. This gave rise to a 25 per cent increase on all tonnages and annual production was estimated to reach 3·78 mtpa on project completion. Costs per GJ with six-day working were estimated to be £1·78 including capital charges (£1·07 without capital charges). The DCF yield was calculated at 8·9 per cent. The total financial commitment at the present time, including £70 million of expenditure already incurred, is £120 million. This amounts to just over a quarter of the 1987 estimates of total out-turn costs.

31. In commenting on the 1987 Review, the Finance Department pointed out that the expected return before risk had reduced from the 11·5 per cent estimated at Stage II to 8·9 per cent, and it estimated that the return on investment fell to

7·7 per cent if account was taken of the further 5 per cent reduction in proceeds then postulated. It considered that at this low level of return the viability of the project was vulnerable to adverse variances to the project or results on completion.

32. In response to the second Annual Review, the CIC decided that the Area should submit a comprehensive review of this project to Headquarters for consideration at its meeting in June 1988. This review, the CIC said, should:

(a) show how the Area intends to improve operating results on those indicated in the second Annual Review;

(b) contain 'best estimates' for future proceeds from the new mine;

(c) refer to the expected costs of the contracts to be let for the next stage of the project; and

(d) show the new mine bearing only a contribution element of Headquarters and Area overhead costs.

33. We asked BC for its current views about the financial appraisal of Asfordby. We were told that the decision to go ahead with the project had been taken on the basis of its financial prospectus. The Stage II approval was conditional upon an improved financial prospectus being obtained: in particular with six-day working, and that the next major contract would only be let when six-day working had been agreed.

34. A further review of the project was under way during our inquiry and BC told us that, although the review had not been completed, it expected that the project would now meet its financial tests after allowing for risk provided that sunk costs were disregarded. If the project marginally failed the financial tests there were wider considerations related to planning procedures, promises given to the local workforce in 1984–85, and the introduction of flexible working which might be taken into account and might still justify continuing with the project.

Third party evidence

35. Although this area of Leicestershire is well known for its unusual deposits of igneous rock, BC told us that had it known of the existence of the igneous rock pile (discovered in 1987) affecting the pit bottom and other designs 'earlier', it would have rethought the project. The British Geological Survey (BGS) provided us with written evidence to the effect that it had made it clear to BC's Area Geologist in 1983 that it considered it likely that igneous bodies might interrupt coal-working as the mine extended. As a result of its involvement in identifying the igneous rocks found, the BGS advised, in 1987, a full-time study of the rocks affecting the Asfordby mine.

36. In view of BC's decision to concentrate upon the production of a single product at Asfordby for supply to the CEGB, we asked the CEGB to give its view on the suitability of Asfordby coal for use in its power stations. The CEGB told us that the latest borehole data received from BC showed that the relatively low calorific value of the coal was unchanged from that indicated in the course of the Belvoir inquiry. However, the accompanying ash analysis for Asfordby showed characteristics somewhat different from the bulk of BC's supplies to the CEGB. The CEGB was concerned that if these characteristics persisted it would raise the need to explore some price adjustment.

APPENDIX 5.3

(referred to in paragraph 5.41)

Central Area

Daw Mill Colliery

Scheme: Capacity expansion

HQ approval:	2 April 1987
Projected completion date:	March 1990
Approved budget:	£23·05 million

Daw Mill Colliery

1. Daw Mill Colliery is centrally located on the concealed part of the Warwickshire coalfield, sited between Birmingham, Nuneaton and Coventry. It is the newest colliery in the coalfield with coal-winding dating from 1965. Capacity expansion projects were approved in 1969 and 1977 at a cost of £0·4 million and £36 million respectively. Total classified reserves allocated to the colliery of 62·7 million tonnes are located in one seam, which has a total thickness at Daw Mill varying between 7·5 metres and 6·2 metres. The colliery employs about 1,400 men and produced about 1·5 million tonnes from three faces in 1987–88. About 35 per cent of the colliery's high-quality coal goes to the industrial and domestic market, with the remainder being sold to the CEGB.

The scheme

2. The scheme is for capacity expansion from the 1·75 mtpa planned for 1987–88 to 2·25 mtpa by 1991–92. The original approval was for £21 million expenditure at 1986 prices (£23 million at out-turn cost). Estimates were revised downwards in March 1987 to just over £20 million at 1986 prices (£22·7 million at out-turn cost).

3. The expansion of capacity was to be achieved by a combination of factors:

(*a*) increase in extraction height to 4·5 metres;

(*b*) increase in face advances by improved technology;

(*c*) increase in the number of working faces; and

(*d*) supporting increases in capacity of coal, dirt and supplies handling both underground and on the surface.

4. Surface works supporting the increase in capacity were to include modifications to the coal preparation plant, and extensions to other pithead facilities. Surface works also covered surface mineral handling, six new bunkers and associated equipment, and a computer control room.

5. Underground works included the installation of a 1,000-tonne vertical bunker, a new conveyor with a capacity of 1,800 tonnes per hour and materials handling improvements.

Scheme's objectives

6. A 1984 report, arising from BC's assessment of the industry's capacity and likely market demands, supported the need for development of the South Warwickshire reserves as soon as was feasible, subject to the achievement of an acceptable rate of return.

7. Examination of alternative ways of developing the reserves resulted in BC's decision to develop existing mines immediately and plan for construction of a new mine by the year 2000. Development of existing mines was to be achieved by expanding planned levels of output to 2·25 mtpa at Daw Mill Colliery and 1·75 mtpa at Coventry Colliery.

Identification of need

8. In pursuit of the objectives contained within the industry's Plan for Coal BC undertook to develop fully the South Warwickshire Prospect. This development was agreed in November 1978 and the first Feasibility Report was considered by the General Purposes Committee in November 1982. That report considered six alternative plans. The Committee agreed the continuation of preliminary work associated with planning the construction of a new mine in the south-west of the prospect. It also agreed that the Feasibility Study be expanded to consider the accessing of new reserves from Daw Mill and Coventry Collieries with a satellite mine to be attached to Daw Mill Colliery at a later date.

9. In 1984 a second Feasibility Report was prepared. In examining options the team established that some £40 million of new investment would be required at Daw Mill and Coventry Collieries to maintain their planned levels of output within allocated reserves. Without a satellite mine to permit exploitation of further reserves, output at both pits would progressively decline leading to the closure of Coventry Colliery in around 20 years and Daw Mill Colliery in about 30 years. To maintain planned levels of output or expand production beyond those dates would necessitate the establishment of a satellite mine in the South-West and its connection to both pits by around the year 2000. The expansion of output at both Daw Mill and Coventry Collieries was examined on this basis.

10. While examination of output combinations including Coventry Colliery were affected by Coventry's geological problems, it was considered that expansion at Daw Mill Colliery would be commercially attractive in its own right.

11. The Headquarters Mining Committee, which received this report in October 1984, considered that it was necessary to develop the reserves urgently especially in view of what was termed the marketing situation. Expansion of Daw Mill's output to 2·25 mtpa was to be pushed forward as soon as possible irrespective of decisions on other options because of a continuing shortage of the grades needed to meet industrial and domestic demand.

12. The Committee requested urgent submission of Stage II proposals for increasing production at Daw Mill to the maximum level which was feasible from within its currently accessible reserves.

13. The Area's Stage I submission was presented to Headquarters CIC in January 1986. It sought approval for expenditure of £17 million for expansion of output from the then planned 1·75 mtpa (1986–87) to 2·25 mtpa by 1991–92. The submission stated that the proposals met BC's objectives of producing low cost, high volume coal, for existing and expanding markets. The proposal was supported by Headquarters Marketing Department on the grounds of strategic need and low marginal cost. In a paper supporting the Stage II submission the Area director stated that the industrial market was expected to expand over the next 15 years as oil-fired plant became due for replacement and oil prices returned to a higher level than they were then.

14. The CIC requested that the Area submit Stage II proposals including a detailed evaluation of expenditure, together with anticipated financial results, to achieve each of the following levels of output:

(a) the maximum saleable tonnage achievable;

(b) 3·0 saleable mtpa;

(c) 2·25 saleable mtpa; and

(d) the maximum saleable tonnage achievable without further capital expenditure ('do nothing').

15. The Stage II submission, which came before the Project Committee in September 1986, considered two alternatives to the option of increasing output at Daw Mill Colliery above 2·25 mtpa. These alternatives were 'closure', and 'do nothing'. The closure option was not considered or evaluated due to the colliery's history of profitability. The do-nothing option would be to maintain output levels using facilities provided under the earlier extension of capacity scheme with continuity of production assured for a further 30 years. This option was used to evaluate the marginal prospectus in the financial appraisal.

Manpower

16. The Stage II submission indicated a programmed increase in manpower from 1,444 at September 1986 to 1,800 by 1990–91. Because of the extremely favourable labour market conditions and increased inter-colliery transfers arising from pit closures it was suggested that this increase in manning levels could be achieved without difficulty from local sources.

Financial appraisal

17. The original Stage I submission estimated total new expenditure during the planned two-year construction period at £8·8 million in 1986–87 and £9·0 million in 1987–88. The Stage II submission cost estimate, which was based on a more detailed specification of costs together with an 'allowance for contingencies', totalled £21·1 million (at 1986 prices). This was compared with the do nothing alternative, which would require expenditure of £5 million. Expenditure would be phased over four years as below:

1986–87	£840,000
1987–88	£4,513,000
1988–89	£10,796,000
1989–90	£4,913,000

18. The Area's Stage II submission included a 15-year DCF appraisal for the colliery which compared the 'with project', 'without project' and 'marginal scheme' effects. In this the scheme was shown to have a marginal net cash flow of some £129·3 million which when discounted at 10 per cent gave a marginal net present value (NPV) of £48·5 million. The marginal DCF yield was assessed at 46 per cent.

19. Various sensitivity tests were carried out at Area level on the marginal cash flows. The base case was tested against a 12-month project completion delay, a 10 per cent project cost increase, 10 per cent marginal output shortfall, 10 per cent marginal operating cost increase, and, to give the worst case, against a combination of all four factors.

20. It was stated that the DCF results indicated a highly profitable scheme well worth the proposed investment. A marginal DCF yield of 30 per cent, after applying a combination of risk factors, indicated to the Area that the project was robust against possible risk. Return on investment was estimated to be 42·5 per cent in the first full year after project completion.

Headquarters departments' comments

21. The Finance Department noted that the colliery had been consistently profitable in recent years. However, at a meeting of the Project Committee on 20 March 1987 it was noted that:

(a) the previous major investment project to increase output to 1·75 mtpa, completed in 1983 at a cost of £36 million, had not yet led to achievement of planned output levels or profitability; and

(b) there was no provision for the estimated new capital expenditure in 1987–88, and that availability in 1988–89 was likely to be limited.

BC told us, however, that when this meeting took place there was Headquarters available revenue in the sum of £12 million, and so had the Committee wished to approve it at that time the funds were available. The Technical Department supported the proposals in principle, but considered that the production pattern proposed in Stage II (six faces working 13 machine shifts) appeared excessive for an annual output of 2·25 mtpa. It appeared to represent a low risk but high cost mining operation, with a degree of 'insurance' built into the estimates. Concern was also expressed over proposed project monitoring and control.

22. The Industrial Relations Department foresaw no difficulty in achieving the manpower build-up and suggested that further consideration be given to increasing profitability by more intensive working. The Marketing Department supported the proposal.

Technical change

23. Following a meeting to discuss the Area's capital allocation for 1987–88, it was decided to defer expenditure on the scheme for 12 months, except for any expenditure already committed. In April the CIC considered scheme modifications and revised levels of expenditure associated with a 12-month deferment. By making modifications to the coal preparation plant, surface layout and sewage plant and cancelling the new office block, the profitability of the scheme would remain substantially the same with only a 4 percentage points reduction in the DCF yield to 42 per cent.

Phasing

24. Because no extra capital allocation would be required for 1987–88 and by rephasing work from 1989–90 only about £7 million might be spent in 1988–89, Stage II approval was given to the scheme in April 1987 but the Area had to reduce proposed expenditure without affecting the date of the project's completion. The rephasing of certain physical and financial aspects of the scheme would result in the project being completed four months later than originally proposed, but with the first year of production unchanged.

25. In October 1987 Stage II approval for £23 million at out-turn prices (equivalent to £21 million at September 1986 prices) was given, phased so that the bulk of expenditure would occur in 1989–90.

North-East Area

Dawdon Colliery

Scheme: Rapid loading station and ancillary arrangements

HQ approval:	16 June 1983
Scheme completed:	August 1986
Approved budget:	£3·5 million
Final cost:	£2·5 million

Dawdon Colliery

1. This is a generally profitable long-life colliery at Seaham, south of Sunderland on the North-East coast of England. It was sunk in 1900 to 1907 and is about 500 metres deep. About £4 million was invested in a major reconstruction at the colliery in 1962. The colliery employs about 1,600 men, and produced about 1·4 million tonnes of coal in 1987–88 from undersea workings. About 90 per cent of the colliery's output goes to the CEGB.

The scheme

2. This scheme is one of two schemes forming a composite project approved by Headquarters on 16 June 1983. This project's approved budget was £4·7 million (of which the capital cost was £4·4 million—the remainder being certain revenue and leased plant costs). The final cost of the composite scheme, on completion, was £3·5 million.

3. The rail 'merry-go-round' (mgr) rapid loading facilities at Dawdon was one element in a programme to provide rapid loading/discharge facilities at a number of locations in the North-East Area[1] as a result of British Rail's (BR's) introduction of large-capacity (33-tonne), high-speed, air-brake wagons to replace its ageing fleet of 21-tonne coal wagons. The main elements of the Dawdon scheme were: rapid loading bunker and ancillary equipment; railway trackwork, including connection to the BR system; the extension of existing coal conveyor system; and electrical equipment.

4. The other element in the composite project was to provide loading facilities for road-borne products. This became necessary because BR had decided not to continue to carry small consignments (such as domestic or industrial coals) over small distances.

Scheme's objectives

5. The Stage II application paper for this project (dated 19 May 1983) gives two objectives for this rapid loading scheme:

(*a*) the provision of rapid loading and associated facilities for part-treated CEGB coals; and

(*b*) manpower saving of 26 (from both schemes in the composite project).

---

[1] Rapid loading stations for Lynemouth and Hawthorn Collieries were given Headquarters approval in June 1982, and one for Westoe Colliery was approved in February 1988. Rapid loading arrangements at Vane Tempest Colliery were approved in June 1986.

Identification of need

6. BR's decision to replace its ageing fleet of mineral wagons was first discussed by BC's Mining Committee in October 1973. Investment in rapid loading was initially concentrated in the Midlands, Yorkshire and Western Areas, where the large CEGB coal-fired power stations came into operation. In 1977 BC thought that BR's policy change would 'cause increasing restriction on the efficient transport of coal in the North-East' by the early 1980s. A working party (with representatives from BR, BC and the CEGB) reported in January 1979 with the recommendations that:

(a) coal distribution in the North-East should be based on the use of 700 larger wagons (replacing the 9,000 or so smaller wagons); and

(b) rapid loading and discharge facilities should be built at the three main power stations in the area, at three coal staiths[1], and at five collieries.

7. These recommendations were accepted by each of the three main parties, and in October 1980 the Mining Committee requested that a Stage I application be prepared which:

(a) outlined the proposals for the North-East Area;

(b) assessed progress by the other two interested parties implementing the recommendations; and

(c) reviewed the alternatives.

8. In June 1981, after consideration of this Stage I submission, a BC working party was set up to re-examine and report on the financial and practical aspects of these proposals, as well as of certain other schemes in the North-East Area's investment strategy. This BC working party reported in January 1982 that, among other things, a 1,000-tonne bunker with conventional stock and reclaim facilities should be installed at Dawdon Colliery at a total cost of £2·098 million (September 1981 prices). This would need to be fully operational by the end of 1984. The Area had proposed to install a 2,000-tonne bunker at a cost of £2 million allowing full rail mgr operation, but the working party concluded that the 1,000-tonne bunker was 'technically preferable'. The saving in the capital cost for the 1,000-tonne, instead of the 2,000-tonne, bunker was estimated to be £542,000. The proposed 1,000-tonne bunker was accepted by the Headquarters Mining Committee on 28 January 1982.

9. The Stage II submission, of December 1982 stated that:

Although both conventional and high capacity wagons can be loaded at Dawdon, the efficiency of the system is dependent on the use of 'buffer sets' (of wagons) and BR has only undertaken to continue providing these until December 1984. Thereafter, no conventional wagons and only a limited number of high capacity wagons will be available. Failure to provide new loading facilities, including bunkerage and stocking, would therefore lead to major problems in the disposal of the power station coal and could place at risk continuity of production.

10. Headquarters Marketing Department was fully involved in both the earlier discussions on the general strategy for loading and discharging facilities for high capacity wagons in the North-East, and in the specific proposal for Dawdon Colliery. The Marketing Department took the view that this Dawdon scheme was necessary to ensure a reliable service to the colliery and a continuing outlet to CEGB power stations in the North-East.

Consideration of options

11. The Area considered the implications of three different sizes of bunker (500-tonne, 1,000-tonne, and 2,000-tonne) in the lead-up to the BC working party's report in January 1982 (see paragraph 8 above).

---

[1] Waterside coal depot equipped for loading vessels.

12. The Stage II submission stated that there was no alternative to the proposed scheme. The Stage II paper (of 19 May 1983) similarly concluded that there was no feasible alternative way of improving rail-loading facilities at Dawdon Colliery. Road transport was considered impracticable because of the large quantities involved, environmental considerations, and the commitment of the power station receiving points to rail transport.

13. The 'do nothing' option was considered difficult to evaluate because of uncertainty about the consequences of the resulting increases in operational and marketing difficulties, including the risk of interruptions to and losses of production. Indeed, the 'do nothing' option was considered in effect to be a proxy for colliery closure as the main alternative to going ahead with the scheme. No options, other than the chosen one, were therefore costed.

Manpower

14. The Stage II submission indicated a resulting net reduction of 14 in the number of jobs concerned with the despatch of power station coal by rail. This reduction would be absorbed by natural wastage. The 14 jobs included 11 job savings which result from both the road loading and the rapid loading schemes. No other manpower or industrial relations issues were addressed and no relevant appendix (estimates of manpower, shifts, productivity and wages costs) was included.

Financial appraisal

15. While the BC working party's estimate (of January 1982) of the total cost of the scheme was £2·098 million (at September 1981) prices, the Stage II submission (of December 1982) estimated the cost to be £2·850 million (at November 1982 prices). The Stage II paper (of May 1983) stated the cost to be £3·2 million (also at November 1982 prices), equivalent to £3·5 million at out-turn prices. The estimated cost of the scheme thus increased (including a revision of price levels) by over 52 per cent between January 1982 and May 1983.

16. The Area's Stage II submission included a 15-year DCF appraisal for the colliery which compared the with and without scheme effects. In this, the scheme is shown to have no effect on projected colliery proceeds, but that it would increase operating costs (including depreciation but excluding interest charges) by £106,000 a year (the effect of the road-borne products project is shown to be a net reduction in operating costs of £165,000 a year, thus giving a combined effect on operating costs of minus £59,000 a year). The interest charge is given as £343,000, thus giving a total increase in costs from this project of £459,000 a year (reduced to an extra £414,000 a year if the effect of the road-borne products project is included).

17. However, with proceeds shown each year to be greater than operating costs (before depreciation and interest payments) the colliery's cash inflow has a positive DCF yield of 59·3 per cent with the scheme and 62·3 per cent without the scheme.

18. The Stage II paper (May 1983) gives the net increase in costs (including interest) resulting from this project to be £413,000 a year—some increases in costs are shown to be offset by an allowance of £120,000 a year arising from an assumed 'contribution' from BR of 12 pence per tonne for 15 years (BR's contribution would take the form of a direct payment to BC).

19. The Stage II contained Headquarters Finance Department's appraisal of the combined project. This showed an overall DCF return on the combined project of four per cent. The Finance Department noted, in relation to its sensitivity analysis, that total colliery cash flow was sensitive to relatively minor variations from planned performance; in particular the colliery net cash inflow would be eliminated by a six per cent output shortfall.

20. The Mining Department confirmed that the colliery was considered a major long-life unit with a continuing role to play in meeting the North-East Area's output and performance objectives. The Marketing Department confirmed the need to maintain Dawdon Colliery as a major supplier of the coals it produced.

Technical Change

21. In March 1984 the Area applied for a Technical Change in relation to Stage II proposals. The main proposed changes were:

(a) increase the rapid loading bunker capacity from 1,000 tonnes to 2,000 tonnes; and

(b) re-position the coal conveyor system.

22. The reasons for the changes were given as:

(a) planning permission (in November 1983) had enabled the colliery to extend its coal-stocking area and so re-position the proposed conveyor;

(b) the 2,000-tonne bunker would eliminate the need for two loading-shovel operators;

(c) tender prices had shown relatively small differences between the capital costs of the 2,000-tonne and 1,000-tonne bunkers; and

(d) savings in the cost of installing the new conveyors offset the cost increases arising from the larger bunker size.

Annual Reviews

23. Two Annual Reviews were conducted, one for the year to June 1985 and one for the year to June 1986. No Annual Review for 1984 was prepared (this was not unusual because of the effects of the 1984–85 strike).

24. The 1985 Annual Review noted that the combined project's latest estimated costs were about £1 million less than the Stage II estimate of £4·7 million, and stated that this was mostly because the costs of contract work had been overestimated. The Annual Review noted that the project was running about eight months late because:

(a) approval had been delayed by three months;

(b) of the need to move stocks of coal to another site;

(c) of the Technical Change application; and

(d) of NUM industrial action.

25. The 1985 Annual Review reported that there were no significant changes to Stage II estimates of benefits from the project, except that BR's contribution had increased to 16·5 pence per tonne for a ten-year period. The paper did, however, report that in comparison with the Stage II prospectus the latest estimates showed that the colliery's results had worsened (saleable output was down by over 8 per cent, with the result that operating profit in 1986–87 was down from £3·882 million to £1·653 million).

26. The 1986 Annual review reported additional project delays resulting from bad weather in early 1986, the late appointment of an electrical sub-contractor by the main contractor, and some additional civil engineering work. The work was completed in August 1986, some 19 months later than originally envisaged (ie December 1984) in the Stage II documents.

27. The 1986 Annual Review also reported that the colliery's performance had worsened, and that the latest estimate for 1986-87 showed an operating profit of £0·4 million before capital charges of £2·7 million.

Completion Report

28. A Completion Report was prepared for the period to June 1987. This showed the combined project's final cost to be £1·2 million less than the Stage II estimate of £4·7 million. The main reasons for the lower costs were that the Stage II estimate had overestimated both the inflation rate and the costs of contract work. The charges made by contractors and suppliers were substantially under BC's estimates. Against a Stage II (out-turn) approved sum of £4·7 million, the total project cost was £3·5 million. The Area's analysis of the difference was as follows:

	£m
Inflation rate change	− 0·37
Estimating	− 0·88
Technical Change	+ 0·04
Slippage	+ 0·01
Total	− 1·20

29. The Completion Report reported few changes to the Stage II paper's assessment of the project's benefits, and effects on manpower. It also reported that the colliery's actual 1986–87 results showed a loss before capital charges of £1·6 million compared with the updated Stage II estimate of profits of £1·9 million (the main reason being a six per cent reduction in saleable output).

30. In commenting on the Completion Report, Headquarters departments noted that:

(a) the project was completed within some 27 per cent of the Stage II cost, and that the project's objectives had been achieved;

(b) the colliery's performance figures for 1987–88 showed substantial improvements over the 1986–87 figures (an operating profit of £8 million was expected); and

(c) the projected manpower saving of 28 had been achieved, although the colliery's total manpower of 1,592 (as at January 1988) was some 456 below the Stage II estimate because of general efforts to reduce costs at the colliery.

Phasing

31. Area's original phasing for the composite project was based on co-ordinating the project works with two key dates:

April 1984 — withdrawal by BR of rail facilities for small consignments of coal; and

December 1984 — withdrawal by BR of buffer sets of rail wagons.

The new facilities would become operational by March 1984 and December 1984 respectively. However, processing the application at Headquarters was delayed because of the need to determine priorities for the Areas' unapproved major projects for starts in 1983–84. This was not completed until June 1983 by which time the phasing of the two Dawdon projects was behind schedule by 4·5 months and three months respectively.

32. At the time of the Technical Change request, in March 1984, the project's completion date was put as March 1985. Between then and the 1985 Annual Review a revised completion date of June 1985 had been agreed with Headquarters. As mentioned in paragraph 25, the 1985 Annual Review gave reasons why the project was then expected to be completed in March 1986, some eight or nine months after the revised completion date of June 1985. The 1986

Annual Review reported further delays (see paragraph 26). The project was completed in August 1986, a further five months late. The sum of these delays is summarized in the table below:

Cause of delay	Delay (months)
Late approval by HQ	8
Removal of stocked coal, Technical Change, NUM action, and other	11*
Bad weather, late appointment of sub-contractor, extra civil works	5

*Includes eight-month delay reported in 1985 AR, and revision agreed by Headquarters between date of Technical Change and 1985 AR.

33. In the meantime BR, being aware of BC's commitment to the project, had agreed to continue providing the facilities previously available.

Cost per GJ

34. This scheme was approved before the cost per GJ criteria were established. Operating costs per GJ at the colliery have fallen from £2·01 in 1985–86 to £1·41 in 1987–88. The budgeted figure for 1988–89 is also £1·41 per GJ.

APPENDIX 5.5

(referred to in paragraph 5.41)

Nottinghamshire Area

Harworth Colliery

Scheme: Expansion of capacity

HQ approval: 11 March 1988
Completion date: September 1989
Approved budget: £22,384,383

Harworth Colliery

1. Harworth Colliery is situated some 12 km to the south-east of Doncaster. The two shafts, each 6·8 metres in diameter, were sunk during 1920–24 and coal production began in 1925. Until 1981 all production was obtained from the Top Hard seam. That is now abandoned and current production is from three faces in the Deep Soft seam. Harworth Colliery has a reputation of consistent profitability, with overall manpower of 760 in 1988–89 budgeted to produce 1·275 million tonnes of saleable output a year (equivalent to 7·13 tonnes OMS). The colliery is regarded as a low-cost long-life source of supply to the CEGB and to general industrial markets.

2. A number of investment projects have been completed since 1981:

(*a*) 1981: development of the Deep Soft seam, including MINOS control of conveyors (cost £6·0 million);

(*b*) 1981: re-electrification of No 1 winder and the provision of 10·5 tonnes capacity lightweight skips cost (£3·0 million);

(*c*) 1982: development of the Haigh Moor seam—including MINOS control of conveyors (cost £4·5 million);

(*d*) 1983: re-electrification of No 2 winder (cost £3 million);

(*e*) 1983: provision of a 1,000-tonne capacity vertical bunker in the Deep Soft seam (cost £3·3 million);

(*f*) 1983: new dirt disposal conveyor system (cost £1·2 million);

(*g*) 1984: a third drift to the Deep Soft seam (cost £2·6 million);

(*h*) 1986: the construction of a surface air-conditioning plant for the Haigh Moor and Deep Soft seams (cost £2·7 million); and

(*i*) 1986: provision of a 1,200-tonne capacity pit bottom bunker (cost £4·2 million).

3. Two further projects have been approved and are currently in progress:

(*a*) new coal preparation plant (to be commissioned September 1988) at a cost of £21 million; and

(*b*) uprating of Deep Soft trunk conveyors (to be commissioned September 1988) at a cost of £2·6 million.

4. The investment programme at Harworth Colliery is considered by Headquarters to epitomize BC's concern to emphasize the need for discrete projects which are in themselves entirely justifiable on a stand-alone basis, but which also form a part of the development of a colliery as a whole.

The scheme

5. This particular project is intended to increase output from 1·275 million saleable tonnes a year (mstpa) to 1·7 mstpa at an estimated capital cost of £21·1 million and £0·5 million revenue expenditure (at January 1988 prices).

6. The main proposals are:

(a) to deepen No 1 shaft by about four metres and equip with a tower-mounted friction winder and uprated skip plant to provide a winding capacity of 800 tonnes per hour;

(b) to uprate the mine infrastructure to provide coal clearance systems compatible with the proposed level of output; and

(c) to increase manpower to 1,100 MOB.

Scheme's objectives

7. The scheme's primary objectives are to expand low-cost output by developing some 180 million tonnes of reserves and thereby reducing operating costs per GJ from £1·17 to £1·12.

Identification of need

8. Harworth's substantial level of reserves have for some years been considered to be well situated for output expansion and to assist in the replacement of output due to be lost through exhaustion in the Nottinghamshire Area. In 1985 it was estimated that operating costs would be £0·95 per GJ, yielding an operating profit of £60 million (£35 million after capital charges) with a DCF yield of 17 per cent. The estimated cost of increasing output to that level, essentially by sinking a third shaft and increasing coal preparation plant capacity, was £120 million at 1985 prices. The Area considered and costed seven alternative options for expanding colliery capacity. A summary of the Stage II submission for the preferred 3·3 mstpa project was circulated in February 1987. A costing of the project at that time estimated costs to be £217·5 million (at December 1986 prices).

9. Whilst the estimation of operating costs and profitability showed no change, the increased project costs over earlier estimates reduced projections of DCF yield from 17 per cent to 9·5 per cent. The Marketing Department expressed doubts about BC's ability to sell increased industrial quality tonnage from Harworth Colliery, notably because the coal produced was not prime-quality free-burning fuel. The Project Committee also noted that as the capital costs had doubled and the returns halved since the original strategy report, the scheme no longer appeared so attractive. The Committee recommended consideration of a scheme option with lower output at lower cost.

10. The lower cost scheme, which was put forward and which was approved in March 1988, arose initially from the need to replace existing winding equipment. This equipment was over 60 years old and, although designed for a duty of 100,000 winding cycles a year, was being required to turn 190,000 cycles a year. Replacement would allow capacity to be expanded to 1·7 mstpa.

Consideration of options

11. The January 1988 Stage II application to expand capacity to 1·7 mstpa considered two alternatives to the chosen option, together with a consideration of six-day working.

12. The first of these options, to maintain the status quo, noted the necessity to invest in the colliery to maintain existing production levels. Probable expenditure required within the following six years was estimated at £19·8 million. Taking 1989–90 as the first full year after such investment, the Area calculated net profit at £5·3 million, based on assumed proceeds of £42·36 per tonne and operating costs of £1·20 per GJ.

13. The second alternative, expanding output to 3·3 mstpa, was estimated to cost £217·5 million. Assuming the first year of full output to be 1998–99, the Area estimated a net profit of £9·4 million based on assumed proceeds of £38·29 per tonne and operating costs of £1·10 per GJ.

14. The option to maintain the status quo was rejected on the grounds that it limited future output and committed the colliery to the continued use of the old mineral winder, thus perpetuating a weakness in the coal clearance system. Expansion to 3·3 mstpa was also rejected, although thought attractive in tonnage and profitability terms, because of its unsatisfactory return.

15. Taking expansion to 1·7 mstpa as the base case, the Area calculated that the introduction of six-day working could increase output to some 2·4 mstpa. Harworth Colliery's particular ventilation problems have been a central consideration to changes in output levels. It was considered that the existing ventilation system could accommodate this level of output with six-day working.

Manpower

16. The total number of MOB in January 1988 was 981. However, the later closure of the Haigh Moor seam reduced the total to 760. An assessment of requirements to develop and work the expanded mine showed a gradual build-up in employment to 1,100 based on five-day working. The increased number of men, BC expects, would be obtained locally and by colliery transfer.

Financial appraisal

17. The Stage II proposal provided three tables of financial estimates:

(a) projections of investment and profitability for each year from 1987–88 to 2004–05;

(b) analysis of changes between 1987–88 and 1990–91, the first year after project completion; and

(c) 17-year comparisons of cash flow projections for the colliery showing the with and without project effects.

Net cash flows showed a 90·7 per cent DCF yield for the colliery without the project, over 100 per cent for the colliery with the project, and a 37 per cent marginal DCF yield for the project. The appraisal assumed proceeds of £38·31 per tonne in 1987–88 and £40·66 per tonne on project completion.

18. Sensitivity tests carried out by the Area estimated DCF yields, comparing them with project, without project and marginal results, for:

(a) a 10 per cent reduction in output;

(b) a 10 per cent increase in operating costs;

(c) a 20 per cent increase in project cost;

(d) a one-year delay in completion; and

(e) (a), (c), and (d) combined.

The 'worst case', (e), estimated a 22·5 per cent yield on the marginal results. In consequence, the Stage II submission concluded that the project showed a very attractive return on capital at low incremental production costs, with considerable safeguard against risk.

19. Headquarters Marketing Department supported the proposals as the most cost-effective in the circumstances. The Industrial Relations Department considered that Harworth Colliery might be appropriate for the introduction of extended working. Technical Department noted that sufficient low-risk reserves were available at Harworth to support profitable production at 1·7 million tonnes

for a period in excess of 30 years. However, the department also expressed concern that the Area had not identified specific proposals for overall project management and control. The Finance Department supported the project on the grounds that it was low-risk, expected to generate low-cost incremental capacity, and offered a quick pay-back. Headquarters' risk assessment for the project in the pessimistic case indicated a DCF yield of 28 per cent. It also commented that further consideration should be given to extended working.

Project timing

20. The timing of authorization was considered to be critical to the successful completion of the project. The new winding equipment was to be built over the existing winding tower to avoid any disruption to production. Once construction was complete, the old equipment would be taken out, and the new tower commissioned. That entire process was scheduled to take no more than three weeks and could only be effected during the period when the mine was closed for its annual summer holiday. Having organized that for September 1989, the colliery must commission the new tower then or wait a complete year for the next summer shut-down.

South Wales Area

Margam

Scheme: proposed new mine

HQ conditional approval:	6 February 1987
Completion date:	Four and a half years after work commences
Estimated cost:	£89·8 million

Location

1. The site of the proposed new drift mine is a few miles north-west of Bridgend, Mid Glamorgan.

The scheme

2. The proposal is that a new drift mine be established at Margam. It is to consist of two retreat faces working for a minimum of six days and 36 machine shifts per week. Full output of 1·2 million tonnes will be achieved in year six using 780 men producing an overall output per man-shift (OMS) of 7·52 tonnes.

Scheme's objectives

3. (*a*) The construction of a new drift mine and coal preparation plant.

(*b*) To provide 1·2 million tonnes a year of high-quality prime coking coal mainly for the steel industry in direct replacement for imports, together with small quantities of housecoal.

(*c*) The provision of major new low-cost coal capacity in South Wales.

Identification of need

4. This scheme has a relatively long history. In 1974–75 an assessment of South Wales coking coal supply and demand identified a need for new capacity. A proposal for a new mine got as far as the preparation of a Stage II submission by early 1980. In March 1980 work on the project ceased due to the weakening coking coal market and capital investment restrictions.

5. In May 1984 the Area felt it appropriate to put forward a new Stage I submission, because the need for high quality coking coal toward the end of the decade was still apparent. Its proposal was for a mine producing 580,000 tonnes a year, using 650 men working on two advancing faces. The cost was estimated to be £85 million, with a planned overall OMS of 4·35 tonnes.

6. Three reasons for the project were set out in this new Stage I submission:

(*a*) coking coals of Margam quality were in short supply, and supplies were likely to decline further;

(*b*) coking coal output from South Wales deep mines would decline beyond the mid–1990s as existing workings became exhausted; and

(*c*) the Margam reserves would significantly increase available prime coking coal reserves in the United Kingdom, and even in the unlikely event of a drastic decline of the coking market within the life of the project, the output could be switched to the CEGB market.

7. By August 1984 the Area had completed a review of its coking coal strategy. This review concluded that, among other things:

   (a) the recession in steel markets had seriously affected the South Wales coalfield;

   (b) local requirements for coking coal had fallen from over 6 million to 4·4 million tonnes a year which, coupled with a demand for consistently high quality coal and a world-wide surplus of cheap coal, gave an urgent need to greatly improve the Area's quality control, productivity and efficiency;

   (c) only by providing high-quality low-cost coal would the Area retain its existing markets;

   (d) the rapid decline in reserves in the east of the coalfield emphasized the urgent need to develop the proven reserves in the western zone; and

   (e) failure to develop Margam would leave the South Wales steel industry totally dependent on imported coking coal following the inevitable exhaustion of the existing coking coal collieries.

8. The Area's Stage I application was considered by the Mining Investment Committee in early August 1984. The mine's operating costs (excluding capital charges) were then estimated to be £31·87 per tonne, giving an operating profit of £16·23 per tonne. Capital charges (at 11 per cent) were expected to be £16·11 per tonne. The Committee agreed that the proposal should proceed to Stage II.

9. The Stage II submission was completed by mid-September 1984. In it the main reasons for promoting the project were stated as:

   (a) 'high volatile coking coal reserves in the area are currently, and will continue to be, in short supply'; and

   (b) 'coking coal production from existing mines in South Wales will decline from the mid-1990s on without the creation of new capacity'.

10. The mine's annual saleable output was now estimated to be 700,000 tonnes (including 70,000 tonnes of low ash house-coal) instead of 580,000 tonnes per annum. It was thought that a higher rate of output than this would require improved ventilation and entail extra work with a capital cost of over £10 million. The Stage II proposal was for two advancing faces (with an additional one on standby), using 650 men, with an overall OMS of 5·25 tonnes. The project's total cost was estimated to be £94·9 million (out-turn prices).

11. The Operations Committee considered the Stage II application at the end of November 1984. It was thought that the marketing case for completing the project as early as possible was strong. The output to the British Steel Corporation (BSC) was considered to displace imports, and house-coal (10 per cent of the mine's output) was also in short supply. The Marketing Department considered the proceeds assumptions to be, if anything, conservative.

12. The Operations Committee provisionally approved the project, subject to planning consent and the Secretary of State for Energy's approval for the new mine. Planning consent was granted in January 1985.

13. In mid-May 1986 the CIC considered a revised Stage II paper requesting full approval for the project. Output was now planned to be 850,000 tonnes per annum from two faces. The cost was put at £98·2 million. The reason for the higher level of output was recent experience in the Area, which showed that the introduction of shield support faces and three-shift working was producing larger daily outputs than originally considered feasible.

14. The May 1986 paper also drew attention to the fact that the basis for assessment of future proceeds from the mine had changed. In previous documents the calculations had been based on scheduled prices and MAF discounts—in the Stage II submission this method was shown to produce a proceeds figure of

£48·79 per tonne. The May 1986 submission figure of £44·62 per tonne for coking coal was, however, based on a world coking coal price of $57·25 per tonne (equivalent to a delivered price at Port Talbot of £40·45 a tonne or at Llanwern of £44·58 a tonne).

15. The Marketing Department noted that a new basis for calculating proceeds for this project had been thought appropriate because Margam was a specific new reserve to be targeted at a specific new potential market at costs and revenues which were fairly clearly identifiable, and with no direct 'knock-on' consequences for existing pits and markets. The marketing risk was the international price of coking coal and the exchange rate.

16. The Finance Department noted that the revised proposals had the effect of raising the project's DCF yield before risk from 12·9 per cent to 15·9 per cent. The most pessimistic assessment of yield, after risk assessment, was 7·0 per cent.

17. The department also noted that the new proposals had reduced the operating cost per GJ from £1·10 to £0·97.

18. A request for project approval was again considered by the CIC in early January 1987. The Area had further revised its proposals. Output was now planned to be 1·2 million tonnes per annum employing 780 men working a six-day week. Output would be from two retreat shield faces working six machine shifts per day on six days each week (ie 36 machine shifts per week). The project cost was estimated to be £89·8 million (about 9 per cent less than Stage II), and overall OMS was put at 7·52 tonnes. Operating costs would be £0·87 per GJ.

19. A summary of the effect of the extended working proposals, compared with the Area's May 1986 proposals, can be seen by comparing the figures in the final two columns of Table 1.

TABLE 1

	Stage I May 1984	Stage II Sept 1984	Revised Stage II Nov 1984	Revised Stage II May 1986	Revised Stage II Jan 1987
Saleable output ('000 tonnes)	580	700	700	850	1,200
Machine shifts per week	25	25	25	25	36
Manpower	650	650	650	600	780
OMS (tonnes)	4·35	5·25	5·25	6·90	7·52
Operating cost per GJ (£)	1·03	1·08	1·08	0·97	0·87
Project cost (£m)	65·0	78·0	79·8	85·2	79·9
	(Apr '84)	(Aug '84)	(Aug '84)	(Mar '86)	(Dec '86)
Operating profit (£m)	9·4	10·7	10·6	14·2	19·7
DCF yield before risk (%)	12·5	14·8	12·9	15·9	23·1
Average proceeds (£/t)	48·10	48·79	48·79	46·94	43·77*

Source: MMC.

* Equivalent to £1·40 per GJ, and incorporating a figure of £41·70 per tonne ($70·89 at $1·70 = £1) for coking coal.

20. At its January 1987 meeting the CIC conditionally agreed that the project be presented to the Board for approval. The proposal was then considered by the Executive Committee in late January, and it also agreed that the project should be recommended to the Board. The paper to the Executive Committee concluded that the proposals provided for the construction of a mine to produce an output of 1·2 mtpa by 1993, at a cost of £89·8 million (at out-turn prices), an operating cost of £0·87 per GJ, a DCF yield of 16·9 per cent (after Headquarters risk assessment), and a profit after capital charges of £10·6 million. The DCF yield reduced to 12·2 per cent if a proceeds reduction of 10 per cent was included.

21. The Board considered the proposal in early February 1987. The paper to the Board noted that the DCF yield reduced to 6·4 per cent if a further reduction in proceeds of 10 per cent was included. Cost per GJ was estimated to be £0·87 before capital charges, and £1·11 after. This compared with the operating costs of the three coking coal mines in South Wales of £2·23, £1·59, and £1·55 respectively.

22. The Board approved the project subject to:

(*a*) a clear commitment from the unions to the concept of six-day working; and

(*b*) obtaining satisfactory arrangements for financing in discussion with the United Kingdom Government and the European Community.

Consideration of options

23. The Stage I submission (of May 1984) noted that various alternatives were discussed in the Stage I and revised Stage I submissions of 1977–78. The major options considered then were not to develop the mine and to develop the reserves in other locations. Minor alternatives to the proposed option were also looked at, including differing mining and surface configurations and drift versus shafts. Because of this earlier assessment, alternatives were only briefly dealt with in the May 1984 Stage I submission.

24. Conclusions, as reported in the May 1984 submission, were:

(*a*) not to develop the mine—coking coal of Margam quality was unlikely to be available from United Kingdom sources after 1988, and the Margam source could displace imports;

(*b*) develop other reserves—Margam was the best remaining reserve;

(*c*) shafts or drifts—in 1977–78 shafts were preferred, but in 1984 drifts were preferred because of the reduced level of output projected, new geological evidence showed that drifts were practicable, and because of the much lower cost of drifts;

(*d*) horizon mining—not preferred because of great initial cost and longer construction period;

(*e*) retreat mining—not preferred for same reason as (*d*); and

(*f*) other sites—three other sites for the mine were considered and rejected.

25. The Stage II submission (of September 1984) more or less repeated the Stage I discussion of alternatives.

Manpower and productivity

26. Consideration of manpower and productivity in the preparation of this project has varied significantly during its history (see, for example, Table 1). It is clear though that a major issue has been the provision, since late 1986, that the project can only proceed on the basis of extended working arrangements.

27. In mid-December 1986 the Project Committee was told that in early discussions with the unions a commitment to the equivalent of 18 shifts per week had been sought. It was then agreed to recommend that approval of the project should be conditional on such a union agreement. In the Area's January 1987 submission it was proposed that a minimum of 36 machine shifts a week be established (based on two faces working three shifts on six days).

28. While it was noted by the Headquarters Industrial Relations Department (IRD) that there are very many different options for achieving more intensive working at Margam, the chosen one is based on the current shift length (18 shifts per week on two faces for 46·6 weeks each year). IRD though was of the view that discussions should not be constrained to any one specific pattern of working, that more than the equivalent of 18 current length shifts might be possible, and that it was likely that more than 46·6 weeks could be available each year.

29. The Area's proposed working patterns were outlined during the CIC's discussion of the project in early January 1987. With an extra production day each week, each man would work 18 shifts in a four-week cycle. Such an arrangement would give an extra 2·5 hours MAT a week. The shift pattern would incorporate one rest week in a four-week cycle.

30. The suggested shift pattern was spelled out in more detail in the paper to the Executive Committee (26 January 1987). The Area proposed to operate Margam on 18 machine shifts per week on each of two faces. Four machine teams would be employed on each face with coal being produced over six days, the seventh day being retained for maintenance. The proposed four-week roster cycle is shown below and is based on each team (or man) working six shifts each week for three weeks and then having a full week off. In any four-week period, therefore, each man would work 18 shifts (compared with the current 20 seven and a quarter-hour shifts) giving an average of 36 hours per week (compared with the current level of 36·25 hours).

Suggested shifting pattern

Team	Week 1	Week 2	Week 3	Week 4
A	Days (6)	Afternoons (6)	Nights (6)	Off (6)
B	Afternoons (6)	Nights (6)	Off (6)	Days (6)
C	Nights (6)	Off (6)	Days (6)	Afternoons (6)
D	Off (6)	Days (6)	Afternoons (6)	Nights (6)

31. [

Details omitted. See note on page iv.

]

32. During the discussion of this paper, the view was expressed that the priority was to secure agreement to six-day rostering rather than to extending the shift length.

Financial appraisal

33. The Area's base case results were tested for the effects of certain technical and marketing risks. The effect on the Area's base case of each of these risks may be summarized as:

	Discounted Area case	
	Net cash flow £m	DCF yield %
Area base case	286·9	23·1
Effect of:		
10% project cost increase	(−) 7·9	(−) 1·9
6-month completion delay	—	(−) 0·8
5% output shortfall	(−) 37·3	(−) 2·1
5% operating cost increase	(−) 21·5	(−) 1·2
Discounted Area case (summation of the above)	220·5	16·9

34. In the light of its experience with the construction of major new mining projects, Headquarters considered that a further risk rating equivalent to a further 10 per cent proceeds reduction should be applied to the above assessment of the Area's prospectus. Allowing for this, in BC's view the best that can be expected to be achieved at Margam is a DCF yield of 12·2 per cent and a net cash flow of £142·5 million.

35. Before adjustment for risks, the production costs of Margam are estimated to be £27·31 per tonne before capital charges (£34·92 after capital charges), with an operating cost per GJ of £0·87 and a cost per GJ after capital charges of £1·11. The only other collieries in South Wales currently producing coking coal (with their respective operating costs per GJ) were:

Six Bells	£2·23
Marine	£1·59
Oakdale	£1·55

36. The cash flow assessment incorporates ongoing routine capital expenditure totalling some £25 million over the 16-year production period assumed in the cash flow (this estimate includes all necessary plant pool equipment). It excludes all money spent on the project prior to 1987. This amounts to some £1·5 million.

37. Headquarters' 'realistic view' of the project was therefore that it would achieve a DCF yield of 12·2 per cent after normal risks. BC recognized that there were great uncertainties in the world price of coking coal and the exchange rate between the pound and the dollar. A further 10 per cent reduction in proceeds as a result of these factors would reduce the DCF yield from 12·2 per cent to 6·4 per cent.

38. BC also noted that a private sector company creating employment for 789 people in a Development Area would be eligible for grant aid. A project such as Margam would probably attract a grant of about £10 million. Additionally an ECSC loan at a 3 per cent rebate would probably be available for part of the project cost. A £10 million grant would increase the DCF yield by 2·1 per cent. A £35 million rebated loan would increase the yield by a further 0·5 per cent.

39. BC thinks that the combination of a grant and loan would provide a cushion against the risks identified in paragraph 37. Project approval is therefore conditional on the case for grant aid and loan rebate being pursued.

Marketing Department's views

40. The Marketing Department supported the project on the grounds that 90 per cent of the output would be sold at a profit to genuinely incremental markets (with about two-thirds going to BSC and the rest to National Smokeless Fuels Ltd (NSF) at the expense of imported coking coal. The remaining 10 per cent (to be produced as a Group 1 house-coal) would be readily absorbed into local markets. It had no doubts about the inherent quality of the coal or its acceptability to the target markets. It did, however, identify two areas of marketing risk:

(a) the price obtainable; and

(b) the future of the target markets.

(a) Price

41. The project assumes net revenue income averaging 140 pence per GJ (£43·77 per tonne) and divided as follows:

Coking smalls	135 pence per GJ (£41·70 per tonne)
House–coal	184 pence per GJ (£62·40 per tonne)

The house-coal is valued at normal saleable proceeds, which in the department's view produces a conservative figure for Margam, because saleable proceeds are net of an apportionment of national special rebates (eg on coal sold in Northern Ireland and Eire), most of which do not directly assist the sale of Welsh coals. However, since house-coal is only 10 per cent of the output, the project was considered to be much more sensitive to assumptions about the value of the coking smalls.

42. Margam coking will be offered to buyers at prices equating to those of imported coking coal at the point of delivery, and taking due account of quality differences according to a formula predetermined by the principal buyer, BSC. It follows that the average price obtainable for Margam coking smalls will vary through time according to the price of imported coking coal (which is traded in US $), to the exchange rate $ against £, to international sea freight rates, and to the proportions of the output that are sold to the different destinations. In the department's view an infinite number of combinations could be constructed, all giving different answers on the average price obtainable for Margam smalls.

43. The department considered (at the end of 1986) international coking coal prices to be extremely low, but still tending to drop at least relative to United Kingdom inflation. While it thought that this might continue for a while, it appeared unlikely that the $ price would have much further to drop before bottoming out. Against this, the £ appeared inherently rather weak against a fairly weak $. If oil prices consolidated around $18 to $20 a barrel the department thought the £ might improve to say $1·50 before weakening again in the face of the underlying weaknesses in the United Kingdom economy and, in the 1990s, the prospect of declining indigenous oil production. On balance, the Marketing Department considered that over the next 10 to 15 years the probability was that any further weakening in the $ price of imported coking coal would be more than offset by a slippage in the £, so that the sterling price of imported coal would tend to rise, both absolutely and in ' real ' terms, ie relative to United Kingdom internal inflation.

44. However, with great uncertainties about all these assumptions, the Finance Department conducted its risk rating on the basis that the ' real ' price of Margam coal could be 10 per cent lower.

(b) Future of the target coking market

45. In the marketing Department's view the second risk to Margam is that the total demand for high grade coking coal in South Wales (currently over 4 mtpa) will reduce to the point that the mine's output cannot be absorbed (or not fully absorbed) into the coking market.

46. To secure Margam without disturbing markets for traditional indigenous supply, a total local coking market of 1·75 to 2 mtpa would be needed, ie a little under half the present market. Thus, Margam would still be secure against the closure of one, but not both, of the two major BSC works.

47. Nevertheless, if both BSC works were to close, then in the department's view Margam would become a general purpose steam coal pit competing in the home market for the established markets of existing mines. The home market would consist of Aberthaw power station (which would take about 25 per cent of the mine's output and where some modification would be needed to assimilate the relatively high volatile content), possibly other power stations (eg Didcot and Uskmouth) in limited quantities, and general industry, especially cement. Whether or not the mine would be able to compete successfully in the market would depend, in the department's view, on its operating costs compared with those alternative supply sources. Current prospects are that operating costs at Margam would be lower than probably any other long-life deep mine in South Wales.

APPENDIX 5.7

(referred to in paragraph 5.41)

Central Area

Markham Colliery

***Scheme: New access with transport facilities into the Oxcroft area
of the Second Waterloo Seam***

HQ approval:	6 March 1984
Re-approved:	26 September 1985
Projected completion date:	1993–94
Approved budget:	£13·5 million

Markham Colliery

1. The colliery is located in North Derbyshire and dates from 1882, when four shafts were sunk to the Top Hard and Deep Soft seams. Two of these shafts were deepened in 1926. Until 1968, Markham functioned as three small collieries operating within one pit yard. In 1976–77 a £10 million reorganization provided additional skip-winding and coal-preparation facilities. Prior to Markham's merger with Ireland Colliery in 1986, the colliery produced 1·7 million tonnes a year. After Ireland Colliery ceased production in 1987 production was 1·6 million tonnes a year. The bulk of Markham Colliery's output goes as blended smalls to the CEGB.

The scheme

2. The project consists of:

(*a*) the drivage of two 1,650-metre roads to access reserves;

(*b*) a new pit bottom, including a material circuit to the two new access roads;

(*c*) provision of a 1,350 tonnes per hour coal clearance system for the new reserves via the intake access road, including construction of a 1,560-tonne vertical bunker; and

(*d*) installation of two 300-horsepower diesel locomotives and equipment for man-riding and materials.

Scheme's objectives

3. The Stage II paper (submitted in June 1983) listed four benefits to be obtained from the scheme:

(*a*) achieving and maintaining improvements in productivity by minimizing travelling time and maximizing MAT;

(*b*) saving 60 jobs (72 men on books) on underground materials transport over a five-year period from 1987–88 to 1992–94 (representing a 50 per cent saving on 123 jobs estimated for 1993–94 without the project);

(*c*) increasing OMS from 3·16 tonnes in 1987–88 to 3·28 tonnes in 1992–93, compared with a projected fall to 2·99 tonnes without the project; and

(*d*) assisting in the management of the social consequences arising from surrounding colliery closures.

Identification of need

4. In March 1983 a paper outlining the investment strategy for North Derbyshire (of which Markham Colliery was then a part) was presented to the Mining Committee for consideration. A central feature of that strategy was the planned closure of collieries within this sector of the North Derbyshire coalfield

and concentration of activity at Markham Colliery. The paper outlined plans to accommodate 20 machine shifts on eight faces at Markham by the early 1990s and stated that within that context, the need was for an efficient transport system to a large area of reserves.

5. The Stage II submission identified the need for the project as arising from this strategy and the intention to maintain output and profit by introducing a more efficient means of access to the reserves. It was thought that without this access the inevitable reduction in MAT would result in a loss of output and consequently a reduction in colliery profitability.

6. Development of the reserves was also a key requirement in the maintenance of capacity at Markham Colliery and of the management of the consequences of exhaustion closures in the North Derbyshire Area. The development of four faces to meet capacity requirements necessitated the provision of additional ventilation roadways to the vicinity of the shafts.

Consideration of options

7. Only the ' minimum investment alternative ' was considered as an alternative to the drivage of two roadways. As the ' do nothing ' alternative, this covered the drivage of only essential ventilation roadways, and the likely cost was estimated at £1 million.

8. Having established that the drivage of two new main roads was the most attractive option, the Area considered options for the provision of an efficient man and materials transport system. Stage II included comparisons between endless rope haulage system, 100 hp unit train system, 300 hp diesel locomotive system, 90 hp battery locomotive, 180 hp battery locomotive, and 90 hp diesel locomotive. The 300 hp diesel locomotive system was found to be the most suited to the conditions and, after a financial evaluation, to be the best alternative.

Manpower

9. An objective of the scheme was to reduce the number of MOB engaged in materials transport by 72 which, on the basis of an assumed rate of absenteeism, equates to 60 jobs. There was no reference in the Stage II submission to how this saving was to be achieved. As a result of BC's 1982 decision to remove all reference to social costs from colliery profit and loss accounts, no calculation of costs associated with the shedding of 72 men was added to estimates of total project costs.

Financial appraisal

10. The Stage II submission estimated the proposed capital investment at £10·5 million (at June 1983 price levels). With inflation assumed to be 6 per cent in 1983–84 and 7·5 per cent thereafter, the estimated out-turn cost was set at £13·1 million.

11. Initially approved in March 1984, the project was delayed by the 1984–85 miners' dispute and was re-approved in September 1985. Revised out-turn costs were estimated at £13·5 million (the inflation rate authorized for use in calculating out-turn costs had fallen to 4 per cent). In October 1986 the out-turn approved cost was reduced to £13·2 million on the basis of a further reduction in the assumed inflation rate to 3 per cent.

12. In 1982–83 the colliery made an operating profit of £5·3 million. Updating these results to September 1983 price levels, and applying the MAF levy, reduced the operating profit to £3·6 million. Interest charges of £5·4 million payable on colliery investment resulted in the colliery accounts showing a net loss of £1·8 million.

13. The Stage II document provided estimates of cash flow and DCF yields based on with project output of 1·475 mtpa by 1988–89 and an operating profit of £5·7 million. This compared with 1·45 mtpa and £5·8 million profit without the project. The with project operating profit was marginally lower than the without as a result of the addition of project depreciation costs. Colliery cash flows from 1983–84 to 1998–99 showed positive net present values when discounted at 10 per cent both with and without the project. The with project cash flows showed an estimated increase of £40·6 million (over the no project) mainly as a result of output lost if the project did not proceed. The marginal cash flow thus showed a DCF yield of 22·5 per cent with pay-back four years after project completion.

14. Since Markham has been identified as an 'ongoing long-life colliery' by the Mining Committee, the primary consideration was considered to be an identification of the need for the project and the estimate that the without project prospectus would result in a minimum £4 million loss. With the project, the colliery would break even. The Finance Department considered that the positive cash flow for Markham before the addition of depreciation and interest charges determined that this was a profitable situation appropriate to the Board's guidelines.

Technical change

15. Since Stage II, changes have been made to the pit bottom layout. It was shortened to reduce project completion time and to avoid problems associated with the impact of hard strata and faulting. As a consequence of technical problems it was necessary to redesign the bunker (to be horizontal rather than vertical). Work on the shaft inset was well behind schedule, but it was expected that the project would be completed by March 1989 (revised completion date), with production from 31 September 1988, although without the bunker. The project would be completed at a saving of £2 million on estimated costs. In 1986 plans to purchase a diesel locomotive were replaced with plans for a battery-operated locomotive of the same capacity. The decision was based on increased reliability and reduced costs.

Annual Reviews

16. All Stage II estimates were based upon the 1983 view of the project and did not include the effect of the merger of the Ireland and Markham Collieries. As a consequence, the Headquarters Project Committee agreed in 1987 that comparisons of then current estimates with Stage II were of limited value because Ireland Colliery was not originally included in the results.

17. Two Annual Reviews have been conducted, one for the year to March 1986, and one for the year to March 1987. The first Annual Review (1986) re-estimated the project's financial prospectus on the basis of the one-year delay due to the dispute. It compared the updated Stage II results with latest estimated results based on 1·75 mtpa. Proceeds were evaluated at £40·12 per tonne. The 1986 estimated colliery cash flow showed a DCF yield of 25 per cent.

18. The increased output for 1989–90 followed a review of the operational plan since Stage II approval and the introduction of new equipment and techniques. The reappraisal of colliery profitability at 1·75 mtpa incorporated additional surface damage and plant hire costs. The estimated operating profit for 1989 was £8·9 million. Capital charges showed an increase of £1·6 million reflecting the higher level of investment planned at the colliery.

19. The second Annual Review estimated a reduction of £0·66 per tonne in proceeds arising in part from a change in the scientific analysis of Markham's output and a shift in other income, and in part from a 1 per cent reduction in proceeds because of the year's delay in completion (part of a 1 per cent a year reduction in each of the five years to 1992–93). However, output estimates for 1989–90 have been increased to 1·9 mtpa.

20. The second Annual Review (1987) compared the updated Stage II DCF yield of 100 per cent with the latest estimate of a zero yield (based upon a net cash inflow of £4·5 million). This represented a £73·5 million cash flow deterioration. Almost all of the deterioration occurred in the four years to 1986–87, and was said to have arisen mainly as a result of the 1984–85 strike. For the remaining 12 years of the cash flow period the latest estimate is in line with the Stage II estimate.

21. In recent years Markham Colliery has recorded operating losses and cost per GJ as follows:

Year	Operating loss £m	Operating cost per GJ £
1983–84	2·80	2·80
1984–85	31·67	5·70
1985–86	9·95	1·87
1986–87	11·03	1·90
1987–88	3.53	1·67

The improved operating results give an increased cash flow of £6 million over the remaining 12 years of the appraisal period. This is more than offset by additional investment of £7 million (not all of which is directly associated with the increased output) to give a net reduction against the updated Stage II of £1 million.

APPENDIX 5.8

(referred to in paragraph 5.41)

North Yorkshire Area

Prince of Wales Colliery

Scheme: Extension to surface drifts

Area approval:	13 February 1986
Scheme completed:	October 1987
Approved budget:	£3·2 million
Final cost:	£3·0 million

Prince of Wales Colliery

1. This colliery, which is located in Pontefract, was nearing the end of its economic life in the mid-1970s when approval was granted for £23·5 million to be spent on a new drift mine to access and work the shallower seams. The final total approved cost was over £69 million and the scheme was completed in early 1984. The planned output was 1·5 mtpa.

2. The colliery employed about 1,100 men and produced about 1·1 million tonnes of saleable coal in 1987–88. Employment had fallen to about 940 by June 1988.

The scheme

3. The project was the extension of the two surface drifts by about 600 metres to access further coal seams. The man-riding and materials conveyances were also to be extended.

Scheme's objective

4. The objective was to access coal reserves and thereby to enable the colliery to continue production at its planned levels of output.

Identification of need

5. The new drift mine had run into an unexpected washout in the first working area to be developed. It was therefore necessary to develop other reserves earlier than had been planned in order to achieve and maintain the colliery's 1·5 mtpa output. Without the proposed drift extension, the colliery's output would decline and would be exhausted by 1994. Not working currently accessible reserves in high subsidence cost areas would reduce the colliery's life by a further three or more years.

6. It was estimated that the proposed access to the first face by means of a drift extension and five-year drivage would cost about £6·5 million. Further expenditure on five-year drivages would then be necessary to gain access to other areas of working. The Area, however, regarded the need as urgent and, rather than put forward a scheme for £6·5 million which would require Headquarters' approval (and so cause two or three months delay to the start of the project), the project was split and only the drift extension proposal was put forward. As such, approval was then within the Area Director's authority. Headquarters was told of the Area's intention to proceed in this way.

Consideration of options

7. The 'do nothing' alternative was taken to mean the rapid rundown of the colliery within eight to 11 years at the then current rates of extraction. One alternative considered was the provision of drifts from existing roadways allowing coal clearance via an extension of the existing facilities. This alternative was considered less efficient than the proposed drift in terms of access and materials supply.

Manpower

8. It was proposed to use outside contractors to extend the surface drifts and to construct the new drivages. Doing this, it was expected, would reduce the colliery's manpower requirements from 1,283 MOB (in November 1985) to 1,188 MOB by 1988–89. No industrial relations issues were identified, and the relevant Appendix was not provided.

Marketing

9. The planned build-up of output at the colliery was not expected to present any marketing problems. All of the colliery's output went to, and was expected to continue to go to, the CEGB.

Financial appraisal

10. The cost of the surface drift extension (without the drivage) was put at £3·1 million (at November 1985 prices). The first full year of benefit was estimated to be 1991–92 when colliery output reached 1·5 mtpa with the scheme (or 1·1 mtpa without the scheme). The 'do nothing' option showed colliery output peaking at 1·45 mtpa in 1988–89 and 1989–90 and falling to nothing by 1994–95.

11. The effect of the scheme (compared with the do nothing option) on the colliery's prospects for 1991–92 was estimated to be an increase in sales of £16·1 million and increased operating and other costs of £6·7 million, giving net profit of £5·7 million with the scheme (compared with an expected loss of £3·7 million without the scheme). A 15-year DCF comparison of the colliery's cash flow prospects with and without the scheme showed that the marginal return on the project would be 51 per cent.

12. Risk assessment consisted of an analysis of the effects of:

(a) shortfall in proceeds of 10 per cent (giving a DCF yield of 46·6 per cent);

(b) scheme cost increase of 10 per cent (giving a DCF yield of 49·8 per cent);

(c) an extra 12 months in scheme completion time (giving a DCF yield of 49·9 per cent); and

(d) a combination of (a), (b) and (c) (giving a DCF yield of 45·6 per cent).

13. The drivage necessary to access the coal on completion of the surface drift extension was to be financed out of the colliery's annual allowance of £2 million for capital drivages.

Annual Reviews

14. An Annual Review was prepared for the period up to February 1987. This reported that the latest estimate of the project's cost was £200,000 below the approved budget. The project was running 11 weeks late because of:

(a) a late start;

(b) a contractor's internal dispute (costing two weeks); and

(c) various other reasons, including flooding and wet conditions, misfires in heading and slow drivage due to sandstone.

15. The first year of full benefit was put back from 1991–92 to 1993–94. This was because of continued problems with one of the seams and the loss of one of the working areas as a result of tighter restrictions on mining in areas prone to high subsidence costs.

16. Instead of a net profit of £5·7 million in 1991–92, the Annual Review showed the colliery making a net loss of £0·7 million. The main reasons given were the reduction in proceeds because of the reduced output level, a reduction in average proceeds (because of the need to increase the ash percentage in the saleable product) and an increase in the MAF percentage [*
] Some of the reduction in proceeds was expected to be offset by a reduction in operating costs. Against the updated Stage II estimate the Annual Review reported an improvement of £2·68 in total profit per tonne.

Completion Report

17. A Completion Report on this project is not due until 1993–94 when the full benefits of the project have been realized.

Cost per GJ

18. The 1987 Annual Review stated that the estimated operating cost per GJ on completion (given as 1991–92) was £1·34 before capital charges and £1·52 after. These estimates are unchanged from those given in notes sent by the Area to BC's Technical Director in November 1985.

19. The colliery's operating costs per GJ declined from £1·96 in 1985–86 to £1·76 in 1987–88. It is budgeted to achieve £1·54 per GJ in 1988–89.

---

* Figures omitted. See note on page iv.

Western Area

Sutton Manor Colliery

Scheme: surface reorganization and installation of skip winding

HQ approval:	10 April 1985
Scheme completed:	Due to be completed in November 1987 but terminated on 15 May 1987 prior to completion.
Approved budget:	£17·3 million
Final cost:	£9·9 million (project not completed)

Sutton Manor Colliery

1. This colliery is located a few miles south of St. Helens, Merseyside. The colliery began working in 1909, and was subject to major reorganization in the early 1950s. Further major investment at the colliery took place in the late 1960s and early 1970s. The colliery now employs about 420 (down from almost 800 in early 1986). It produced about 306,000 tonnes of saleable output in 1987–88, and is budgeted to produce some 510,000 tonnes in 1988–89. Since 1970 the colliery has made continuing losses despite large manpower reductions. The main reasons appear to have been problems in keeping up output because of washouts, and heavy costs of maintaining obsolete plant.

The scheme

2. The colliery was old, with outdated and inefficient equipment. It was, however, seen as a long life colliery with substantial accessible reserves sufficient to maintain output for 30 or more years.

3. The main elements in the final scheme were:

   (*a*) reconstruction of winding equipment for No. 1 shaft with new skip winding, new electric winder, and undergound access drivage;

   (*b*) reconstruction of No. 2 shaft with a refurbished electric winder, and surface airlock with men and materials handling facilities;

   (*c*) new fan house, drift and electric fan;

   (*d*) replacement of steam-driven compressors by electrically driven compressors;

   (*e*) new run of mine (ROM) stockpad;

   (*f*) new control room and the installation of a MINOS control system;

   (*g*) new boiler house and boilers; and

   (*h*) surface roads and weighbridges.

4. Final approval was for a project cost of £15·4 million (at April 1984 prices), which was considered to be equivalent to £17·3 million at out-turn prices.

Scheme's objectives

5. The main objectives were stated to be:

   (*a*) to enable the colliery to achieve a stable and profitable position by raising output from the existing level of 410,000 tonnes a year (of mainly CEGB fuel) to 550,000 tonnes (of mainly industrial and domestic fuel, for which an increasing demand in the North-West was forecast); and

   (*b*) to maximize colliery output by fully utilizing available shaft capacity to reduce costs, and to improve efficiency and productivity.

Identification of need

6. Sutton Manor was one of a group of three collieries (the others being Cronton and Bold Collieries) in the west of the Lancashire coalfield whose future was being considered in the early 1980s.

7. The Stage I paper in particular noted that, with the likely closure of nearby collieries and the unions' knowledge of the extent and quality of workable reserves at Sutton Manor, then some direct confrontation with the unions was to be expected if the closure of Sutton Manor Colliery was announced rather than investment in its reconstruction. Closure of Sutton Manor Colliery would have led to a minimum of 576 compulsory redundancies of men under 50 years of age. Sutton Manor Colliery had a history of poor industrial relations, but a series of good monthly performances in 1983 suggested that investment there would be worthwhile. BC therefore arrived at an understanding with the colliery's workforce which effectively linked the proposed investment to the colliery's continued satisfactory performance.

8. It was also noted that by 1984–85 Sutton Manor's output was expected to be exclusively obtained from coal seams, the quality of which would enable it to resume production of domestic house coal and increase its output of industrial coals to meet an expected growth in demand. This in turn would entail a reduction in the colliery's supplies to the CEGB to a minimum.

9. The continued operation of the colliery without the proposed investment was considered to be too expensive in annual maintenance and repair costs. The existing steam engines and winding plant in particular were considered to be inefficient and extremely labour-intensive.

Consideration of options

10. The initial strategy report and draft Stage I proposals suggested a scheme costing about £40 million for the construction of a surface drift from Bold Colliery to the Sutton Manor seams, together with a complete surface reorganization at Sutton Manor Colliery. These proposals were rejected by the Project Committee on cost grounds.

11. The Area's Stage I submission (dated January 1983) proposed a £13·8 million scheme to increase the colliery's output to 450,000 tonnes a year and 'a significant working profit'. The scheme involved the electrification of the two winding shafts, the use of No. 1 shaft to raise coal, and the installation of new electric fans. This scheme was expected to reduce manpower requirements by 34.

12. The proposal was discussed by the Project Committee in May. It was noted that the Area had not provided feasible alternatives to its first preference. The committee agreed, however, that apart from the Area's proposal, and the 'do nothing' and 'closure' options, there were no alternatives open for the colliery. At a later meeting that same month, though, it was noted that one alternative would be just to replace the winder.

13. A Stage I paper was presented to the Mining Committee in September 1983. This proposed the same cost (at £13·8 million) and scheme (though now given in more detail). The Mining Committee commented on the absence of consideration of options and agreed to request the Area to submit fresh Stage I proposals.

14. In October the Project Committee was informed that the Area was now considering proposals that would raise the colliery's output to 550,000 tonnes a year with a manpower saving of 35. The committee was sceptical about whether this output increase could in fact be achieved.

15. A revised Stage I submission was prepared in November and this discussed the following alternatives:

    (a) do nothing—expensive in maintenance repairs and replacement costs, in lost revenue from mine-gas sales and a new fan was thought to be essential anyway;

    (b) closure—resulting in the loss of substantial reserves, of 410,000 tonnes a year of good quality coal, a confrontation with the unions and the end of coal mining in South-West Lancashire;

    (c) surface drift—estimated to take nine years to complete and to add £9·6 million to the cost but with no additional benefits;

    (d) satellite shaft—solely to wind men and material, with coal-winding continuing at Sutton Manor, at an estimated cost of £52·7 million over ten years plus additional expenditure of £14·2 million at Sutton Manor; and

    (e) skip installation—the proposed scheme, and estimated to cost £14·2 million.

16. The Stage II proposals confirmed these as the only alternatives, with the additional cost of the surface drift revised downwards to £8 million and satellite shaft cost revised upwards to £54·6 million. The Stage II submission, however, made the additional point, in respect of the 'do nothing' option, that the colliery was excellently placed to serve the growing industrial market in the area and that any failure to increase output would mean a growing proportion of industrial coal would have to be brought in at a higher cost (about £2 per tonne), so jeopardizing the prospects for new industrial sales.

17. Apart from the addition of MINOS, the finally approved proposals (of April 1985) for the reconstruction of Sutton Manor Colliery appear not to be significantly different from the Area's original proposal in its Stage I submission of January 1983.

Manpower

18. The scheme was expected to reduce manpower requirements by 35 (from 777 to 742) as a result of the skip-winding, coal clearance and MINOS elements. The main benefit was, however, seen as the planned 34 per cent increase in the colliery's annual output, with an increase in overall OMS from 2·40 tonnes to 3·38 tonnes.

Proceeds

19. The market assessment at Stage II (August 1984) was that the industrial demand for singles and washed smalls would increase substantially over the following few years. Even if the colliery's output were concentrated in this market it was thought that some of the demand in the east of area would still have to be supplied from Yorkshire and the Midlands. Closures of other Lancashire collieries reinforced this need to increase output at Sutton Manor Colliery.

20. As a result it was expected that the effect of the scheme would be to enable the colliery, by 1987–88, to produce about 550,000 tonnes of industrial and domestic coals at an average price of £46·97 a tonne (November 1983 prices), in comparison with 310,600 tonnes of largely CEGB fuel in 1983–84 (affected by national strike) at about £43·78 per tonne (November 1983 prices).

Financial appraisal

21. The proceeds figures used in the project's financial appraisal, the derivation of which is outlined above, were as follows:

Output in first year of full benefit (1987–88)	550,000 tonnes
Average selling price	£46·87 per tonne
Approximate proceeds	£25·8 million
Miscellaneous income	£1·2 million
Total proceeds	£27·0 million

22. Total proceeds were shown to rise slightly in 1993–94 and 1994–95 and then as staying at £27·4 million to 1999–2000. These figures compared with expected proceeds in the absence of the project of slightly over £20 million.

23. A 15-year DCF analysis of the colliery's cash flow results showed the colliery's DCF yield with the project to be 30·5 per cent. The Area's base case for the project showed a marginal DCF yield of 36 per cent compared with 'do nothing', and 45 per cent compared with closure. The key to achieving these yields was considered to be the expected increase in ROM output (by 57 per cent compared with 1983–84) but with the same number of faces and one extra machine shift.

24. The financial appraisal in the Stage II submission noted that the project consisted of a number of aspects which could be constructed independently and improve efficiency without committing BC to the full project proposals. A DCF analysis of the colliery's results for all elements of the project except the skip winding showed a very poor result, and further limitations on the project were expected to reduce performance further. The only other DCF analysis reported was on the MINOS element alone, which showed a marginal DCF yield of 31·5 per cent.

Risk assessment

25. The colliery's cash flows were tested for the following risks:

(a) project costs:
    (i) completion delayed by one year;
    (ii) costs increase by 5 per cent;
    (iii) new coal preparation plant (CPP) (£8 million).

(b) operating costs:
    (i) an extra £0·3 million on operating cost increases resulting from project;
    (ii) an extra £0·2 million a year for extra maintenance on CPP if not replaced;

(c) output:
    (i) shortfall of 5 per cent; and

(d) proceeds:
    (i) incremental tonnage priced at export prices.

26. The results were summarized as follows:

DCF yields

		per cent*
	Colliery	Marginal
Base case	31	36
Most likely case	25	34
Worst case	Nil	11

* Based on current prices.

In the most likely case the only risk identified was the possible increase in colliery operating costs of £0·5 million a year to cover repairs to the 58-year-old CPP.

27. The proposed project was supported by the Marketing, Finance and Industrial Relations Departments.

28. The Mining Department supported the scheme, but it felt that the reserves of sufficient quality to justify the investment were limited, suggesting a colliery life of about 20 years. The department also suggested that in progressing the scheme, the Area should give careful consideration to:

(a) likely increase in subsidence damage and/or costs as the workings in some seams were completed;

(b) a long-term solution to the dirt disposal problem at the colliery; and

(c) the adequacy of the coal preparation facilities at the colliery.

Annual Reviews

29. There were two Annual Reviews; the first covered the year to October 1985, and the second to October 1986.

30. The 1985 Annual Review concluded that the project was proceeding satisfactorily and that the completion dates would be met. The Review did note, however, that the latest estimates of colliery results on completion showed a shortfall in proceeds. As a result in February 1986 the Annual Review was referred by the Project Committee to the Accountability procedure.

31. The 1986 Annual Review noted that as a result of a review of the colliery's results, the second half of the project had been suspended, and that the November 1987 completion date could not therefore be met.

32. Work had been completed (at a cost of £9·2 million) on:

(*a*) No. 1 shaft;

(*b*) new surface fan and fan house;

(*c*) new surface cable duct and cabling;

and work was outstanding (at a cost of £8·2 million) on:

(*a*) No. 2 shaft;

(*b*) boiler plant; and

(*c*) surface roads and weighbridge.

The manpower savings attributable to the project had been 12.

33. The Annual Review noted a reduction in proceeds against updated Stage II expectations of £2·10 per tonne, of which £1·94 was a result of failure of the industrial market to materialize (due largely to the collapse of the oil price). In order to maintain disposals the colliery had continued to produce blended smalls for the CEGB. The DCF yield had declined to 1·7 per cent.

34. The 1986 Annual Review was considered by the Project Committee in early March 1987, when the poor results of the colliery were commented on. At the next meeting of the Project Committee (on 20 March) it was noted that work on the project had been suspended. It was also noted that not only had the expected industrial market failed to materialize, but that poor quality coals had also contributed to lower than expected proceeds per tonne. The committee agreed to recommend closure of the project. The project was considered by the CIC in late April 1987, and it was agreed that the project should be formally closed at its present stage, so cancelling approval for the outstanding expenditure of £7·5 million.

35. The outstanding investment is still considered necessary by BC for Sutton Manor Colliery to continue to operate, and it is likely to be undertaken in the next few years if the colliery maintains its present good performance.

Developments at the colliery

36. Output at the colliery failed to pick up satisfactorily after mid-September 1985 (in the aftermath of the strike), and by November performance at the colliery was causing sufficient concern for the workforce to be warned that the project would be stopped if results did not improve.

37. In April 1986 the Area Director announced the suspension of the project until the colliery showed profits. In October agreement was reached at the colliery to go to single-face working and to reduce the manpower by 310 to 480.

38. In October 1987 the colliery was told that unless output of 12,500 tonnes a week was achieved it would be closed. By April 1988 the colliery was producing coal at a rate equivalent to 510,000 tonnes a year and its budget for 1988–89 calls for an annual output of 510,000 tonnes.

Cost per GJ

39. The scheme was approved before the current cost per GJ criteria were established. The colliery's operating cost per GJ has declined from £2·41 in 1985–86 to £2·18 in 1987–88. A figure of £1·38 is budgeted for 1988–89, and during the first quarter of this financial year the colliery achieved £1·27 per GJ.

Central Area

Warsop Colliery

Scheme: MINOS system for monitoring and control of conveyors, pumps and auxiliary fans

Area approval:	20 December 1985
Completion date:	December 1986
Approved budget:	£1,179,640
Final cost:	£981,500

Warsop Colliery

1. Located in the North Derbyshire coalfield, Warsop's shafts were sunk in 1893, and the surface layout reorganized in 1954. In 1987–88 the colliery was re-planned, concentrating production on two faces. This reduced MOB to 848 and reduced annual production to 789,000 tonnes.

The scheme

2. The mine operating remote control and monitoring system (MINOS) proposed for Warsop Colliery consisted of two main parts:

(*a*) Conveyor automation—selective plant monitoring of 25 conveyors and one crusher. The costs of implementing the scheme were £473,000 capital and £470,100 revenue with an estimated payback in year two after completion.

(*b*) Pumps and fans automation—controlling and remote monitoring four pumping stations and five fan installations. The cost of implementing the scheme was estimated at £94,600 capital and £141,900 revenue with payback in year two after completion.

Costs for the total scheme were £567,600 capital and £612,040 revenue. The scheme would be completed 15 months after authorization. The capital/revenue split demonstrated within this project arises from BC's capital/revenue code. All installation costs are treated within the code as 'revenue' and not capitalized irrespective of what it is that is being installed.

Scheme's objectives

3. The primary objective of all BC's MINOS installations was the reduction of total manpower. Most conveyors at Warsop Colliery were previously manually driven and relied on manual observation of spillage, chutes, braking systems and bearings. Stopping and starting conveyors was also manually controlled. With three men at each of 11 transfer points, the scheme's objective was to save 33 men on the coal clearance system. Applying MINOS to the continuous monitoring and control of pumps, fans and air sampling removed the necessity for 43 man-shifts to perform these tasks at weekends. A second objective of the MINOS system was to increase safety and control of the coal clearance and environmental systems. The third objective was to achieve a more rapid start-up of equipment.

Identification of need and manpower aspects

4. The installation of a MINOS system for the remote monitoring and control of conveyors, pumps and auxiliary fans was aimed largely at: (a) improving safety by continuous automatic monitoring; (b) improving efficiency by achieving better control with less down-time; and (c) reducing manpower with the elimination of expensive weekend shifts for manual inspections.

5. In 1985 BC's Method Study Branch indicated a need for three fans to be examined twice in each eight-hour shift and considered that two deputies were sufficient. However, their inspections required seven other men to be employed to

facilitate those inspections. Thus nine men had to be paid premium rates for inspections on Saturday afternoon and night and Sunday afternoon. The total saving to be achieved by remote monitoring of fans was calculated in 1985 at nearly £1,500 per weekend or £77,909 per year. In the same exercise it was estimated that the manpower required for weekend pumping duties cost BC £735·44 per weekend or £38,242 per year (at 1985 prices). Introduction of MINOS would save 43 man-shifts per weekend and 33 MOB, these savings covering the monitoring of conveyors, pumps and fans.

Financial appraisal

6. Costs associated with the environmental system (pumps and fans) together with a 10 per cent contingency totalled £236,500. Savings in manpower on inspection of pumps were calculated at 16 shifts per weekend (equivalent to £38,500 a year). Savings in manpower on fans inspection were calculated at 27 shifts per weekend (equivalent to £78,000 a year), bringing total annual savings to £116,500. The net annual benefit was calculated at £94,025 over eight years giving a DCF yield of 43 per cent over the same period. Costs associated with the conveyor system totalled £943,100 including a 10 per cent contingency. Total saving in manpower was set at 33 men to give a DCF yield of 40 per cent over eight years.

7. No sensitivity tests were applied to the financial appraisal as the project was considered to be 'risk free', applied only to manpower savings, and involved the application of well-proven technology.

8. Authority for expenditure of £1·2 million under delegated authority was agreed by Headquarters on 20 December 1985, subject to the 1985–86 capital expenditure being contained within the Area's existing overall capital allocation.

Headquarters departments' comments

9. Headquarters departments were not required to comment on the project. It was submitted to Headquarters for agreement because the project was not included within the Area's 1985–86 Business Plan and consent from Headquarters for it to be authorized under delegated authority was therefore needed.

Completion Report

10. Because working at two seams ceased, not all the conveyors originally proposed were installed. The system was installed without technical problems. The project was completed three months earlier than envisaged at Stage II (December 1986), at a total cost of £981,500. Savings were achieved as a result of reuse of some existing equipment at the colliery. There was some over-estimation of costs in the original submission. Contingency provisions were not called on.

11. The target manpower saving of 33 men per day (coal clearance system) and 2,236 weekend man-shifts (pumps and fans) was achieved in full. The installation of computerized monitoring equipment allows the manager to close the colliery completely at the weekends when no maintenance is being carried out.

12. Overall colliery results in 1987–88, updated to September 1987 prices, showed a colliery net profit of £1·5 million with operating costs at £1·44 per GJ and DCF yield over a 13-year period estimated at over 100 per cent. The results for 1987–88 were below those estimated at Stage II. This was said to be because of geological difficulties depressing operating results for the first quarter. Results in the third quarter exceeded the Stage II estimates.

	Stage II estimate 1986–88	Actual results 1987–88
Saleable output ('000 tonnes)	1,070	789
Face OMS (tonnes)	18·15	16·77
Overall OMS (tonnes)	4·82	4·21
Average manpower	1,007	848

APPENDIX 5.11
(referred to in paragraph 5.41)

A: Creswell Colliery, Nottinghamshire Area

Scheme: Proposed new mine fans

Area approval:	17 November 1982
HQ approval:	May 1983
Scheme completed:	September 1985
Approved budget:	£1·4 million
Final cost:	£1·25 million

A1. The Stage II prospectus was drawn in November 1982, and proposed the replacement of two surface fans and three underground booster fans by two new surface fans. The purpose of this was to increase ventilation (thus providing adequate ventilation as the underground workings extended further), and to improve the reliability of the ventilation system as a whole. The elimination of booster fans and the removal of their associated airlocks also permitted man-riding facilities to be improved, with a favourable effect on machine available time.

A2. The programme for the project anticipated Headquarters approval in May 1983, and completion (ie commissioning the second fan) in April 1985. It was expected that Headquarters would agree to tenders being invited for the mechanical equipment in December 1982, some five months prior to Stage II approval. In the event this was not agreed to, although a memorandum in March 1983 still referred to a completion date of March 1985.

A3. The programme shown in the Stage II presentation gives the first activity (prepare specifications and build up quantities) as October 1982, the Stage III authorization for the two mine fans in May 1983 (presumably following an expected Stage II approval in April 1983), physical work on site (ie following manufacture of the mechanical equipment) in April 1984, and the commissioning of the last of the two fans in April 1985.

A4. The project was in fact completed in September 1985, some five months later than expected in Stage II. The Completion Report states that this was entirely due to the delay in going out for tender. In so far as judgments may be made about project management and control, the evidence indicates competent management on the ground.

B: Merthyr Vale Colliery, South Wales Area

Scheme: Installation of skip-winding facilities

Area approval:	28 November 1985
Scheme completed:	September 1986
Approved budget:	£3·4 million
Final cost:	£3·2 million

B1. This was a £3·2 million project approved by the Area Director under delegated authority. The colliery was to be brought to profitability by increasing face output, and the improved skip-winding facilities were required in order to handle the higher product volume through the shaft. The project showed a positive colliery DCF yield of 63 per cent and marginal yield of 42 per cent.

B2. The Stage II submission was approved for submission by various Area officers in the course of November 1985, and was approved by the Area Director on 28 November. The expected commencement date for the project was November 1985, and the expected completion was September 1986. The first Annual Review was as at July 1987 (not, as might have been expected, in November 1986), and it was approved on 18 September 1987 by the Area Director.

This Review showed that the main skip changeover had been completed successfully, but the skip speed was 35 feet per second as opposed to the expected full speed of 38 feet per second.

B3. Colliery operating profit was estimated at Stage II to be £2·4 million at £5·46 per tonne (on an updated basis) at the completion of the project. The estimate in the Annual Review was £1·34 million at £3·35 per tonne on completion, and saleable output was not expected to be as high as the Stage II estimate (400,000 tonnes as opposed to 440,000 tonnes). Face OMS was expected to be higher than the Stage II estimate (16·39 tonnes as opposed to 14·3 tonnes), but the overall OMS was going to be lower (at 3·33 tonnes as opposed to 3·6 tonnes).

B4. The approved out-turn cost of the project was £3·379 million, and the actual cost of completion was £3·175 million — a saving of £204,000.

B5. The Annual Review implied that the Area's management regarded the project as having been completed within time and cost. Whether or not the project can be regarded as complete when the equipment was not at that time running to specification is open to question.

B6. The project papers did not show any failure in project management or control of costs. Colliery profitability did not reach the levels expected at the time of the Stage II prospectus, mainly because of poor geological conditions.

C: Cynheidre Colliery, South Wales Area

Scheme: installation of chock shield supports

Area approval:	12 November 1986
Completion date:	August 1987
Approved budget:	£3·8 million
Final cost:	£3·8 million

Cynheidre Colliery

C1. This anthracite colliery is five or so miles north of Llanelli, Dyfed. Two seams are worked and in 1986 work began on a £30 million new drift project to access 7 million tonnes of anthracite in the Carway Fawr seam.

C2. The colliery produces high-quality coal with average proceeds of about £75·00 per tonne (which is equivalent to over £2·30 per GJ). In 1987–88 it produced 193,000 tonnes saleable output (down from over 230,000 tonnes in previous years). In March 1988 it employed 656 men compared with almost 1,000 in 1985–86. Conditions in the anthracite seams are difficult to work. Thin seams restrict the ability to produce bulk saleable output and, as a result, operating costs per GJ are high.

The scheme

C3. The proposal was to install 162 chock shield supports at the 240-metre F4 advancing face of Felin seam. The face is 1·1 metre high. The cost of the heavy duty supports was estimated in the preliminary submission to be £2·8 million, and other face and revenue equipment was estimated to cost £1·0 million.

Identification of need

C4. Three reasons for the shield supports were given in the Area's preliminary submission:

(a) preliminary training for the Carway Fawr drift mine;

(b) ability to work longer faces with heavy duty AFC; and

(c) improved production and productivity for thin seam working.

C5. The scheme was expected to result in an estimated saving of 42 man-shifts a day by concentrating production on two rather than three faces. This saving was assessed to be equivalent to 50 MOB, yet colliery output was planned to increase from 1,000 tonnes to 1,400 tonnes a day.

Consideration of options

C6. The option considered was the use of conventional supports.

Financial appraisal

C7. Comparisons were made between the prospects with heavy duty and with conventional supports for both the face results and the colliery results. The comparison showed that saleable output from the face would improve from 600 to 1,000 tonnes a day, giving a face OMS improvement from 12·50 tonnes to 17·54 tonnes. The installation cost of conventional supports was put at £2·1 million compared with £4·0 million for the heavy duty supports.

C8. Total face costs were estimated to fall from £18·34 per tonne to £17·54 per tonne after capital charges. The face operating profit was therefore estimated to increase from £58·83 per tonne to £58·13 per tonne (after capital charge).

C9. The colliery's saleable output was estimated to increase by 40 per cent to 326,000 tonnes a year. The higher output and lower operating costs resulted in an estimated colliery operating profit of £9·16 per tonne (compared with a loss of £10·73 per tonne if conventional supports were used). DCF analysis of the colliery's cash flow showed its yield to be 25·6 per cent, and the project's marginal yield to be 32·8 per cent.

Cost per GJ

C10. The colliery's cost per GJ was estimated to be £2·07 with the scheme and £2·69 with the alternative conventional supports.

Approval

C11. As the proposed heavy duty face was projected to produce only 233,000 tonnes a year with a colliery cost of £2·07 per GJ, the Area Director did not have authority to approve it. The Area therefore made a submission to Headquarters in April 1986 and this was approved subject to capital availability. Formal notification that £2·5 million capital had been allocated followed in November 1986.

D: Daw Mill Colliery, Central Area

Scheme: installation of heavy duty shield supports

HQ approval	March 1985
Projected completion date:	March 1988
Approved budget:	£3·8 million

Daw Mill Colliery

D1. Daw Mill Colliery is located in the South Warwickshire coalfield and produces coal from four faces. The colliery is affected by problems of spontaneous combustion.

The scheme

D2. The scheme was for the installation of 134 heavy duty shield supports on a face due to be brought into production in 1985. The supports were to facilitate advance working on the face. They would extract a 3·66 metre section of coal to produce 837 tonnes of saleable coal per shift. The capital cost of the supports, with associated equipment, was estimated at £4·8 million with £1·8 million revenue expenditure (at September 1984 price levels).

The scheme objectives

D3. The scheme identified two prime objectives:

(a) to maximize output and effect optimum support stability; and

(b) to control waste flushing at 3·66 metre extraction height.

Identification of need

D4. The installation of heavy duty supports on this face was first conceived in November 1983 and was included as part of the then five-year plan. They were to be installed July 1985 with full face production scheduled for November 1985. The interruption of colliery production by industrial disputes between 1983 and 1985 resulted in the scheme being re-scheduled and included in the March 1985 colliery Action Programme, with installation planned for April 1986.

Technical change

D5. Unexpected events resulted in the necessity to replan the colliery. One face was lost 12 months earlier than expected, and another face stopped short of its planned target. Both events resulted in the decision to bring forward the planned production date of an adjacent face.

D6. The need to deal with further problems on other faces meant that the installation of the new supports was put back. The supports were finally in place and in full production in June 1988.

Consideration of options

D7. In its application, the Area compared shield supports against an 'alternative specification if funds are not available from the national programme'. The comparison of face characteristics showed the alternative specification to result in lower levels of coal extraction, and shorter advances per shift. Daily output was expected to be 2,310 tonnes per day with shield supports and 1,970 tonnes per day with the alternative specification.

D8. A method study assessment of standard face performance comparing shield supports and non-shield supports showed shield supports to reduce ancillary time by 13 minutes and operational time by nine minutes, and to reduce by two the average number of men required each shift. Shield supports reduced the average number of manshifts per day from 84 to 78.

Financial appraisal

D9. Total capital cost set out in the colliery application was £4·849 million. Added to this was £1·781 million to be spent on new revenue equipment allied to the project, bringing the total cost of the scheme to £6·630 million (of which £5·853 million required Headquarters authorization). Within the formal financial appraisal appended to the application, the total cost of the project was calculated at £6·630 million before the addition of £980,000 working capital (at September 1984 price levels).

D10. The proposed investment was compared with the alternative non-shield support specification:

	Preferred specification	£'000* Alternative Specification
Powered supports	3,744	2,004
Other face equipment	1,105	266
Revenue equipment	1,781	307
Total cost of project	6,630	2,577
Working capital	980	769
Total investment	7,610	3,346

* At September 1984 prices.

D11. No sensitivity tests were applied but, as a result of projected higher output, lower wages costs and higher proceeds, profits after interest for the year to December 1986 were estimated to be £4 million higher with the preferred specification than without. The appraisal estimated 4·1 months to pay back. No DCF calculation was carried out.

(referred to in paragraphs 7.65—7.70)

Project Control Performance

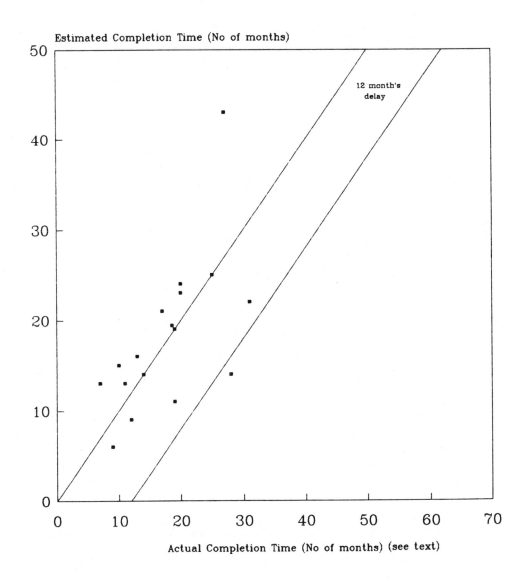

Source: MMC from BC Information.
* Times adjusted to allow for 84/85 strike.

APPENDIX 7.1(ii)

(referred to in paragraphs 7.65—7.70)

Project Control Performance

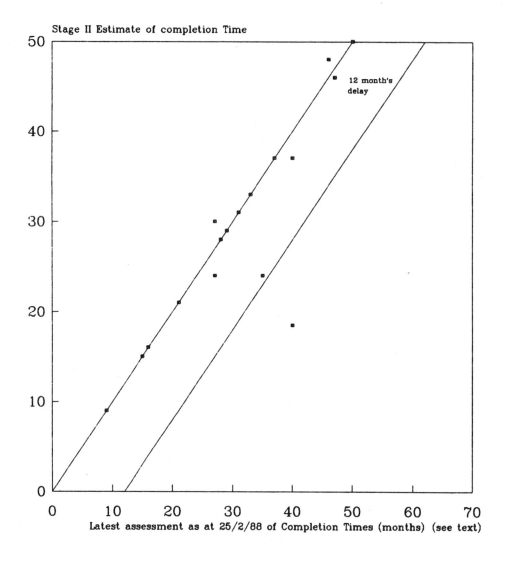

Stage II Estimate of completion Time

Latest assessment as at 25/2/88 of Completion Times (months) (see text)

12 month's delay

Source: MMC from BC Information.

* Time after adjustments to allow for 84/85 strike.

152

APPENDIX 7.1(iii)

(referred to in paragraphs 7.65—7.70)

Project Control Performance

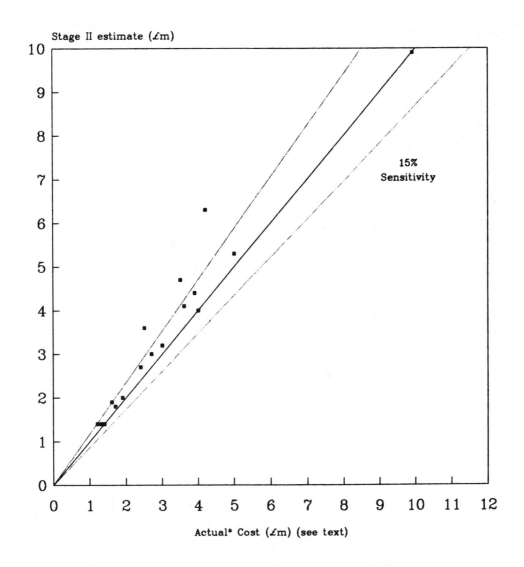

Source: MMC from BC Information.

* Actual cost after adjustments to allow for effects of 84/85 strike.

Printed by Her Majesty's Stationery Office

Dd 050383   C20   1/89   3182588